Guide to Ministering
to Alzheimer's Patients
and Their Families

Guide to Ministering to Alzheimer's Patients and Their Families

PAT OTWELL

Routledge
Taylor & Francis Group
New York   London

Routledge
Taylor & Francis Group
270 Madison Avenue
New York, NY 10016

Routledge
Taylor & Francis Group
27 Church Road
Hove, East Sussex BN3 2FA

© 2007 by Taylor & Francis Group, LLC
Routledge is an imprint of Taylor & Francis Group, an Informa business

Printed in the United States of America on acid-free paper
10 9 8 7 6 5 4 3 2 1

International Standard Book Number-13: 978-0-7890-2903-4 (Softcover) 978-0-7890-2902-7 (Hardcover)

Library of Congress Cataloging-in-Publication Data

Otwell, Patricia Anne.
Guide to ministering to Alzheimer's patients and their families / Pat Otwell.
p. cm.
Includes bibliographical references (p.).
ISBN: 978-0-7890-2902-7 (hard : alk. paper)
ISBN: 978-0-7890-2903-4 (soft : alk. paper)
1. Church work with the mentally ill. W. Alzheimer's disease--Religious aspects--Christianity. I. Title.

BV4461.O89 2008
259'.4196831--dc22   2007034358

Visit the Taylor & Francis Web site at
http://www.taylorandfrancis.com

and the Routledge Web site at
http://www.routledge.com

To the glory of my Heavenly Father

To the memory of my mother
Dorothy Hamrick Otwell
and earthly father
James A. Otwell, Jr.
and brother-in-law
Donald Creamer

To the honor of my family
Deanie, Zac, and Blaire Creamer
Carmen, Charlie, Caroline, and Jack McQueen
Janet and Jim Otwell
James, John, Joseph, and Jacob Otwell

To my former employers
Charles and Larry Greb
whose financial support enabled me to minister
to Alzheimer's patients and families

To those who have died with Alzheimer's disease
those who live with Alzheimer's disease
and those who love Alzheimer's disease patients

ABOUT THE AUTHOR

Pat Otwell, DMin, is the author of *A Chaplain-Led Ministry to Families of Alzheimer's Disease Patients Through the Development and Utilization of a Support Group,* "A Hobby That Ministers," and "Reflections." She has been on the cutting edge of Alzheimer's ministry for more than 20 years and has experience in virtually every aspect: assisting in nursing facility  placement and adjustment, providing day-to-day spiritual care for patients and families, providing crisis ministry during hospitalizations, developing and facilitating Alzheimer's support groups, and officiating at funerals.

CONTENTS

Foreword

Many of the great preachers of today and days past have had the blessing of a research assistant—one who would bring together all the pertinent materials needed for good exposition, thus saving the preacher hours of time and yet allowing him or her to minister the Word in his or her own unique style.

That is what Dr. Otwell has done for busy pastors in *Guide to Ministering to Alzheimer's Patients and Their Families*. Her work provides all the basic material needed for successful, compassionate ministry in this special area. Unlike the "sermonic" researcher, Dr. Otwell has not only brought together the important material but also put it into practical use during her many years of chaplaincy ministry and therefore offers counsel from a "been there, done that" experience.

Faith is frequently "tested" during difficult times. Persons diagnosed with Alzheimer's and their families have questions about God and other aspects of spirituality. It is common for them to search for "reasons" why this is happening and why at this point in their lives. This book assists ministers in helping patients and families find meaning through a relationship with God, prayer, worship experiences, and rituals.

Dr. Otwell reminds readers that ministry is foremost being physically present during times of need. Effectiveness of ministry isn't necessarily contingent on the minister's brilliance and expertise but rather on empathic understanding and willingness to be involved.

The Ten Commandments for Friends of Alzheimer's Patients and Families, which concludes Chapter 1, is a concise tool that can be applied by pastors for their personal use when ministering, or in training others in the congregation to minister. When these "commandments" are shared with family members, they, in turn, can share them with friends to help make their journey more bearable.

Dr. Otwell has the ability to put ministers "at ease" and even interjects humor into such a serious subject. Specifically, I found this statement to be quite humorous and yet encouraging: "Alzheimer's ministry can be your 'easiest' ministry! . . . If you happen to say or do something you regret, the patient likely will be unable to tell anyone about it!" It speaks volumes of truth.

This book addresses issues pertinent to Alzheimer's ministry, and it serves as a valuable resource when ministering to those affected by dementia caused by other illnesses or conditions. Alzheimer's disease has been referred to as "a long journey into night." *Guide to Ministering to Alzheimer's Patients and Their Families* enables caring ministers to spread the light of God's love to those who suffer and struggle for years because of the illness. As Dr. Otwell emphasizes, "Hope is available in the midst of what seems to be tragedy. Yet, God can, and does, bring good as a result of Alzheimer's disease." As ministers, may we be thankful God uses us as His servants to accomplish His awesome work in the lives of Alzheimer's patients and families!

Dwight Eldeen, Pastor
First Baptist Church
Hanover, Pennsylvania

Preface

Perhaps the sentiment of most religious leaders* is, "I know Alzheimer's patients and their families need and deserve ministry. I really would like to help, but I just do not know how." Good news—you can learn!

Many of us have little knowledge about Alzheimer's disease unless we have been personally involved. My "reason" for learning about the illness was that I served as a chaplain in three nursing facilities for fourteen years. During that time, I had the privilege, responsibility, and challenge of ministering to countless Alzheimer's victims. Not only is the patient a victim—family and friends are all affected by a loved one's illness.

Alzheimer's patients and their families are spiritual beings and have spiritual needs even though they may be unaware of them or not feel comfortable sharing them. Yet, these people cannot be helped maximally unless their spiritual needs are met through ministry. My purpose in writing this book is to communicate the thoughts, feelings, and needs of patients and families to you, and other ministers, who are in a prime position to help.

According to Ephesians 4:11-16, every Christian is to be a minister; therefore, this book is designed for *all* Christians. Clergy alone cannot provide a comprehensive ministry to Alzheimer's patients and families. Talents, gifts, and abilities of parishioners must also be utilized. "Clergy," "pastor," "preacher," "chaplain," "priest," and "rabbi" will refer to persons who are ordained, whereas "minister" (as a noun) will generally be used to designate ordained *or* laypersons.

Guide to Ministering to Alzheimer's Patients and Their Families is unique in that spiritual journeys were shared through questionnaires

---

*Although this book is written from a Christian perspective, adaptations can be made to meet the spiritual needs of people embracing other faith traditions.

by the "real experts"—family members who are living, or have lived, through this awesome ordeal. Of approximately 600 questionnaires distributed, 67 were returned. (Appendix A contains the questionnaire, and statistical data are recorded in Appendix B.) Due to factors such as personalities, beliefs, and timing, respondents' comments may be contradictory. Personalities of participants account for the manner in which they perceived, interpreted, and reported their experiences. Answers to ethical questions vary considerably according to personal beliefs. Respondents' remarks naturally could be predicated only upon their experiences at that point in time. For example, a respondent whose loved one was in the "early Alzheimer's" stage may have answered questions differently if the patient had reached the "severe Alzheimer's" stage.

This book is based on the author's experience in ministry, extensive reading, and knowledge gleaned from the questionnaires. (For ease in readability, certain respondents' comments are woven into the text, whereas other ideas, words, or thoughts are highlighted in block quotes or lists.) A number of responses address several issues and could be placed appropriately in more than one section. Information is included intentionally to assist in your role as educator to patients and families as well as for your own educational purposes. Suggestions presented for family members will be helpful to you, if you encounter the same situation in ministry.

To minister effectively to Alzheimer's patients and families, you must have these assets:

- Knowledge of the nature of Alzheimer's disease and its ramifications in the lives of patients and families
- Desire to minister to Alzheimer's patients and families
- Theological understanding of God, Alzheimer's patients, Alzheimer's family members, and self as minister
- Understanding of grief and guilt as related to Alzheimer's disease
- Ability to communicate with Alzheimer's patients
- Knowledge of the role, responsibilities, and record-keeping of an Alzheimer's ministry coordinator
- Knowledge of spiritual needs and implications of spiritual care for patients and families
- Understanding of ethical issues and the role of ministry in helping patients and families make crucial decisions

- Knowledge of models for ministry
- Ability to create, encourage, facilitate, and sustain faith, hope, and love in patients and families
- Acknowledgment of blessings that occur as a result of Alzheimer's disease and ministry to patients and families
- Knowledge of resources

As much as I wish I could offer a "how to" manual for what works every time when ministering to dementia patients, numerous variables do not permit "tried and true" formulas. Alzheimer's ministry is not a "one size fits all" approach, but rather a "trial and error" ministry with each individual during every encounter. Suggestions are made with the hope that *some* will work *sometimes* with *some* people. Always rely on the Spirit of God to be your guide, teacher, and helper!

Medical knowledge and treatments will progress as research continues; however, spiritual care to Alzheimer's patients and families is not expected to change significantly. Until the illness is eradicated, there will be a need for this ministry, with love being the basis and motivation.

Guide to Ministering to Alzheimer's Patients and Their Families is presented as a labor of love in behalf of Alzheimer's patients and families everywhere.

Acknowledgments

A very sincere "thank you" is expressed to everyone who had a part in making this book a reality. I never cease to be amazed at how willing and eager you, family members, are to be of assistance to others who share your plight. Not only were the detailed answers to the questionnaire, long letters, and booklets appreciated, but especially your prayers and words of encouragement. To maintain your privacy and confidentiality, I regret being unable to reveal your names. However, you know who you are. Your knowledge and experience will enable us to minister more effectively to Alzheimer's patients and families in the future. May God continue to bless you richly throughout your pilgrimage!

What a blessing you, the excellent staff at The Haworth Press, have been. Thank you for recognizing the need for this timely publication and being God's instrument in bringing my dream to fruition. An extra special word of appreciation goes to Senior Production Editor Amy Rentner. You truly went beyond the call of duty in patiently, promptly, proficiently, and professionally answering all my questions in such a reassuring manner. Throughout the long process, you treated "my" book as "your" book!

Most of all, I express my gratitude to God, without Whose help this publication would have been impossible. You provided every resource I needed and just when I needed each one! Now, I commit this book to You, Heavenly Father, trusting You to use it to help ministers, patients, families, and friends in Your timing and ways.

Chapter 1

Help!

"Come over and help us"—the call of the ancient Macedonians—is basically the same modern-day plea of Alzheimer's patients and families. Today's cry may be spoken or silent. But, truly all people affected by this disease need all the help they can get.

Receiving a diagnosis of Alzheimer's disease is devastating and life changing for those involved; yet, the resounding message is that no one has to face this illness alone. Help is available for patients, families, friends, and EVEN ministers!

Regardless of the recipients of our ministry, we can identify with the young pastor in the following parable by E. T. Eberhart[1] and be motivated to learn more about providing pastoral care to challenging patients.

The Fledgling Pastor
Who Did as Well as Could Be Expected

I was sick and you visited me.
Matthew 25:36b

A newest member in the ranks of the ordained got a nervous stomach whenever he thought of making a hospital call. In seminary he had sparred with spiritual comforting by way of approved textbooks. But now he was inside the ropes and expected to take on the real thing.

The closest he'd ever come to experiencing pain was a penicillin shot; and in the art of binding up wounds, it was Band-Aids, iodine, and a kiss to make it well.

Nevertheless, there was a command burning inside him: "As you did it to one of the least of these my brethren, you did it to me." And his professor in Pastoral Care 256 Section B had told him of the unspeakable joys in being God's vessel.

So being a man of faith he swallowed hard and advised his flock that in their moments of pain and loneliness God's help was as near as the phone. He put his prayer book at the ready and waited for his moment of truth.

One evening, parishioner Johanson drove down the street and made an unexpected exit through the windshield, landing in the hospital's emergency room. His life was intact, but several bones needed realignment.

Hearing of the accident the young pastor grabbed his prayer book and, en route to the hospital, dress rehearsed several comforting thoughts designed for such occasions. He came through the rehearsal as a tower of spiritual strength and a messenger of great compassion. It was opening night and he was ready.

Now his seminary books had neither pictures nor sound tracks, so what he was to see was a first for him. There stretched out with guy wires and pulleys like a repair job in a machine shop was Johanson. Tubes, needles, and gadgets protruded conspicuously from all over his body. His face was the color of sunset patterned with a black embroidery.

From the opening curtain it was stage fright. The pastor's mouth dried out; instead of his comforting thoughts he remembered he should be home preparing Sunday's sermon. His spirit fled. His body would have gone too except Mrs. Johanson was there watching.

A strange power held his tongue. He felt his pounding heart, the perspiration on his head, and his stomach shifting into reverse. Then the patient rolled his eyes, opened his mouth, and groaned something awful.

The symbol of God's presence cried "Amen!" and fled.

Late the next morning he stumbled out of bed and went to the kitchen to tell his wife he was leaving the ministry. But before he could open his mouth, she told him that Mrs. Johanson had called and said how his visit had helped them greatly. They had gained composure through his quiet, sensitive mood and found strength for the night through his silent prayer.

Providing pastoral care to Alzheimer's patients presents a real challenge for amateur *and* seasoned ministers. Expect the unexpected! Expect to encounter unexpected sights, sounds, and smells. Expect there will be times you do not know what to say or do. Expect moments of frustration and despair—maybe to the extent you want to leave the ministry. But, likewise, expect a patient, family member, or friend along the way to gain support from what you said or did. Then forge ahead to assist others in finding help through God, God's Word, the church, prayer, clergy, other professionals, resources, support groups, and friends.

GOD

The Alzheimer's journey is too overwhelming for anyone to travel alone. God is the greatest source of help. He wants to dwell within, walk beside, and bear the burdens of patients and families throughout the long, arduous pilgrimage.

Alzheimer's disease has the potential to cause those affected to seek God through faith in Jesus Christ, if they have not already done so. God and His resources are readily available to all who confess their sins, ask forgiveness, repent, and place their trust in Jesus. "God is our refuge and strength, a very present help in trouble" (Psalms 46:1). Testimonials by respondents include such affirmations of God's faithfulness:

✧ I know God is with me.
✧ God has given me what no one else could.
✧ God is always there to comfort and see me through when I ask Him for help.

Virtually every Alzheimer's family member to whom I have ministered appeared to have a strong faith in God and recognized the need to depend on Him. These respondents' comments support my observation:

✧ Only with God's help can you endure this dreadful disease.
✧ I am a Christian and go to church every Sunday. I find comfort in talking to God. I ask Him to take over and guide me.
✧ God has taken care of me.
✧ God has never given me more than I can bear. He will help me accept the things I cannot change.

GOD'S WORD

Although "Alzheimer's disease" is not mentioned in the Bible, the same words of encouragement given to people facing other adversities can strengthen and sustain those affected by this illness as well.

As noted by this respondent, patients often amazingly recite Bible verses learned years ago:

✧ My husband quotes, "I am the way, the truth, and the life," at least three times during Sunday School. He really believes it and grasps this verse.

Quoting favorite scriptures is an excellent intervention to try when dealing with agitated or hostile patients. Familiar passages can have a calming and comforting effect.[2]

In addition to quoting or reading Bible verses, passages can be shared through other creative ways such as music, drama, needlework, calligraphy, and written correspondence. Scriptures that family members found helpful are recorded in Appendix C.

THE CHURCH

The whole Body of Christ (the church) is affected when a member has Alzheimer's. If one person suffers, everyone shares the pain. Congregations have the opportunity, responsibility, and privilege to care, sustain, support, nurture, and love all who are touched by the disease. One respondent expressed the following perspective:

✧ The church can be supportive as a place to "weep" and a place to "heal."

Respondents' experiences regarding their church's ministry ranged from "have not found any help" to "one of my best supports":

✧ The church is failing families when it should be their *best* support. I have not found any help within the church. People seem afraid to broach the subject.
✧ I started a support group at our church and have counseled hundreds of caregivers.* Many become isolated when they can no longer attend church due to their loved ones' condition. It is sad that families are forgotten in their time of need.

---

*A caregiver is one who provides or arranges care for a patient. Often, the caregiver is a family member but can be someone who volunteers or who is paid. Care may be provided in the patient's home or in a care facility that would include a nursing facility, assisted living facility, adult foster home, adult day care center, or hospital. Care facility staff, other professionals, and clergy may be considered caregivers also.

✧ I would like to see more overall church support for Alzheimer's disease.
✧ My church has shown me lots of love. It has been one of my best supports. I have never had to walk alone.

As we avail ourselves of opportunities to learn more about Alzheimer's ministry, great hope exists that all families will be able to report favorable experiences in the future. Respondents suggested the church be supportive in these ways:

✧ Let the church not forget Alzheimer's patients and their families.
✧ Congregations can come to caregivers' aid with visits and phone calls. It takes so little to brighten our day.
✧ Ministering to Alzheimer's patients and families is *too big a job for one person,* but parishioners can assist after proper training. If a church member has (or had) a loved one with Alzheimer's, it would be helpful for that person to visit families of newly diagnosed patients.
✧ I believe the church can fill the role of friendly visitors. Members are an important contact with the outside world and can provide much support to homebound caregivers and patients.

PRAYER

Congregations have various ways to communicate prayer needs— spoken requests during worship services, telephone calls, e-mail prayer chains, bulletins, and newsletters. Use all opportunities to pray for patients and families because it is so significant to them. A number of respondents acknowledged prayer as their "lifeline":

✧ Who but the Lord understands what we are experiencing? Prayer is essential. It is the only way I would have made it. God is aware even before I talk to Him.
✧ We are in God's hands. Prayer is a real solution to the here and now. It has sustained and comforted me.
✧ To me, the most important help of all is prayer. It gives me a sense of peace and comfort.
✧ Prayer helps me face each day—one day at a time.

Intercessory prayer (talking to God in behalf of another person) is one of the manifold blessings of being a Christian. Naturally, you can pray for patients and families when you are away from them as well as when you are in their presence. These family members shared the value of intercessory prayer in their lives:

    ✧ My greatest need is prayer from everyone.
    ✧ Knowing that others pray for us keeps me going.
    ✧ We always need to know people care and are praying for us.

An excellent way to pray for others is during a telephone conversation. "Telephone prayers" enable patients or families to know you are praying for them at that moment. Also, a telephone prayer ministry is an excellent way to involve homebound church members in Alzheimer's ministry.

    ✧ When telephoning, check to see whether it is a convenient time for the caregiver to talk. Ask how the caregiver is doing as well as the patient. Pray for the patient and family during the conversation.

Families do not always know how to pray for their loved ones. A few respondents honestly and courageously shared their difficulty in talking to God:

    ✧ Many times prayer has been difficult.
    ✧ It was difficult to know how to pray for Mother during her illness.
    ✧ I would not have survived without my faith even though the Lord and I did wrestle a few times. Those were the days my prayers only made it to the ceiling! When I finally came to grips with the situation, I would try to start my day by saying, "I cannot do this alone. So, Lord, I am turning the day over to You!"

Giving thanks is an important form of prayer. This family member acknowledged her thankfulness to God for His help:

    ✧ I am fortunate to have had a strong-minded mother who raised me with "faith" that the Lord would provide a way. In trying times, I ask the Good Lord to give me the physical strength I need to cope. He has helped me do what has to be done. I thank Him daily.

Researchers constantly need prayer for guidance and wisdom as they seek the cure for Alzheimer's. One respondent captured the heartfelt petition of all who are affected by the illness:

    ✧ Let us pray that our Lord leads researchers to a cure for this cruel affliction.

CLERGY

Parishioners, in times of need, often turn to their clergyperson. One respondent observed:

✧ I have given a great deal of thought to the role of clergy in the Alzheimer's cause—finding it somewhat disappointing but in *many* instances very inspiring.

Clergy have an ideal vantage point in helping Alzheimer's patients and families because of their

- faith resources in sharing God's love;
- trustworthiness in safeguarding confidences;
- understanding of the nature and remedy for grief and guilt;
- interpersonal skills;
- professional relationships;
- knowledge of community resources;
- positive example in encouraging the church to be "the Church";
- opportunities to educate the congregation about the illness;
- responsibility to train members for ministry;
- knowledge of patients' and families' needs as well as knowledge of spiritual gifts of those within the congregation; and
- knowledge of scriptures to offer encouragement, support, and comfort.

Ministers wear many hats when providing Alzheimer's ministry. The major responsibilities are (1) sharing the gospel with those who are not Christians and (2) supporting those who are Christians. Within these responsibilities are numerous roles. Depending on the needs of the moment, the role might be listener, educator, encourager, facilitator, communicator, advocator, or reconciler.

OTHER PROFESSIONALS

Patients and families need the expertise of other professionals—physicians, attorneys, law enforcement officials, social workers, home health providers, adult day care staff, nursing facility personnel, hospital staff, and funeral directors—during the lengthy duration of the illness. As much as possible, work cooperatively with these people to provide for the welfare of patients and families.

RESOURCES

Organizations, agencies, programs, and services to assist Alzheimer's patients and families vary from one geographical location to another. Patients and families may request information from you about resources to meet their needs. Respondents shared the following comments:

✧ Be knowledgeable of local, state, and federal resources to assist Alzheimer's patients and families.

✧ Finding someone to help is so important. Ministers can inform families of agencies or organizations that might assist. "Easter Seals" has daytime sitters where I live. Some communities have "Meals on Wheels," which enables patients to live at home longer.

✧ There is not an "Elder Assessment Program" is our area. So, we made appointments with various specialists as well as consulted an accountant and attorney. We read and floundered and read some more.

With the help of your congregation, community leaders, and the Alzheimer's Association, proactively work to develop new services as needed. Nevertheless, bear in mind that just because a particular service or program worked well in another location, it may not be the best solution for your area or at that time.

Due to the high cost of health care and the length of the illness, savings can rapidly dwindle if expenses are not covered by insurance or other assistance. Although patients and families may not acknowledge it to their family of faith, many have financial concerns:

✧ A constant concern of many caregivers is how to survive after so much money is spent on catastrophic care for the patient. There is almost nothing left for the spouse.

✧ I could have used more financial help. Our small savings were soon depleted after my husband had to be hospitalized and put in a nursing home.

✧ Pastors and churches need to address the issue of financial support for chronic medical care. Our free enterprise system is not doing its job in this respect. Christian people need to realize their love and concern can be exercised in seeking a society that cares for its sick and elderly. It is not enough to rely upon volunteers. This whole matter is difficult for all involved.

✧ If money is available, assist with nursing home or home care expenses.

Individuals within the church, Sunday School classes, or mission groups may desire to contribute as needs arise. Financing a portion of respite care expenses or Safe Return registration and annual fees might be considered. Assistance should be offered sensitively and, preferably, anonymously.

For more information about financial concerns, see the pamphlet *Money Matters: Helping the Person with Dementia Settle Financial Issues,* by the Alzheimer's Association.

Numerous organizations and publications are listed in Chapter 16, "Resources."

SUPPORT GROUPS

Establishing and facilitating a support group was the most rewarding aspect of my Alzheimer's ministry. I did not have to have all the answers! We learned from one another. Through a support group, a maximum number of people can be helped in a minimum amount of time and with minimal effort. Members are helped as they help others:

✧ Support groups are such powerful avenues of mutual help.
✧ My only salvation was when I heard of, and attended, an Alzheimer's support group. I finally found people who knew exactly what I was experiencing. I could talk to them. We gave each other moral support and swapped ideas about how to cope and care for our loved ones.
✧ I helped organize our local chapter and had the hotline in my home. Support group members helped me as much as I helped them.

One respondent put this truthful twist on the value of a support group:

✧ Hearing others' problems caused me to realize mine could be worse.

Someone suggested "prayer time" be included in the meetings. When members share prayer requests, others know of current concerns. Therefore, bonding occurs within the group, and an opportunity exists to express love between sessions through calls, cards, and prayers.

Certain times are more difficult for families than others:

> ✧ A support group for family members at the time of nursing facility placement could be helpful. My father's nursing home placement was harder for me than his death.

> ✧ Family members might find a "Life After Alzheimer's Disease" support group meaningful in the early days and weeks following the death of their loved one.

It is not advisable for Alzheimer's patients to attend family support groups because they can easily become agitated, confused, disruptive, and depressed. Also, members and guest speakers might not share everything they would like, if patients were present. However, some communities have support groups designed for patients in the early stages of the illness.

Many localities have only one support group, whereas metropolitan areas may offer several groups that enable members to have a choice of time, location, or special need interest (e.g., children, teenagers, male caregivers, spouses, or adult children). If special interest groups are not available in your area, consider providing sessions periodically to help family members deal with specific issues unique to their situation.

If you are involved in establishing a support group, an important factor to consider is location. Some people prefer to attend sessions in a neutral facility rather than in a church:

> ✧ When I joined, my group met at a church. The preacher's wife was the leader, and I found it valuable. Later, I invited an acquaintance who thought meeting at the church gave it a "denominational flavor." She never came. Now we meet in a hospital's wellness center, and I have not encountered this attitude.

On the other hand, probably more people prefer to attend meetings within a church setting—especially when they are among friends.

Churches may have opportunities to establish a support group as a ministry, if there is a need and interest.

✧ Contact the Alzheimer's Association for information. Large churches may have enough people to start their own group and invite others to join. Smaller churches could offer space and provide knowledge-able leaders who are *qualified* to give guidance.

If a congregational support group is not available through your church, encourage participation in a community group.

Family members may have erroneous concepts of support groups and offer excuses for not attending. A small, but significant, act of ministry is for pastors to go with parishioners:

✧ My pastor attended a support group meeting with me.

Should family members continue to attend a support group following the loved one's death? This depends on the individual's needs and involvement within the group. Each person will know. Some choose not to return. Others find it meaningful to remain in the group for these reasons:

1. It is comforting to receive love from this "family" where one is known.
2. The group enables the grieving process that was begun following the loved one's diagnosis to continue.
3. Family members who have completed the cycle from "diagnosis to death" are in a better position to help others.

The Alzheimer's experience should not define anyone's life at any time. Alzheimer's is only a part, not the totality, of life. At some point following their loved ones' death, families need to put the past behind and move forward. This will probably mean saying good-bye to the support group; however, you can encourage parishioners to become involved in other ministries.

For additional information about support groups, consult the article "It Doesn't Just Happen: What Makes a Support Group Good?" by Vicki Schmall, and the professional project report *A Chaplain-Led*

Ministry to Families of Alzheimer's Disease Patients Through the Development and Utilization of a Support Group, by Patricia Otwell.

FRIENDS

Regrettably, many people do not know how to relate, and be help-ful, to Alzheimer's patients. Yet, these patients and their families des-perately need true friends—those who will stand by them *no matter what!* Real friends genuinely care and meet needs without being asked.

The following (source unknown) provides excellent suggestions for anyone willing to be a friend.

Ten Commandments for Friends
of Alzheimer's Patients and Families

1. Thou shalt learn as much as possible about Alzheimer's disease and how it affects patients and families.
2. Thou shalt offer a listening ear.
3. Thou shalt call frequently and visit as often as possible.
4. Thou shalt help the patient by supporting the family.
5. Thou shalt be sensitive of patients' and families' needs and feel-ings.
6. Thou shalt not be afraid or embarrassed to be with patients and families.
7. Thou shalt remember the illness causes patients to say and do things that cannot be helped.
8. Thou shalt treat patients and families as thou would want to be treated.
9. Thou shalt make specific offers to help.
10. Thou shalt pray often for patients and families.

Let us therefore come boldly unto the throne of grace, that we may obtain mercy, and find grace to help in time of need.

Hebrews 4:16

Chapter 2

Alzheimer's Disease

Excellent materials abound on Alzheimer's disease and its ramifications in the lives of patients and families. For detailed information, readers can refer to the books listed under General Information About Alzheimer's Disease in Chapter 16, "Resources." Knowledge contained in the following synopsis focusing on such aspects of the illness as history, diagnosis, nature, heredity, cause, cure, statistics, stages, and characteristics will be beneficial when providing pastoral care.

HISTORY

In 1906, Alois Alzheimer (a German physician) described the disease that now bears his name. He treated a patient in her early fifties who exhibited behavioral symptoms normally present in older people. When an autopsy was performed, numerous tangles and plaques were discovered in the brain, and these have become characteristic of the illness.

For years, it was assumed all elderly folks would eventually become senile, if they lived long enough. Today, we know people can live functionally for more than a hundred years unless Alzheimer's or other debilitating illnesses develop. A significant breakthrough occurred when Alzheimer's was recognized as an illness rather than a consequence of aging.

DIAGNOSIS

Patients may know something is wrong or deny that anything is the matter, if they become forgetful or notice a change in their behavior.

A variety of emotions, including anger, frustration, sadness, anxiety, and fear, may be experienced during this time by patients and families. No one can tell by observation alone whether a person has Alzheimer's disease; therefore, it is important for a diagnosis to be sought when the illness is suspected.

Dementia (loss of memory and abilities to the extent of interfering with daily living) can be caused by many illnesses or conditions; however, the most common type is Alzheimer's disease. To determine the cause of dementia, various tests must be performed, including a medical history review, mental status and mood assessment, physical exam, laboratory tests, and a neurological exam.[1]

With greater awareness of the illness and more effective diagnostic tools, patients are diagnosed earlier in the disease process than previously.

Never assume a person has Alzheimer's disease. Certain causes of dementia are treatable or reversible, and the patient gets better. I ministered to a resident who exhibited classic symptoms of the illness. Although tests were not performed, family members and staff assumed he had Alzheimer's. It turned out he was not getting proper nutrition. After a feeding tube was inserted, his symptoms disappeared and his quality of life drastically improved! Granted, this is a rare success story, but it is a perfect example of the importance of seeking a diagnosis to eliminate other reasons for dementia.

When the diagnosis is Alzheimer's, the patient's condition is irreversible. Abilities, skills, and functions will further deteriorate as the illness progresses.

For additional information, consult the pamphlets *About the Alzheimer's Association* and *Basics of Alzheimer's Disease: What It Is and What You Can Do,* by the Alzheimer's Association, as well as *Alzheimer's Disease* and *Alzheimer's Disease: Unraveling the Mystery,* by the National Institute on Aging and National Institutes of Health.

NATURE

Alzheimer's disease has been described in various ways—"the disease of the century," "the forgetting disease," "a never-ending funeral," "a living death," "another name for madness," "the long good-bye," "the silent epidemic," "loss of self," "the disease of the soul," and "the theological disease." One of the earliest and most popular books written about the illness is appropriately titled *The 36-Hour Day,* by Nancy Mace and Peter Rabins, because a caregiver's day seems like thirty-six hours instead of twenty-four.

J. Thomas Hutton and Jerry L. Morris write:

> No other chronic medical condition is more devastating to the quality of life. It strips away the personhood of the individual: those human aspects that are held most dear—the ability to think, to plan, to remember, and to function as a productive member of society—are taken away.[2]

Initial symptoms of Alzheimer's disease will likely be forgetfulness, personality changes, or bizarre behavior. These changes may be so subtle that family members and friends tend to overlook them. In time, however, symptoms occur more frequently and are so evident they can no longer be denied. Family members feel helpless and embarrassed when a loved one displays undesirable behaviors:

✧ I strongly believe the minister's most helpful role is to be knowledgeable about the disease and sensitive to families' needs. Then family members will feel comfortable discussing their loved one who is exhibiting behavioral changes. Alzheimer's can cause a patient's personality to change entirely.

✧ I found it difficult to talk to my pastor because of my husband's accusations, behavior, insane sex ideas, and cussing. Although he has been a Christian for years, he says and does things you would not believe.

Reassure families that problematic behaviors ensue as part of the disease process. Patients are not intentionally being mean but are unable to control their feelings and behavior. Because of limited ways to express anger, patients may resort to words and actions never otherwise used. Scolding or shaming patients should be avoided.

Another sad, yet common, aspect of the illness is that patients may accuse their spouses of having an affair. If this occurs, it is better for the non-Alzheimer's spouse to listen rather than become defensive or argumentative. Humor may help relieve the tension. Patients also may accuse families, residents, or care facility staff of stealing their belongings when items are misplaced. Actually, patients tend to hide and hoard articles. Whoever is accused of stealing should help find the items without being defensive, argumentative, or offering rational explanations.

Since it becomes impossible to reason with patients, logical explanations do not make sense. Listen to what is said without correcting or contradicting. Arguing will agitate them and make matters worse. If safety issues are involved, take necessary actions to protect patients.

As the illness progresses, patients lose their inhibitions. However, what *appears* to be inappropriate sexual behavior *may not be* that at all. Patients may disrobe in public without realizing they are doing anything socially unacceptable. Disrobing can be an attempt to communicate a need to use the bathroom or that clothing is uncomfortable. Care facility patients may attempt inadvertently to perform sexual acts on persons other than their spouses because they are unable to differentiate their mates from others of the opposite sex. The book *Sexuality and the Alzheimer's Patient,* by Edna Ballard and Cornelia Poer, provides helpful information for families, care facility staff, and ministers regarding sexual issues. For additional insight, the reader can refer to the pamphlet *Sexuality,* by the Alzheimer's Association, and the article "The Changing Face of Sexual Intimacy in Alzheimer's Disease," by Daniel Kuhn.

Often, patients maintain their social facade as the illness advances. This is especially evident when they are asked questions or faced with choices. Patients sometimes have an uncanny ability to hide their mental deficiencies when they can no longer make decisions. If you ask, "Would you rather hold the hymnal or the Bible?" the patient may smile and graciously say, "You decide" or "I do not care." General responses allow the person to save face without admitting inability to make the decision.

Long-term memory usually remains intact far into the disease process. Patients can relate events that occurred many years ago—and, often, with amazing accuracy. It is short-term memory that is affected. Patients may not know what they ate for breakfast, or they may not remember a visit from the previous night. It is difficult when families visit faithfully in a care facility, and their loved ones are unable to remember the visits. Patients may tell you their families never come to see them when, in fact, they do.

Word to the wise: Do not believe everything an Alzheimer's patient says!

Patients are not intentionally telling untruths when their memory fails. Whatever they say seems real and right to them. Their stories may even sound credible! However, there may be times you need to verify what is said.

An example: A resident related an elaborate account of renting a car to drive herself to a doctor's appointment. She even provided answers to my questions! I thought her story to be strange, but she normally was lucid during my visits, so I questioned a nurse about the accuracy of the account. The nurse told me an employee drove the resident. Confession: I was so accustomed to being able to believe this resident I even asked one of her relatives about the incident. The relative confirmed the nurse's version!

Another aberration is patients do not realize they are as old as they are. This manifests in such ways as (1) being unable to recognize themselves in current photographs, (2) calling for Mama or Daddy during difficult moments, and (3) saying they have to take care of their babies.

Patients may reach a plateau and remain at the same level of functioning for quite a while. Yet, for reasons unknown, some patients decline more rapidly than others do.

Many patients experience "sundowning" (reversal of day and night patterns) as the illness progresses. In the evening and at night, they are more alert, restless, and agitated than in the morning. Turning on additional lights in the room during the evening and night may help. Caregivers must always ensure the environment is as calm as possible.

It is difficult, if not impossible, for patients to learn new skills; however, they may maintain skills previously learned for a long time. An example: Soon after a dementia resident was admitted to the nursing facility, a deacon from her church came to visit. Knowing she had been the pianist at their church and had played for worship services in another nursing facility for as long as—*actually longer than*—she was mentally capable, he told her she could practice on the piano in the lobby. The dear lady curtly let him know she did not practice— *she played*. And play she did. Her repertoire consisted of about ten songs that she artistically and *repeatedly* played for years!

Patients may pass through a period when they experience unique idiosyncrasies. One patient might cry for seemingly no reason every afternoon at four o'clock. Another patient may urinate in the trash can instead of the toilet. Such behaviors cease as the illness progresses or may be replaced by other irrational behaviors.

Patients ultimately become unable to handle their personal and business affairs. Trustworthy persons need to make decisions in the best interest of patients.

It is amazing what patients sometimes "know" without being told. One dementia resident could tell when it was Friday although she did not know the other days of the week. Friday was the day her daughter took her home for the weekend!

I like to wear jewelry with religious symbols—a cross or an angel on a necklace—to help dementia residents identify me as a minister. One evening, I saw an Alzheimer's patient sitting in the lobby and walked toward her. During our conversation, I held out the cross on my necklace and asked what she thought about when she saw it. She responded, "My Lord."

On another occasion, I broke one of my own rules: Never ask an Alzheimer's patient who I am. A gentleman was transferred from another facility to the Alzheimer's and Related Disorders Unit due to mental deterioration. I happened to be on the unit the day he moved and visited him because he was among unfamiliar faces. When I asked whether he knew me, he answered affirmatively but did not say my name nor give any other indication that he recognized me. I continued to inquire, "Who am I?" After my third attempt, he uttered, "You are the nun here." I smiled and replied, "Yes, that is right, except I am Baptist instead of Catholic!"

Frequently, elderly non-Alzheimer's spouses seem to provide better care for their Alzheimer's spouses at home and for a longer duration of time than their adult children do. Non-Alzheimer's spouses compensate incredibly for patients' losses. In fact, mental deficits may be hidden so well that close family members do not realize the extent of the disease process unless the non-Alzheimer's spouse becomes ill or dies. This could be due to family members' denial, additional stress on the patient, or the non-Alzheimer's spouse's trying to hide the reality of the situation. With God's grace, strength, and help, the spouse may well have kept the patient at home for years. However, it may be only days, weeks, or months after the non-Alzheimer's spouse's illness or death until the patient is placed in a care facility. Of course, adult children often have other family responsibilities and may have illnesses themselves.

Some patients become hostile as the disease progresses. If this happens, adjustments may be necessary. One respondent shared how she handled the situation:

> ✧ My husband became so hostile it was dangerous for both of us. At that point, his twin brother cared for him until he became incontinent. Then I placed him in a domiciliary.

For additional information on hostility, read the pamphlet *Behaviors: What Causes Dementia-Related Behavior Like Aggression, and How to Respond,* by the Alzheimer's Association.

Patients can appear, and even act, normal *at times* far into the disease process. An example: One day the husband of an employee stopped to see her at the nursing facility. As he was leaving, he saw a former neighbor near the front door. They chatted briefly, and the resident asked the man to take him home. He obliged, not knowing his former neighbor lived in the nursing facility!

Toward the end of the disease process, patients may yell, "Help me, help me," without realizing they are doing so. The screaming may cease, at least momentarily, if you stand by the bedside and calmly speak the person's name.

Patients usually become bedridden and helpless, if the illness runs its normal course. They require constant supervision and depend on others to provide for their basic needs.

Patients may have Alzheimer's for years before it is diagnosed and are likely to live many years after the diagnosis. Ironically, in the later stages, they may have few, if any, major medical complications. They die *with* the disease—not *from* it. Death is often due to an infection or injury.

HEREDITY

Family members of Alzheimer's patients often wonder whether they and other family members will develop the illness. These respondents' comments indicate their concern:

✧ I hope I do not get Alzheimer's disease nor pass it on to my children.

✧ The thought that my children may have to deal with this disease has been a real problem for me.

✧ I hope a cure is found for this devastating illness before it strikes any of our nine children.

According to the Alzheimer's Association, "Those who have a parent, brother, or sister with Alzheimer's are two to three times more likely to develop the disease. The risk increases if more than one family member has the illness."[3]

Although children or siblings of patients may desire to have genetic testing, I think this is generally inadvisable because

- there is no cure,
- such knowledge could lead to depression,
- the person may be unable to obtain insurance,
- the person may be unable to gain desired employment,
- quality of life may be greatly diminished,
- death could result from other causes, and
- a cure may be found before the person is affected.

You can help family members who express fear of developing Alzheimer's by (1) listening to their concerns, (2) sharing accurate information, and (3) praying with them.

For additional information, see the pamphlets *Genes and Alzheimer's Disease* and *Ethical Issues in Alzheimer's Disease: Genetic Testing,* by the Alzheimer's Association, as well as *Alzheimer's Disease Genetics,* by the National Institute on Aging and National Institutes of Health.

CAUSE

Although researchers are diligently working and have tested many theories, the cause of Alzheimer's is still unknown.

Risk factors identified by the Alzheimer's Association may include the following:

- Being sixty-five years old or older
- Family history
- Genetics
- Head trauma
- Heart disease, diabetes, stroke, high blood pressure, or high cholesterol
- Being Latino or African American[4]

For additional information, see the pamphlet *African-Americans and Alzheimer's Disease: The Silent Epidemic,* by the Alzheimer's Association.

CURE

Although there is no cure for Alzheimer's disease, treatments are available to attempt to alleviate symptoms and behavioral problems. It is not easy to ascertain whether behavioral problems are caused by the illness, environment, adverse reaction to medication, or other factors.

Medications and dosages can be tricky. Periodically, physicians may need to make adjustments. An example: A resident on the Alzheimer's and Related Disorders Unit became uncontrollable. I asked his wife whether she had considered having him hospitalized so his medications could be adjusted. She decided to give it a try. When he returned to the facility, he was like a different person—much more subdued and manageable.

God is all-powerful and can heal all diseases; however, the nature of Alzheimer's is that patients get worse as the illness takes its toll. Therefore, ministers should not give false hope of healing.

✧ Do not offer glib clichés or make promises of healing.

STATISTICS

Alzheimer's is not a new disease, but it is more prevalent because the average life span has increased through the years. It was estimated that 4.5 million people in the United States had Alzheimer's disease in 2000. By 2050, the projected number of these patients is expected to increase threefold.[5] According to one study, approximately 10 percent of persons over sixty-five years of age had "probable Alzheimer's disease" compared with approximately 47 percent of those over eighty-five years old.[6]

However, Alzheimer's does not strike *only* older people. Persons in their thirties can have the disease. When younger people are afflicted, there are unique issues.

For additional information, see the pamphlets *Early-Onset Alzheimer's: I'm Too Young to Have Alzheimer's Disease, Alzheimer's Disease Statistics,* and *Alzheimer's Disease Growth: U.S. Will See Average 44 Percent Increase in Alzheimer's Disease by 2025,* by the Alzheimer's Association.

STAGES AND CHARACTERISTICS

Your mental picture of Alzheimer's patients may be at a certain stage of the illness—anywhere on the spectrum from forgetfulness to being bedridden. Actually, in the course of the disease, patients experience several stages of decline. So, there is not just one stereotypical image.

Although it is not necessary to identify the stage a patient is experiencing, it is important to have an understanding of the progression of decline, as noted by the following respondents' comments:

◇ Ministers should be knowledgeable of Alzheimer's behavior in its various stages.

◇ Clergy need to be familiar with the progression of the disease so they can be more understanding and helpful.

Literature varies regarding the number of stages and symptoms. Stages are not always clear-cut and may overlap. Patients will likely not have every symptom; yet, symptoms may change in a patient throughout the day or week. While no one knows how long a patient will live with the illness, it could be twenty years or more. To indicate the progression of decline, I am using the manual *Caring for People with Alzheimer's Disease: A Manual for Facility Staff* (Second Edition), by Lisa P. Gwyther, as a *guideline* for what can be expected.[7]

Early Alzheimer's

- Recent memory loss affecting work performance
- Confusion
- Gets lost when driving
- Verbal communication difficulties—devises words if unable to say desired ones or says words opposite those intended
- Disoriented
- Judgment problems—makes inappropriate decisions
- Unable to think abstractly
- Misplaces items
- Change in mood, behavior, or personality
- No initiative in conversation or tasks
- Unable to perform routine chores

Mild Alzheimer's

- Memory loss and confusion are more noticeable
- Difficulty managing finances—forgets to pay bills or pays more than once
- Unable to learn new skills
- Withdrawn
- Talks less
- Short attention span—cannot stay focused long on a task
- Unable to organize thoughts
- Unable to rationalize
- Repetitive words and movements
- Unable to cope with change
- Insensitive to others' feelings
- Easily angered when frustrated or tired
- Avoids making decisions
- Change in eating habits—forgets to eat, eats ravenously, or eats only a certain food
- Needs more time to complete tasks
- Hides belongings or puts them in unusual places

- Searches for objects or people
- Hoards items

Moderate Alzheimer's

- Lack of concern for appearance and hygiene
- Changes in sleep patterns—stays awake most of night and naps during day
- Confuses identity of family and friends
- Requires supervision for safety and well-being
- Takes others' belongings, mistaking them for own
- Restlessness at evening and night—paces and fidgets
- Unable to follow spoken or written directions (even if words are read correctly)
- Unable to understand explanations
- Compensates memory loss by making up stories
- Falsely accuses others—spouse of having an affair, family or facility staff of stealing, and so on
- Curses, screams, hits, bites, or kicks
- Inappropriate social and sexual behavior—disrobes or masturbates in public, mistakes someone else for spouse
- Unable to differentiate reality—thinks what is seen on television is real
- Movement difficulties when walking and sitting
- Unable to recognize self in mirror
- Needs assistance with toileting, bathing, feeding, dressing, and walking
- Hallucinations

Severe Alzheimer's

- Unable to recognize family and friends
- Unable to speak or makes gibberish sounds
- Swallowing problems
- Chokes easily
- Touches objects
- Groans
- Incontinent
- Weight loss

- Skin easily torn
- Screams when touched or moved
- Seizures
- Infections
- Susceptible to falls if still walking
- Sleeps much of the time
- Requires total care

Implications of spiritual care for patients and for families, based on this four-stage model, are found in Chapters 9 and 10, respectively.

> Cast me not off in the time of old age; forsake me not when my strength faileth.
>
> Psalms 71:9

Chapter 3

Desire to Minister
to Alzheimer's Patients and Families

Wanting to minister is a prerequisite for effective Alzheimer's ministry. Regardless of the extent of your knowledge, it is useless unless you *want* to serve these people. Ministry puts knowledge into action.

Patients and families readily sense when ministry is performed out of *desire* rather than *duty.* These respondents acknowledged appreciation for their clergy who went beyond the call of duty:

◇ My pastor was so good to me. It was easy to talk to him because he was understanding, supportive, and loving. He prayed for my husband at every church service and visited him at least once a week for three years in a nursing home fifty miles from where we lived! He missed prayer meeting the night before my husband died and was by my side in the nursing home when death occurred in the early morning hours.
◇ Our rabbi was always there for us. He stood by for fourteen years and was our "rock."
◇ I was fortunate to have a very concerned preacher. He was the first person I saw in the hospital after receiving the sad news of my husband's diagnosis.
◇ My minister told me I could call him day or night, if I needed to talk. Believe me, I have done this.

If you truly desire to provide pastoral care to Alzheimer's patients and families, you must be willing to overcome obstacles, reach out, and acquire additional knowledge.

OVERCOME OBSTACLES

What stands in your way of ministering to those affected by Alzheimer's may be different from the hindrances faced by other ministers. Therefore, explore your personal obstacles and creatively find solutions so these barriers will no longer prevent you from sharing God's love with these patients and families. Common obstacles that impede Alzheimer's ministry include (1) myths, (2) excuses, and (3) fear.

Myths

Two popular myths related to Alzheimer's ministry must be dispelled: (1) ministry to Alzheimer's patients is difficult, and (2) nothing can be done spiritually for Alzheimer's patients.

Ministry to Alzheimer's Patients Is Difficult

Fact: Alzheimer's patient ministry is *not difficult—just different!*
Probably the most common misconception of ministers regarding Alzheimer's patient ministry is that it is difficult. Many tend to make it more difficult than it is. Think *simple* and *easy!* Be fully present, listen, and just do what comes naturally!

Alzheimer's ministry can be your "easiest" ministry! With one-on-one patient ministry, no in-depth Bible study or exegesis is required—use children's Bible stories to convey biblical truths. If you happen to say or do something you regret, the patient likely will be unable to tell anyone about it! Furthermore, you do not have pressures associated with other ministries, such as preparing sermons, handling administrative tasks, counseling, preaching, raising gigantic offerings, and reaching lofty attendance goals.

Although ministry to Alzheimer's patients is not difficult, it can be challenging due to these variables:

- No two patients are alike.
- Personalities and situations differ.
- Patients can be in one of several stages.

- What is effective with one patient may not be effective with another patient.
- What is effective with one patient at one time may not be effective with the same patient at another time.
- Illness likely will last many years.
- Communication techniques for Alzheimer's patients are different from those used with patients who have other diseases.

Nothing Can Be Done Spiritually for Alzheimer's Patients

Fact: Much can be done to minister to the spirit of Alzheimer's patients.

When I taught elementary school, it was my task to find a way in which all my students could learn. These methods varied according to each individual learner and the type of material being studied. Some pupils learned best visually—others by listening. A combination of seeing and hearing worked well for many students. Likewise, as ministers, it is our task to seek a way that connects the spirit of each Alzheimer's patient with the Spirit of God. Ideally, during every visit we will find at least one way to accomplish this goal. Ways to assist patients in making a connection with God include quoting a familiar Bible verse, observing communion, singing a hymn, watching a sunset, talking, listening, or praying. More than one of these acts may be used during a visit.

A patient may indicate a spiritual connection has been made by repeating a Bible verse or singing a hymn, or the response may be as negligible as a smile or a tear. If a certain act of ministry does not evoke a visible response in the patient, try another act. Yet, remember some spiritual connections may be invisible to the human eye, but God sees beyond what we can see!

Alzheimer's ministry requires patience as you search for ways to put the spirit of these patients in touch with the Spirit of God!

Excuses

Countless excuses have been offered for not visiting Alzheimer's patients. Perhaps the most common is, "They will not know or remember I came." Granted, that may be true. However, the issue is not,

"Will the patient know you came or remember you came?" You will know—family and friends might know. Far more important, God knows.

Visits can be meaningful and appreciated even if not *remembered.* Patients can enjoy the moment you are there and *may* remember more than you realize. Seemingly insignificant visits can become treasured memories for families.

Excuses never nullify God's commands! However, legitimate reasons for not visiting Alzheimer's patients may include having (1) chronic, debilitating conditions which interfere with mobility and could cause injury and (2) contagious diseases. *Never visit when you have a contagious illness because Alzheimer's patients are highly susceptible to infections.*

Fear

Emotions can be contagious! If you are afraid, patients may become anxious. Therefore, it is important for you to confront and control your emotions rather than allow them to interfere with your ministry.

If you experience fear related to Alzheimer's ministry, determine the source. Are you afraid patients might physically hurt you? If so, take necessary precautions to try to prevent that from happening. Watch your stance and stay out of patients' range of motion. When they feel their space is invaded, they may become frightened and hit or kick.

Are you afraid you will not know what to say or do when visiting Alzheimer's patients? Many ministers are unduly concerned about *what* to say:

> ✧ I did not find that what my pastor said made that much difference in ministering to me during Mother's illness and following her death. His attitude and concern were more important. What he did rather than what he said mattered to me.

Fear of not knowing what to say or do can easily be overcome as you gain greater knowledge of the disease and how to minister to these patients. The more you visit Alzheimer's patients, the more at ease you should feel in their presence, and, hopefully, the more comfortable they will feel in your presence.

Regardless of the source of your fear, the solution is to trust God.

REACH OUT

Clergy and family members may feel awkward when taking the first step in discussing an Alzheimer's patient's illness. You may experience a dilemma about bringing up the subject because you do not want to appear confrontational nor invade the patient's and family's privacy. Lack of energy, embarrassment, depression, pride, or not knowing what to say or do may keep those affected by Alzheimer's from seeking you out. Therefore, patients and families may be without ministry during this critical time in their lives unless you (1) take the initiative and (2) teach by example.

Take the Initiative

An excellent way to initiate contact is to visit in the home. You do not have to mention "Alzheimer's disease." Still, your visit assures the patient and family of your concern and provides an opportunity for them to privately discuss the situation with you.

◇ Ministers need to take the initiative. Provide an opportunity for patients and families to express their grief and doubts. Empathize and offer reassurance of your concern, availability, and desire to help.

◇ Clergy should *always* be reaching out to family members! Ask about them and offer a listening ear. Families need encouragement, help, support, and understanding.

◇ The most meaningful thing ministers can do to help families is to let them know you care. Just be there.

Timing is an important factor for patients and families when dealing with the diagnosis. If they are not ready to discuss the illness during your first visit, continue to provide opportunities to gain their trust through more visits and telephone calls. Make yourself available to minister in ways acceptable to them and in their timing.

Teach by Example

Seeing someone minister helps motivate others. Subtle messages are given when you provide spiritual care to Alzheimer's patients and families: (1) These people and their needs are important. (2) It is all right to minister to them. (3) Let us minister together.

You must know how to share God's love with Alzheimer's patients and families before you can train others and offer guidance when problems are encountered.

ACQUIRE ADDITIONAL KNOWLEDGE

You will never "arrive" in the sense of knowing everything there is to know about Alzheimer's ministry! However, your general knowledge about the disease and ministry to one patient will help you minister to others.

Excellent ways to learn more about the illness and ministry include the following:

- Reading
- Watching TV programs and videos
- Observing patients
- Talking to family members and facility staff
- Visiting patients
- Attending and participating in support groups
- Attending seminars
- Attending seminary
- Offering church-sponsored workshops, displays, and informal discussion groups
- Presenting verbatims and case studies
- Role-playing
- Keeping an Alzheimer's ministry journal
- Relying on the Holy Spirit

Reading

Families can assist ministers in learning more about Alzheimer's disease by sharing helpful literature with them. One respondent reported thus:

✧ I gave my pastor *The 36-Hour Day.*

As a learning tool, reading is advantageous in that you can read alone and at your convenience. Only an article or book is needed. To gain more from personal reading, peers could read the same material for discussion in a group setting.

Watching TV Programs and Videos

Special television programs and news segments are aired periodically to highlight the latest information about Alzheimer's disease. You can watch TV programs and videos alone or with peers. If you listen alone, you may be able to multitask; however, a peer group enables ideas to be reinforced or clarified. Videos can be effective for educational purposes with peers and the congregation. Watching TV or a video is easier, quicker, and more enjoyable than reading a comparable amount of material.

Contact the Alzheimer's Association for information about rental videos.

Observing Patients

It is amazing what you can learn by watching a patient. Initially, observe one patient at a time. Focus on behavior, expressions, and sounds. Notice if something in the environment or within the patient seems to spark a change in behavior. Try to determine what stage of the illness the patient is experiencing.

On the same day you observe just one patient, try to gradually include other patients—especially if you are in a care facility. Watch for differences when patients are alone and in a group setting—dining room, worship service, or lobby. Observe patients you know and those you do not know, if possible. Note any differences. Also, be aware of differences in patients who are living at home and those who reside in care facilities.

You can learn much by observation when you are alone. However, you will learn more if a peer is observing the same patient(s) at the same time, and you share impressions of your observations later.

Talking to Family Members and Facility Staff

Family members are excellent teachers, as they have learned from experience and traditional methods. Spend time with them. Let them provide information about their loved one's religious preference, beliefs, and practices as well as the disease. Family members feel useful when they share their knowledge with you:

✧ Caregivers can give ministers, priests, and rabbis a wellspring of information which will not necessarily be found in books.

Family members and facility staff are your best sources for specific information about an individual patient. They can tell you when the patient is most likely to be lucid. Plan your visits accordingly and when the patient will not be eating, taking a bath, participating in activities, or sleeping.

Visiting Patients

Visitation allows you to put into practice what you have learned. There are no short-cuts. Practice, practice, and practice to become more confident and competent!

Preparation for pastoral visits begins long before you arrive at the home or care facility. It may begin as a prayer is breathed seeking the Spirit of God's guidance in knowing what to say and do. Training through seminars and instructional materials is also part of preparation. Another aspect includes locating worship aids to be utilized during the visit—Bible, hymnal, pictures, church bulletins, and other objects.

Attempt to set a positive tone for each visit. If you have any doubt the patient may not recognize you or remember you, introduce yourself. You do not want the patient to be embarrassed by not knowing who you are. Also, if the patient knows your identity, the communication may be more appropriate and you may learn more.

Make brief, but intentionally pastoral, visits. Ten-minute visits can be successful and not taxing on the patient or you. Long visits tend to agitate a patient and, ultimately, you.

For routine visitation with your parishioners who are affected by Alzheimer's, you may set aside a certain day of the week or week of the month, or you may prefer to visit one patient and family a day. Develop a visitation schedule that meets your needs as well as the needs of patients and families. As a reinforcement to stick to your plan, make a tentative standing appointment at the same time every week or month. Patients need routine and structure. Of course, crisis visitation must be done when needs arise.

If you serve in a multistaff church or health care institution, you can find a peer to visit with you from time to time. Occasionally, it would be interesting and informative to visit with a colleague of another denomination.

Pastoral visits can have unusual by-products. An example: A pastor shared his reluctance and frustration about visiting an Alzheimer's parishioner in a care facility. He wondered whether he was wasting his time until one day the patient's wife remarked, "I always know when you visit my husband." Incredibly, she *knew without being told.* Her way of knowing was he ate every bit of his lunch! What an unexpected benefit of a pastoral visit!

Alzheimer's patients teach in ways—through silence and behavior—that are not our traditional methods of learning. Immanuel—God comes to us. *Whatever happens during the visit happens—make the most of it!* The encounter is to be what God wants it to be. Ministry is not up to us—it is up to God.

Ministers, family members, and friends will find useful tips in the pamphlet *Visiting,* by the Alzheimer's Association.

Attending and Participating in Support Groups

Clergy and support groups can be mutually beneficial. Participating in a support group is an excellent way for you to learn more about the illness as well as the needs of patients and families. Occasional sessions may be held when families share meaningful ministry ideas with clergy. Periodically, a clergyperson (or panel of clergy) could speak about faith issues. Pastors can also serve as resource persons for the group:

⬧ I highly recommend ministers attend frequently to learn and share.
⬧ Clergypersons should sit in on a support group from time to time. Members "let it all hang out" and discuss lost expectations, anger, family problems, financial stresses, as well as other issues.

✧ My pastor did not know what my family and I were facing. I helped him learn more about Alzheimer's disease. We started a support group at our church.

✧ My pastor spoke at one of our support group meetings.

Attending Seminars

You may have opportunities to suggest or coordinate an Alzheimer's clergy seminar. One respondent made the following comment:

✧ I think it would be great if the Alzheimer's Association would offer special training for clergy based on suggestions from support group members.

Depending on community resources and to maintain minimal costs, the seminar might be sponsored by a local chapter of the Alzheimer's Association, a ministerial association, community colleges, day care centers, retirement homes, hospitals, and nursing facilities.

The planning committee (preferably composed of clergy, lay ministers, family members, and representatives of the Alzheimer's Association) is responsible for various decisions:

• When will the seminar be held? Date? Morning, afternoon, or evening? Month? (November is Alzheimer's Disease Awareness Month and Family Caregiver Month.)

• Where will the seminar be held? (Attendance may be better if the seminar is held at a neutral location, such as a college, civic center, or hospital, because some pastors are reluctant to attend events in churches of other denominations.)

• Who will be the speaker(s)? (Program participants should be secured several months in advance so the event can be publicized appropriately.)

• Will the seminar (or a portion) be designed for laity as well as pastors, chaplains, and pastoral counselors?

• To more fully utilize a guest speaker's expertise, will a separate seminar be held to help families deal with spiritual issues?

• What is the registration fee? Does this cost include a snack or meal? Will attendees be given a free book or other material about Alzheimer's ministry?

Try to schedule an Alzheimer's clergy seminar at least every two years because (1) ministers who have not had special training for this ministry may move into the area, and (2) ministers who have had training and experience can always learn more about the latest research and resources.

Appendix D contains a sample Alzheimer's Clergy Seminar Agenda.

Attending Seminary

Seminaries offer courses on various aspects of aging. Some classes may be designed to provide hands-on training through hospital, care facility, or in-home visitation.

If you are unable to attend formal seminary classes, perhaps you can enroll in online pastoral care courses or obtain training in other ways. Many churches provide general pastoral care training for members utilizing Stephen Ministries materials. For additional information about Stephen Ministries, see Chapter 16, "Resources."

Offering Church-Sponsored Workshops, Displays, and Informal Discussion Groups

Educational workshops, displays, and discussion groups enable clergy, congregation, family, and friends to have the same information. Sessions can cover a variety of topics based on participants' needs:

◇ A nurse spoke about Alzheimer's disease to key groups in the congregation.
◇ One week we had a display of information at the church.
◇ At regular intervals, offer sessions on grief and the grief process. People do not know in advance when this information will be needed. I am grateful I knew what to expect before the crisis of Mother's illness.

Presenting Verbatims and Case Studies

Verbatims and case studies are valuable learning tools for ministerial meetings, clergy seminars, and clinical pastoral education groups. Preparation of these documents is worth the effort because learning occurs during patient visitation, writing of the document, and discussion during the presentation.

Role-Playing

A fun way to practice what you have learned is role-playing various scenarios in a group setting. One minister plays the role of the patient, and another minister plays the pastoral role. Role-playing can be done as part of clergy seminars, ministerial meetings, or other training events. The audience discusses the effectiveness of the minister's responses. Suggestions are offered to improve future visits.

Learning with, and from, others is better than one's own reflection. When you reflect upon your visits, you may repeat ministry patterns that are not the most effective, whereas peer groups provide insights for changes in ministry.

Role-Play Scenarios for Clergy Seminars and Other Ministerial Peer Groups can be found in Appendix D.

Keeping an Alzheimer's Ministry Journal

Record your Alzheimer's ministry experiences. Take notes of visits made, articles and books read, TV programs and videos watched, seminars attended, and peer group sessions held. Indicate strengths and weaknesses of each. If you have questions, consult with another minister. Answer the self-examination questions in Chapter 4, "Theological Understanding," and Chapter 12, "Models for Ministry." Periodically, refer to these questions and discover your progress in Alzheimer's ministry!

Relying on the Holy Spirit

Let the Spirit of God help you. Ask Him to bring to your remembrance what you have learned. Pray for wisdom in knowing what to say and do. Trust Him to lead you to specific individuals in His timing. Always obey the promptings of His still, small voice.

Time and time again I walked into the "right" room at the "right" moment during a crisis situation. Who but the Holy Spirit could have so directed? It was truly phenomenal considering the hundreds of people entrusted to my spiritual care.

Therefore seeing we have this ministry, as we have received mercy, we faint not.

II Corinthians 4:1

Chapter 4

Theological Understanding

Unfortunately, many people today regard Alzheimer's patients in the same manner lepers were treated in biblical times—as outcasts having no value. When others approached lepers, they were required to yell, "Unclean!" People did not want to be near them partly because they were afraid of contracting leprosy themselves.

Although we know Alzheimer's disease is not contagious, frequently these patients are neglected or ignored by some family members, friends, health care professionals, and even ministers. Families report that such avoidance contributes to isolation and increased emotional pain:

✧ My husband and I used to attend our monthly senior group social. As his illness progressed, people started avoiding us when he did not make sense, laughed at the wrong time, or did something "normal" people do not do. It was heartbreaking. I was hurt and angry. Patients and family members do not want to be treated as though they have a contagious disease.

✧ People stop phoning and visiting. You feel so alone. We need friends and encouragement rather than the usual avoidance.

✧ Isolation is difficult for caregivers. More than anything, ministers need to care enough to be there. One's presence speaks eloquently!

✧ There is a "stigma" associated with Alzheimer's disease, but this is improving.

You can be instrumental in enabling your congregation to extend Christian love to patients and families:

✧ Urge church members to visit patients and families. We become avoided by prior friends. Caregivers suffer greatly.

✧ A cope class could help the congregation understand Alzheimer's disease and how to relate to patients. Many people withdraw instead of giving support.

✧ Please overlook and accept these broken-hearted people. Educate the congregation about ways to help and accept Alzheimer's patients. Ensure patients and families feel welcome as long as they can attend church. They will not be wanted elsewhere. To quote one minister I know, "If we cannot make them welcome, we need to close our doors."

In his excellent article "Caring for the Confused," Kevin Ruffcorn shares the transformation that occurred in himself and his ministry with Alzheimer's patients. Initially, he rationalized his neglect of visiting these people, but after some soul-searching, he decided to learn about the illness and special needs of those affected. Finally, Kevin came to see ministry as a "calling to be with people, no matter what their situation in life, and to remind them of God's loving presence."[1]

QUESTIONS FOR MINISTERS

Ask the Holy Spirit to guide you in your exploration process and reveal areas in which change is needed. Then ask Him to help you make these changes so you will be the vessel God wants you to be. Utilize the following questions in your self-examination as you reflect upon your theological understanding of God, Alzheimer's patients, Alzheimer's family members, and self as minister.

God

- Who is God to you?
- Do you believe "all things are possible with God"?
- Are you willing to be obedient to God's commands and minister to Alzheimer's patients?
- Is God able to penetrate the minds of Alzheimer's patients when your efforts seem unable to do so?
- Do you believe God can use you as His instrument to help Alzheimer's patients and families? If so, how?

- Are you willing to minister to Alzheimer's patients and trust God for the results?
- What does God teach you during each visit with an Alzheimer's patient?
- What does God teach you during each visit with an Alzheimer's family member?

Alzheimer's Patients

- How do you view Alzheimer's patients?
- Is an Alzheimer's patient "one of the least of these" to you?
- Are Alzheimer's patients important to you or do you want to ignore and neglect them?
- Do you think you are wasting your time when visiting Alzheimer's patients?
- Do you believe Alzheimer's patients are created in the image of God?
- Do you love Alzheimer's patients? If so, what is the basis of your love for them? Do you love them because of their acts or their past acts? Do you love them because of physical characteristics or past physical appearance? Do you love them because of their personality—or former personality? Do you love them because of their being? Do you love them because they are made in the image of God? Do you love them because you are commanded to do so by the Word of God? Can you love them—like God loves all of us—in spite of our acts?
- Do Alzheimer's patients need reassurance of God's love and presence? If you do not offer this reassurance, who will?
- Can you see a person behind the illness or does the illness get in your way of seeing the person?

Alzheimer's Family Members

- How do you view Alzheimer's family members?
- Are Alzheimer's family members important to you or do you want to ignore and neglect them?
- What is your attitude toward Alzheimer's family members?
- Do you grow weary of listening to Alzheimer's family members' woes?

- What kind of help do Alzheimer's family members need?
- What kind of help can you provide Alzheimer's family members?
- Have you sought to connect Alzheimer's family members with others in the congregation who can offer support, encouragement, and love?
- Do you find it easier to minister to Alzheimer's patients or family members? Why?
- What differences do you notice when ministering to Alzheimer's patients and family members?

Self As Minister

- How do you feel when you are with Alzheimer's patients? Comfortable? Uncomfortable? Afraid? Sad? Frustrated? Impatient?
- How do you feel when you are with Alzheimer's family members? Comfortable? Uncomfortable? Afraid? Sad? Frustrated? Impatient?
- If you feel uncomfortable in the presence of Alzheimer's patients or family members, what can you do to be more comfortable?
- If you are sad when you are with Alzheimer's patients or family members, what causes your sadness? What can you do to overcome your sadness?
- If you are afraid of Alzheimer's patients, what causes your fear? How can you overcome your fear?
- Do you feel "threatened" by Alzheimer's patients, thinking that some day you could have the illness?
- Would you feel comfortable if you had more experience in ministering to Alzheimer's patients and family members?
- Do you dread visiting Alzheimer's patients and family members or do you look forward to visiting them?
- Do you believe the Holy Spirit can create a desire in your heart to minister to Alzheimer's patients and family members?
- Do you believe the Holy Spirit can transform your attitude toward Alzheimer's patients and family members?
- What can you do to make Alzheimer's ministry more enjoyable?
- Are you confident in knowing what to say and do when you are in the presence of Alzheimer's patients and family members?
- Are you willing to learn more about Alzheimer's ministry by reading? Watching TV programs and videos? Observing patients?

Talking to family members and facility staff? Visiting patients? Attending and participating in support groups? Attending seminars? Attending seminary? Offering church-sponsored workshops, displays, and informal discussion groups? Presenting verbatims and case studies? Role-playing? Keeping an Alzheimer's ministry journal? Relying on the Holy Spirit?

- Would you visit with another minister and critique visits?
- What are your weaknesses in ministering to Alzheimer's patients and family members?
- What are your strengths in ministering to Alzheimer's patients and family members?
- Can you motivate and train others in your congregation to minister to Alzheimer's patients and family members?
- What differences do you notice when visiting an Alzheimer's patient you have never met and an Alzheimer's parishioner you know?
- What is your mood before, during, and after visiting Alzheimer's patients and family members?
- Can you plan to do something fun and uplifting after visiting Alzheimer's patients and family members?
- Are you faithful in visiting Alzheimer's patients and family members even when they reside in a nursing facility?

For additional information regarding theological reflection, read the article "A Model for Theological Reflection in Clinical Pastoral Education," by Joe Gross; the book *Let Ministry Teach: A Guide to Theological Reflection,* by Robert Kinast; and the book *How to Think Theologically* (Second Edition), by Howard Stone and James Duke.

Can a woman forget her sucking child, that she should not have compassion on the son of her womb? Yea, they may forget, yet will I not forget thee. Behold, I have graven thee upon the palms of my hands . . .

Isaiah 49:15-16

Chapter 5

Grief

Alzheimer's disease causes patients, families, and friends to encounter countless losses throughout the lengthy illness. Each loss is a grief experience. Patients lose their memory, abilities, skills, and functions. Family members and friends grieve the loss of hopes and dreams for their loved ones and themselves. The magnitude of grief and its impact in the lives of family members is revealed in this respondent's response:

✧ My greatest need is coping with my grief.

Due to the nature of Alzheimer's, patients may be unaware of their losses and unable to grieve these losses. However, families are fully cognizant of the losses and, generally, have the ability to express their grief. Some losses are shared by patients *and* families. Other losses are experienced by the patient *or* family.

✧ Grief is a normal reaction to loss. Therefore, family members should not feel shamed to express their grief. Do not say, "Be strong." Too many of our friends told me that for so long. I could not cry at my husband's funeral because I was "too strong." Four months after he died, I had a stress-related heart attack. One who can express emotions is much better off.

Expressions of grief may be the same or different for patient and family. Upon learning of the diagnosis, tears are a normal way to show sadness. Words may be spoken or written to convey grief. Art forms and music can be utilized to depict feelings. Patients gradually lose their ability to express grief in socially acceptable ways and may resort to inappropriate behavior, including hitting, kicking, biting, or screaming.

To help patients and families cope with grief, you must have an understanding of the (1) stages, (2) types, (3) additional grief-related issues, and (4) role of ministry.

STAGES

Dr. Elisabeth Kübler-Ross interviewed many dying patients and discovered similarities in what they suffered. In her well-known book *On Death and Dying,* she identified five stages dying patients experience—denial and isolation, anger, bargaining, depression, and acceptance. Anyone who sustains any loss will confront these stages of the grief process every time a loss occurs.

Denial and Isolation

Usually, a diagnosis of Alzheimer's does not come as a surprise because symptoms have been evident for a while; yet, confirmation of the suspicion is devastating. It is too much to absorb all at once. Time is needed to face reality:

✧ Families are in shock following the diagnosis. They do not fully understand what will happen and are overwhelmed by all that must be learned. The whole family is experiencing a crisis which may last many years.

✧ In the early stage, no one knows how confused the patient is and how stressful the situation is for the family. Patients may look and sound "normal." I received such comments as, "Your mom seems to be doing so good. I think she is better." Or, my favorite, "Are you sure she has Alzheimer's? She seems fine to me." Little do others know what is really going on! The family is in the awkward position of trying to cover up the patient's losses.

Anger

Perhaps, the most obvious and difficult stage is anger. Patients and families may feel anger in general or target their anger toward anyone who is there, anyone who is not there, and even God.

✧ I wish my priest would reassure me that it is all right when thoughts of anger arise regarding the situation. I am angry because the repetition of conversation is very trying—not at Mom. Grief never goes away.

✧ When my husband was diagnosed, I did not go to the Bible. I was mad at the world.

✧ After seven years of caring for my husband's every need, I had to place him in a nursing home. This was extremely difficult. I was depressed, suffering, and needed help. I was angry at God.

✧ Why was this happening to me? I had done nothing wrong. Why was I being punished? This was a strange feeling because deep down inside I knew God did not punish. But, I was mad at Him for a while.

Sadly, Alzheimer's patients often express anger toward those who love them most—their family. No one likes what is happening. Patients may blame family members for what is not right in their world, while families are trying desperately to do what is best for the patients.

If the patient resides in a care facility and becomes angry with a family member during a visit, the family member can calmly say, "I love you," and leave. Otherwise, an argument would likely ensue and words spoken that would be regretted. By leaving, the family member may be spared unpleasant memories, and the incident will probably be quickly forgotten by the patient. Handling anger consistently in this manner may prevent outbursts during visits. Incidentally, patients are often more pleasant to the staff and others than they are to their families.

If a fit of anger occurs in the home, the caregiver may ignore the behavior or try to focus the patient's attention on something else. Help families understand that episodes of anger are to be expected with this disease and encourage them not to take their loved ones' anger personally.

Although patients, and even families, consciously or unconsciously drive others away, this may not be what they want or need. Bitterness, hurt, and anger might be avoided, if needs are shared with the appropriate person(s) at the right time and in the right manner. You may have opportunities to direct families to resources for assistance.

Unfortunately, Alzheimer's patients and families may become angry at their pastor or other ministers for various reasons. If this happens to you, try to rectify the situation. Ask what you have done to offend, listen without being defensive, and ask forgiveness. Keep the lines of communication open. However, if your ministry is rejected in spite of your efforts, respect their right of refusal, but be available to minister later, if they desire. In the meanwhile, you may have opportunities to assist others in ministering to them.

Patients and families bear a heavy load; therefore, do not take their negative reactions personally. Hopefully, most people will forgive when we fail to say or do the "right" thing in their eyes, if we sincerely convey our concern. Never be judgmental nor speak unkindly to, or about, patients or families. Always be sensitive, patient, understanding, loving, mature, and *forgiving!* Alzheimer's patients and families need ministry too desperately to be abandoned in their time of need.

Acknowledging and dealing constructively with grief may prevent inappropriate anger later. For example, participating in a "Care Facility Memorial Service" after a loved one's death provides an opportunity to grieve among loving staff, other family members, and friends. This may circumvent feelings and expressions of anger associated with the care facility. See Appendix D for a sample Care Facility Memorial Service.

For additional information, consult the pamphlet *Feelings,* by the Alzheimer's Association; the booklet *"Hit Pause": Helping Dementia Families Deal with Anger,* by Edna Ballard; and the book *Pressure Points: Alzheimer's and Anger,* by Edna Ballard, Lisa Gwyther, and T. Patrick Toal.

Bargaining

None of the respondents reported any incidents of bargaining with God.

Depression

Due to the nature of Alzheimer's disease, depression is a common and serious problem of many patients and family members.

> ✧ When my mother was diagnosed, I was very depressed and sad. I could only talk to God.

Factors such as the disease, stress, fatigue, grief, guilt, despair, depression, lack of assistance, and feelings of hopelessness may cause patients and families to think irrationally. Murder or suicide can occur, if the proper help (counseling, "Meals on Wheels," respite, and other services) is not provided at the proper time. One family member stated he had considered murder. Another respondent replied:

> ✧ I would have blown my brains out years ago, if I had not had faith and hope.

Not only the *fact* of having Alzheimer's but also just the *fear* of having the illness can cause depression and suicide. Watch for signs of depression in patients and caregivers. Always take suicidal comments seriously. Never agree to keep this information confidential, but instead share statements with appropriate persons so help can be obtained. Acknowledge the limits of your expertise and always recommend psychological or psychiatric assistance, when warranted.

For additional information, consult the pamphlets *Depression and Alzheimer's Disease,* by the Alzheimer's Association, and *Depression: Don't Let the Blues Hang Around,* by the National Institute on Aging and National Institutes of Health.

Acceptance

To accept the diagnosis of Alzheimer's disease and resultant losses involves admitting each loss is a reality. In fact, with each loss, there is a new reality. The situation is different from the way it was—this is the way it is now. When family members accept the new reality, energy and effort are no longer expended on denial but rather can be focused on coping with the current situation.

Accepting a loss is never easy. Grieving major losses requires more time than grieving minor losses. Grief cannot be rushed and must be handled in each person's own way and timing. Accept people where they are in the grief process and minister at their point of need. Respondents offered these comments pertaining to acceptance of grief:

> ✧ Offer support at the pace of the caregiver.
> ✧ It usually takes at least a year to level out emotionally after a major grief experience.
> ✧ When my mother was diagnosed with Alzheimer's, I needed loving support as I worked through acceptance.

✧ When my wife was diagnosed, I needed to accept the "situation" and determine to live with it. Life goes on.

✧ My mother-in-law's faith helps her accept her disease. Her religious background is her greatest source of comfort. She is still active in Bible study. Her illness is part of God's plan, and He has a purpose that will be served.

Each loss needs to be fully grieved. Yet, due to concurrent losses, one loss may not be "accepted" before another loss occurs. Therefore, families can be overwhelmed by the backlog of grief in their lives:

✧ Until you experience the devastation of Alzheimer's, you cannot truly understand the frustration, weariness, loneliness, and fear it brings. When patients have Alzheimer's, you "lose" them and keep "losing" them. There is a grieving process all the time.

TYPES

Alzheimer's families experience three kinds of grief: (1) ongoing, (2) anticipatory, and (3) end point.

Ongoing

Grief occurs repeatedly for families and friends before the time of diagnosis and continues after their loved ones' death. Respondents' comments indicate ongoing grief associated with the illness is more difficult than the end point, or "final," grief associated with death:

✧ Once a clergyman spoke to our support group on the topic "grief after death." At the conclusion of his talk, he asked if there were any questions. I raised my hand and told him that I did not think he understood our situation. I stated, "I feel like my husband died years ago when he became a vegetable. I am going through my grief. Every day, when I look at my husband, I pray the Lord will be merciful and end his suffering. It is like a funeral that never ends. Death will be a relief and blessing. My grief will be brief." Everyone else in the room knew exactly what I was saying and nodded their heads. The clergyman had never looked at grief in this way before. He thanked me for letting him know what it is like to live through this endless nightmare.

✧ Every time I see my grandfather, he is slowly dying. That hurts.

✧ Families of Alzheimer's patients are devastated. Looking at our loved ones is like seeing someone who looks familiar—someone we used to know. I dealt with this for fourteen years. My husband was only fifty-three years old when he became ill.

✧ At this point, I feel like I am grave-tending. Grief has no end point.

✧ We chose to place "No Heroic Measures" on Mother's chart at the nursing facility. Her physical body remains but she has been missing a long time. The grief of losing her and loneliness exists for years.

Many non-Alzheimer's spouses feel like their lives are "on hold" for years. Although they grieve while their spouses are alive, they do not have freedom to move forward. Death brings freedom. One family member noted this distinction between ongoing and end point grief:

✧ During the illness, you lose your loved one over and over. There is somewhat of a grief process all the time. But, when death comes, you grieve and go on with your life.

Anticipatory

Families expect other losses throughout the disease process before the final loss of death occurs. No one knows when or what the next grief experience will be. Patients may have numerous infections and injuries before succumbing to death. During each episode, family members may experience one or more stages of grief. Going through the grief process repeatedly is exhausting and heartbreaking.

Patients can live many years with the illness; yet, they can die unexpectedly as a result of choking, infection, or injury. Therefore, it is difficult for families to be prepared for an imminent as well as a far-distant death of their loved ones. As much as they have prepared mentally, emotionally, physically, financially, and spiritually, when death comes, it is likely that there will be more grief than they anticipated:

✧ I have never talked to my minister about my mother's death. I guess I try not to think about it. But, I truly feel I will not cry at her funeral because I have cried so often at each loss through the years. There should not be any tears left, but I know I will shed some.

✧ There will be no grief process when my mother dies. She is "still alive" but is also dead now. I am just waiting for the funeral. Sadistic? No! I am just facing reality and being truthful.

✧ My mother-in-law is in a nursing home because my father-in-law can no longer care for her at home. She requires feeding, uses a wheelchair, responds very little to her environment, and is incontinent. My wife says, in many respects, the mother she has known and loved has died. So, some of her grief work is past. Yet, there is still much sorrow about the situation and the toll it is taking on her father.

End Point

Death of their loved ones represents the "final" grief experience families face in the Alzheimer's journey. That finality brings mixed emotions and many adjustments:

✧ Most families feel grief and relief when loved ones with Alzheimer's die because we know firsthand how great the loss of self is. I will be sad, but I shall also find joy in the fact that Mother's illness is over. I will remember the days before Alzheimer's.
✧ After ten years, you are glad for death to come.
✧ I will not grieve too much when my wife dies because I know she will be better off. I will be suffering mostly from loneliness.

Respondents, whose loved ones have died, shared these comments:

✧ I had pretty well finished my grieving by the time my wife died.
✧ Now that Mother has died, I feel sad. Yet, I am glad she is at last at peace.
✧ Spiritually and emotionally, I felt like I was on a roller coaster. I was happy and excited when my husband had a few lucid days, but drastically depressed when he became disoriented and forgetful. Death brought relief from the roller coaster feeling and worry. My emotions are leveled out, and I remember the good times.

ADDITIONAL GRIEF-RELATED ISSUES

Other issues related to grief and the Alzheimer's situation include (1) family members in different stages, (2) job loss of patients or family members, (3) patients' inability to recognize loved ones, (4) loss of routine for family members, and (5) grief of clergy.

Family Members in Different Stages

Ministry is further complicated by the fact that family members may be in different stages of grief at any time—especially when dealing with several losses concurrently.

The following quote illustrates a husband's denial of his wife's need for constant supervision and his daughter's realization or acceptance that her mother could not be left alone safely:

> ✧ Fighting with Dad over Mother's inability to stay by herself was very hard. My minister, doctor, and social worker were unable to help. This has since been resolved due to her worsening condition.

The following response indicates a wife's acceptance of her husband's approaching death, while other family members have not reached that point:

> ✧ I wanted my minister to support my decision not to have a feeding tube inserted in my husband nor to place him on a respirator in spite of other family members' opposition.

Job Loss of Patients or Family Members

If Alzheimer's patients have not retired before the illness takes its toll, likely they will become unable to perform the necessary tasks required for employment. Also, one or more family members may decide to quit a job in order to provide more extensive care for the patient.

Adjustments must be made when either the patient or a family member is no longer employed. Losing a job is a significant loss. Many people tend to equate their self-worth with what they do. Job loss includes other losses as well, such as the loss of socialization with co-workers, loss of income, and loss of an established routine.

Employers should sensitively handle situations when patients are unable to carry out their job responsibilities. If a patient is "forced" to retire or is fired, embarrassment and depression may result, compounding the feelings associated with the loss of a job. When termination is necessary, family members can play a key role by supporting the employer yet nurturing the patient.

The task and timing of getting a self-employed patient to retire is often relegated to family members. The wife of one patient shared:

✧ My husband was a physician. One of the most difficult decisions I faced was getting him out of the practice of medicine.

Patients' Inability to Recognize Loved Ones

Perhaps the saddest loss for families is when their loved ones no longer recognize them. This loss represents other losses as well—loss of memories, loss of associations, and loss of the ability to express love. Patients have nothing to build on—no past recollections. Therefore, family members are like strangers. Families often sacrificially express their love to patients through words and deeds, even though that love cannot be reciprocated.

Loss of Routine for Family Members

Families likely developed a routine during their loved one's illness. If the patient resided in a care facility, certain hours of the day and days of the weeks may have been devoted to visiting. Following the loved one's death, there will be a void during those particular times:

✧ In the days following the funeral, help families adjust to the void and loneliness after total caregiving. Ask periodically, "How are you adjusting?" Be sensitive and express love. Stay in touch to see whether anything is needed. Respect family's need to grieve but also encourage participation in activities.

Grief of Clergy

You need to acknowledge that you, too, grieve in the course of ministering to Alzheimer's patients and families. Because of the length and depth of this ministry, you may feel like you are part of the family. Take care of yourself and find ways to grieve appropriately. The husband of an Alzheimer's patient offered this wise counsel for pastors:

✧ Be yourself. Show empathy, not sympathy. You are human and hurt, too, when something happens to a member of your congregation.

ROLE OF MINISTRY

Ways you can help with grief issues include the following:

✧ Visitation.
✧ Be there to listen to feelings of anger, sadness, and fear. Alzheimer's is drawn out, sad, and frustrating. What can anyone say except, "I am sorry"?
✧ Be knowledgeable of the grief process and available to discuss it.
✧ Prepare families for the wide range of emotions and mood swings they will experience related to Alzheimer's and caregiving. Reassure them that loss, anger, and confusion are normal.
✧ Present educational programs at regular intervals on the topic "understanding the grief process." So, as I go through it, I will know I am not losing my mind, too.
✧ Offer spiritual support by reading scriptures related to grief, praying, and encouraging a positive representation of the church family.

For additional information, consult the pamphlet *Grief, Mourning, and Guilt,* by the Alzheimer's Association.

Blessed are they that mourn: for they shall be comforted.

Matthew 5:4

Chapter 6

Guilt

Alzheimer's patients probably do not feel much, if any, guilt during their illness. Even if they do, it is unlikely they would be able to sufficiently formulate their thoughts and words to express these feelings. But, feelings of guilt can be a constant companion of family members, if not dealt with in God's way.

To help families deal with issues of guilt, you must have an understanding of the (1) purpose, (2) types, (3) situations which may cause families to feel guilt, (4) prevention, (5) additional guilt-related issues, and (6) the role of ministry.

PURPOSE

Frequently, guilt is portrayed with negative connotations; however, it actually serves a positive purpose—to lead to confession, repentance, and forgiveness. Guilt is a unique bad feeling that is difficult to describe but is universally known. No one wants to feel, nor be, guilty. Yet, guilt is the Holy Spirit's way of convicting a person of sin (John 16:8). When someone is guilty of sin, that person needs to confess, repent, and seek forgiveness from the person sinned against and from God. Without guilt, there can be no forgiveness. And, ironically, forgiveness is what absolves a person of guilt. A forgiven person is no longer guilty in God's eyes—the albatross has been lifted. It is as though the sin never occurred. When God declares a person "not guilty," that person is truly "not guilty" indeed.

TYPES

Perhaps it is conceivable that people can feel guilty without being guilty. There may be times you will need to help families distinguish between the two types of guilt: (1) false and (2) real.

False

Wrongdoing does not occur with false guilt. Therefore, as sin was not committed, forgiveness is not needed and cannot be given nor received.

Real

When a person sins, guilt is real. As previously mentioned, God's remedy for guilt is forgiveness.

SITUATIONS THAT MAY CAUSE FAMILIES TO FEEL GUILT

It would be impossible to list every situation about which Alzheimer's family members could feel, or be, guilty. Common situations that often involve guilt feelings include the following:

1. Diagnosis
2. Expression of negative emotions toward the patient
3. Nursing facility placement of the patient
4. Not visiting the patient more in the care facility
5. Not being present when the patient experienced a tragedy
6. Making health care decisions for the patient
7. Relief regarding the patient's death

Diagnosis

A few family members feel guilty because their loved one developed Alzheimer's disease. They want reassurance they did not cause it and could not have prevented it:

◇ Following my mother's diagnosis, I wish my minister had told me there was nothing I could have done to prevent her from having it.

◇ As a result of my mother's illness, I have experienced guilt, anger, frustration, and hopelessness.

Expression of Negative Emotions Toward the Patient

Due to resultant behavior from patients' memory loss, families frequently feel frustrated, impatient, and angry. One respondent stated thus:

◇ My greatest need is to have patience with my mother-in-law because of her forgetfulness, repetitious questions, and misplaced items.

Although negative feelings are about the illness and situation, they may be expressed toward the patient. Sadly, verbal and physical abuse may occur. Then family members feel guilty for their "out-of-control" emotions and behavior.

Caregivers are human and have limits to what they can tolerate. Respite care is desperately needed to help them cope with the intensity of the situation. To prevent patient abuse, caregivers must take care of themselves physically, emotionally, and spiritually.

Nursing Facility Placement of the Patient

Various living arrangements may be necessary throughout the illness. When a patient can no longer live alone safely, a family member or paid caregiver may move into the patient's house, or the patient may move into a family member's house or care facility. In many cases, the initial care facility could be an assisted living center or adult foster care home that provides minimal supervision.

Guilt associated with placing a loved one in an assisted living center or adult foster home may not be as intense because patients' losses are not as severe as those necessitating nursing facility care.

Although a nursing facility is often a "last resort" care option, families frequently report feeling guilty about their loved ones' placement. Respondents shared these comments:

✧ Placing my husband in the nursing home was another step in losing him. I knew he would never return home. Guilt is a common emotion when placing a loved one in a facility. I think those who have strained themselves to the maximum physically and emotionally need to know they have no reason to feel guilty.

✧ Most people feel a sense of guilt over nursing home placement even though they know it is necessary. Ministers can reassure families it is the best, or only, thing they can do and help them not have guilt feelings.

✧ When I placed my husband in a nursing home, my pastor supported me. He knew what was going on. I did not feel guilty. Clergy need to keep in touch and be aware of what is happening in the lives of the entire family.

While guilt is commonly associated with nursing facility placement, perhaps the feelings actually are sadness and a sense of failure rather than real guilt. Family members are sad when they are unable to live up to their superhuman expectations of providing care for their loved one at home indefinitely.

For more information, see Nursing Facility Placement (under Common Ethical Dilemmas) in Chapter 11, "Ethical Issues."

Not Visiting the Patient More in the Care Facility

Families need to understand and honor God-given priorities in relationships. The primary earthly relationship is that between husband and wife (Genesis 2:24). A spouse is to put the needs of the other above those of parents and children. If the primary relationship is not honored, life can get out of balance. Resentment and other problems can develop. Time and energy must be shared within the family circle. Hopefully, when crises occur, everyone will work cooperatively to do what needs to be done.

While the quality of time spent with the patient may outweigh the quantity, perhaps *love* is the issue rather than *time.* Pursuing outside interests may enable time spent together to be more enjoyable. Love endures whether in the presence or absence of those loved, and it does not mandate family members spend every waking moment in the care facility:

✧ I feel guilt from anger, misunderstanding progression of the disease, and not being with Mother as much as she wants. It is difficult to do something for myself without feeling guilty since I am not giving all my free time to Mom.

Not Being Present When the Patient Experienced a Tragedy

Family members may feel guilty if they were not there when their loved one became ill, had an accident, or died. It is easy to blame someone—even oneself—when a tragedy occurs. People sometimes erroneously think nothing bad will happen if they are there. Granted, being with a patient at the right moment may prevent an accident, at times. However, stress, fatigue, lack of sleep, and depression can cause families to have irrational thoughts and focus on guilt feelings rather than realistically seeing the situation. A loved one can become ill, have an accident, or die while family members are standing by the bedside at home or in a care facility.

Making Health Care Decisions for the Patient

If the patient did not make health care decisions before being diagnosed with Alzheimer's, family members may be left to guess what would have been desired. Often, such decisions must be made quickly while under duress. Since no one can foresee the outcome of surgery, life support, or other medical procedures and treatments, family members could feel guilty if the results are not favorable.

The best scenario is for the patient, prior to the time of need, to make health care decisions based on the teachings of God's Word. If an Advance Directive is signed, emotional trauma related to making these decisions would likely be eliminated for family members. Families and physicians would know in advance the type of care and treatments desired by the patient.

A Declaration of Freedom from Guilt form is contained in Appendix D. Clergy can encourage parishioners to sign this tangible document indicating they do not want their loved ones to feel guilty about health care decisions made on their behalf.

Relief Regarding the Patient's Death

You can help family members realize death is not the worst thing that can happen to a Christian. In fact, it is the best thing. Death ushers a Christian into God's presence forever. In heaven there will be "no more death, neither sorrow, nor crying, neither shall there be any more pain" (Revelation 21:4).

> ✧ My mother's death will be a relief to me. But, I will have to deal with guilt about my relief.
> ✧ We may feel grief and relief when our loved ones die. I think we must be able to express this, know it is normal, and not feel guilty.

PREVENTION

Caring for a loved one who has Alzheimer's disease is difficult enough without the burden of guilt. Therefore, preventing guilt is far better than having it and having to deal with it. When guilt can be avoided, family members have more energy to focus on important tasks at hand.

In a nutshell, the only way to prevent guilt is to live in accordance with biblical teachings. To obey God's Word, family members must know what it says and means. Sermons, Bible studies, counseling, scripture reading, and prayer can assist with this.

Countless teachings could be discussed in light of Alzheimer's families and guilt. However, two specific and significant areas in which families can spare themselves guilt feelings are (1) telling the truth and (2) expressing love while the patient is living.

Telling the Truth

Not only to avoid guilt, but also primarily to obey God, family members should be careful that every word they speak is truthful. However, they do not have to tell the *whole* truth—just enough to answer patients' questions. Families need to anticipate questions and be prepared to respond. If unable to think of a truthful response, they can remain silent or turn the question back to the patient, "What do you think?" Such approaches are better than giving an untruthful answer that would be regretted.

Two common situations in which families may be tempted to be untruthful include (1) nursing facility placement of the patient and (2) death of a relative.

Nursing Facility Placement of the Patient

Promises should never be made to keep loved ones out of a nursing facility. No one can know what unforeseen circumstances are ahead. If a loved one must be placed in a nursing home, in spite of promises to the contrary, the person who made the promise will feel, and be, guilty of telling an untruth. Forgiveness must be sought by the one who was promised and by God.

Families find it traumatic to place their loved ones in a nursing facility. Out of their own denial, they may be tempted to say the facility is another hospital or anything but a nursing facility. However, there are two factors in families' favor when their loved ones have to go to a nursing facility: (1) many Alzheimer's patients are disoriented with regard to places by the time nursing facility care is needed, and (2) patients often adjust to care facilities better and more quickly than do families.

After admission to a nursing facility, residents commonly will plead, "I want to go home." Fortunately, these words may neither be understood by patients as we understand them nor be intended to mean their literal residence before placement. I once heard about an Alzheimer's patient who said he wanted to go home when he was at home on a visit from the nursing facility.

These emotionally charged words—"I want to go home"—are difficult for families to hear when they are already upset about placement. Naturally, they wish their loved ones could be home, too. Yet, family members realize their loved ones need nursing care, whereas patients do not rationally understand this need. Families must anticipate what to say when their loved ones say they want to go home. Responses should be short, firm, nondefensive, nonargumentative, and as unemotional as possible. Such a response might be, "That is what I want, too." Be prepared to discuss a pleasant subject quickly.

Death of a Relative

As the illness progresses, patients may become agitated and cry because they think a loved one *just* died—not realizing the death occurred a long time ago. Again, families need to anticipate what to say. A rational reply stating the person died many years ago will not satisfy, but the patient may find it calming and reassuring to talk about the person.

When a death does occur in the family, surviving family members have a choice of telling the patient or withholding this information. Certain factors need to be taken into consideration: How often did the patient see the deceased? Will the patient miss the deceased? If so, for how long? Will the death affect the patient? If so, how? If the patient asks about the deceased later, how will the situation be handled?

Generally, it is probably best to tell patients about deaths of close relatives or friends because (1) they may accept the news better than anticipated, (2) the whole family can openly support one another, and (3) there will be no guilt as a result of not informing them.

If the patient is able and wants to go to the funeral home to view the body of the deceased, I suggest a private viewing for the patient and a few close family members. A public viewing can be held during other hours. Attending a funeral would likely be too confusing, emotional, and upsetting, especially if the patient is in the later stages of the illness.

Even if patients are told of deaths and view the bodies, they may not remember. That is all right. At least the family did what they could and will have no guilt from hiding the truth.

Expressing Love While the Patient Is Living

To faithfully love and express that love while the patient is living helps family members avoid regrets and, ultimately, guilt following the death. It is a good feeling to remember, and be reassured, that all was done that could realistically be done while there was an opportunity.

ADDITIONAL GUILT-RELATED ISSUES

Other issues pertaining to guilt and the Alzheimer's experience include (1) motivation for visits, (2) past sins, (3) colluding on untruths, and (4) reassurance from clergy.

Motivation for Visits

Motives and attitudes are easily detected. Patients and families want visitors who want to visit. One respondent offered advice regarding this aspect of guilt:

✧ Get caring visitors—not ones who are visiting just to keep from feeling guilty.

Past Sins

God can use Alzheimer's to cause family members to remember sins committed against the patient and others in the past. Remembrance of a sin that has not been thought about in years may surface. This is a God-given opportunity for family members to seek forgiveness and be relieved of the burden of guilt:

✧ I have guilt because I was a workaholic in my early years. I regret not spending more time with my wife and children back then.

If family members sinned against the patient and have not asked for forgiveness, they should do so to absolve their guilt. The response of the patient does not matter. In fact, the patient may not be able to respond verbally.

Colluding on Untruths

In desperation, some family members may ask you to join them in their scheme to be untruthful. This is an indication they have not accepted the situation. *Never agree to tell patients untruths!* Instead, prayerfully and sensitively help family members deal with their denial. "Honesty is the best policy" because there is no guilt when the truth is told.

Reassurance from Clergy

Especially with issues of grief, guilt, and ethical decisions, the "authority" of the clergy may come to the forefront. Families tend to believe what their clergyperson says. One respondent stated thus:

✧ You trust your pastor.

You may encounter family members who have difficulty forgiving themselves, perhaps even after God has forgiven them. Pray with them and share scriptures pertinent to assurance of God's forgiveness.

Families often want reassurance from their pastor that what they are doing or have done is right. They want their minister to say what they want to hear:

✧ I would like reassurance from my pastor that I have nothing to feel guilty about.
✧ I have done my best and so has my husband.

Always be truthful and uphold biblical principles. When family members disagree about decisions to be made for their loved one, you will not always be able to say what each one wants to hear. Still, you can be instrumental in helping the family make decisions that can be lived with *without guilt.*

ROLE OF MINISTRY

You can help families deal with guilt through the following ways:

✧ Listen to expressions of guilt feelings.
✧ Through counseling, help us "let go" and deal with the terrible guilt.
✧ Preach sermons on guilt, anger, and fear.

• Present seminars and Bible studies on the topics of guilt and forgiveness.
• Assist in exploring options for loved ones.
• Help family members seek forgiveness from those sinned against, themselves, and God.

- Offer to go with family members to visit their loved one in the nursing facility, if they are not visiting.
- Present seminars with physicians and attorneys to help parishioners make health care decisions prior to need.

May love—not guilt—serve as the motivation of all ministries to Alzheimer's patients and families!

For additional information, see the pamphlet *Grief, Mourning, and Guilt,* by the Alzheimer's Association.

For if ye forgive men their trespasses, your heavenly Father will also forgive you: But if ye forgive not men their trespasses, neither will your Father forgive your trespasses.

Matthew 6:14-15

Chapter 7

Alzheimer's Patients
and Communication

Christ's death made it possible for everyone to have relationship and fellowship with God. When a person confesses sins, seeks forgiveness, repents, and trusts Christ as Savior, relationship or "connection" with God originates.

As long as faith can be expressed by attending worship services, praying, reading the Bible, meditating, singing, marveling at God's creation, finding meaning and purpose in life, and living a life devoted to Christ, ministry is relatively easy. However, if Alzheimer's strikes, patients lose their ability to use and comprehend words.

Various changes regarding verbal disability are evident throughout the disease process. Initially, patients may be unable to think of the word or name they want to say, or they may use a certain word when they intend to use the opposite word (e.g., "yes" for "no" or vice versa). They may invent words. Gradually, patients reach a point when they do not initiate conversation but simply reply when someone speaks to them. Ultimately, they become withdrawn and say little, if anything.

Therefore, as the disease takes its toll, ministers face a *real* challenge in communicating with these patients to nurture their faith connection. To meet this challenge, you must have an understanding of (1) the importance of communicating with Alzheimer's patients, (2) differences in communicating with Alzheimer's patients and other patients, (3) validation therapy versus reality orientation, (4) how to help Alzheimer's patients communicate, (5) how to communicate with Alzheimer's patients, and (6) additional communication-related issues.

IMPORTANCE OF COMMUNICATING
WITH ALZHEIMER'S PATIENTS

Because Christians are entrusted with the responsibility of sharing the greatest message on earth, you must do everything possible to ensure the message is not only sent but also received. The gospel of evangelism is "God loves you so much that He sent His Son, Jesus Christ, to die on the Cross to pay the penalty for your sins. Forgiveness is available by confession of sin, repentance, and trusting Christ." The gospel of spiritual care for those who have trusted Christ as their Savior is "God loves you and is with you at all times."

DIFFERENCES IN COMMUNICATING
WITH ALZHEIMER'S PATIENTS
AND OTHER PATIENTS

Most patients can relate their experiences using spoken or written words, but Alzheimer's patients become unable to convey to others what it is like to have this disease. In the severe stage of the illness, it may seem patients speak a different language than we do on our way to finding a common language. We even tend to impose on them what we think their situation is like and how we ought to respond. Yet, their stories or vignettes are theirs regardless of the veracity from our perspective.

Encourage patients in their role as teacher. Never stifle their communication by ignoring them or correcting what they say. Focus on patients' strengths and all they have remaining rather than their losses. Expect to learn from every encounter you have with them.

Because Alzheimer's patients have difficulty using and understanding words, it will take time, patience, and a lot of practice to make necessary adjustments to communicate effectively with them. But remember, communication with Alzheimer's patients is possible even though you have to search for effective methods.

Thomas St. James O'Connor offers these suggestions for ministering to Alzheimer's patients:

> Another way of thinking, relating, and using religious symbols is required when ministering to these patients. A gentle touch

may evoke more response than words. Attempt to find meaning in gesture and gibberish. Traditional religious symbols that can be touched, seen, heard, or smelled might trigger spiritual memories or associations. If a patient sees someone wearing a clerical collar or cross, he or she may think of a preacher or God's representative. Pictures and object lessons are excellent aids when presenting Biblical truths. Patients may still be able to recite familiar prayers and sing well-known hymns. Ministry is in the "here and now" because visits will likely not be remembered. Therefore, a long-term pastoral relationship is needed involving presence and being, not progress or change.[1]

A fun and beneficial exercise is to practice communication skills with fellow ministers. At first, your attempts may seem awkward and require concentration, but, in time, changes in communication necessitated by Alzheimer's should become natural and automatic.

When conveying messages to Alzheimer's patients, (1) focus on nonverbal communication, (2) use the familiar and original, and (3) delay notification of forthcoming events.

Focus on Nonverbal Communication

You are accustomed to ministering to people who can understand and remember you and your spoken words. Verbal communication involves the use of words in conveying the message and is an easy form of communication for most people.

However, because of the nature of Alzheimer's disease, patients may not remember you, much less your words. Therefore, nonverbal communication—body language, tone of voice, and gestures—is often more effective when sending messages, especially if patients are in the later stages of the illness.

Interactions between you and patients may involve verbal and nonverbal communication. When you supplement words with nonverbal cues, be sure these cues support your spoken words. Verbal and nonverbal messages should be congruent rather than conflicting.

An example of appropriately combining verbal and nonverbal communication is to close your eyes, bow your head, fold your hands, and kneel while praying aloud. These gestures reinforce the fact that you are praying.

Constantly seek similar ways to incorporate nonverbal cues into your conversations with Alzheimer's patients to give them additional clues for understanding your words.

Use the Familiar and Original

Since Alzheimer's patients have short-term memory loss, they are more likely to recall and understand what was learned long ago rather than recently. When reading or quoting scripture, use the King James Version due to its familiarity because modern versions and paraphrases may not be recognized as the Bible. Similarly, if a patient embraced more than one faith tradition, use the symbols and practices of the original tradition. Likewise, if a patient spoke more than one language, try to find someone who speaks the original language and can interpret.

Even use a patient's most familiar name. An example: I once addressed a newly admitted resident on the Alzheimer's and Related Disorders Unit by her surname. She acted as though I had not spoken to her. When I used her first name, she immediately knew I was talking to her and responded. Later, I learned she had been married twice. That meant she had had three last names including her maiden name. No doubt she had forgotten her most recent surname. Naturally, she was more apt to remember her first name because she had had it all of her life. Addressing elderly patients by their first names may seem disrespectful; however, the advantage potentially gained in eliciting a response will compensate for poor etiquette.

Delay Notification of Forthcoming Events

Generally, most people find it beneficial to plan ahead, but since Alzheimer's patients have little, or no, conception of time, it is wise to wait as long as possible to inform them of church attendance, physician appointments, activities of daily living, nursing facility placement, or even visitors who are planning to come. Otherwise, they may become upset because they do not understand what is to happen or when. If they are told of approaching events in advance, they will probably not remember anyway. Additional turmoil, agitation, and confusion can be spared by telling them only once and delaying this notification.

VALIDATION THERAPY
VERSUS REALITY ORIENTATION

Two major techniques have been used to communicate with Alzheimer's patients: (1) validation therapy and (2) reality orientation. Validation therapy is often more effective in communicating with Alzheimer's patients than is reality orientation. When reality orientation is used, it is wise for ministers to supply information rather than ask questions. Patients are unable to enter our "reality"; therefore, we must try to see the world from their viewpoint as best we can. Attempt to understand why they are saying and doing what they are—look for hidden meaning in behavior. Validate them and their reality without arguing or correcting. When patients are understood, accepted, and validated, the potential exists for positive behavioral changes.[2]

For additional insight, read the chapter "A Practical Theological Model for Worship with Alzheimer's Patients: Using the Validation Technique," by Dee Ann Klapp, in the book *Practical Theology for Aging*.

HOW TO HELP ALZHEIMER'S
PATIENTS COMMUNICATE

Witness in the Christian community involves telling what happened or relating experiences of faith. Although Alzheimer's patients may be unable to verbally explain an encounter with their living Lord, a smile, nod, tear, or twinkle in the eye can be revealing. Just because these faith experiences cannot be articulated, it does not mean they do not, and cannot, occur at every stage of the disease. After all, words are inadequate to articulate "holy moments" that transpire between anyone and God. Isn't that characteristic of faith? Faith cannot be explained or rationalized and is a personal, private journey for many people.

Trying to understand what patients are attempting to communicate may seem like a game of charades. Although you may not always comprehend their words, take time to listen. Learn as much as you can from others about their work history, family, interests, and spiritual preferences. Use this knowledge as clues for what is lacking in their communication efforts. Be a good detective. Mentally fill in the gaps as best you can. Are their words and behavior communicating something about their work history? Family? Other interests? Physical needs? Spiritual needs?

It is amazing what patients communicate through their words, behavior, and even silence:

✧ Listen—even to unspoken words.

The Alzheimer's Association offers these suggestions for ways you can help patients communicate:

- Be patient and supportive.
- Show your interest.
- Offer comfort and reassurance.
- Give the person time.
- Avoid criticizing or correcting.
- Avoid arguing.
- Offer a guess.
- Encourage unspoken communication.
- Limit distractions.
- Focus on the feelings, not the facts.[3]

HOW TO COMMUNICATE
WITH ALZHEIMER'S PATIENTS

When you send a message to Alzheimer's patients, you want a response. What you say and do will likely affect patients' responses.

Think in terms of "effective" or "ineffective" communication rather than "right" or "wrong." If your words or actions are effective, you are more likely to elicit a desirable response. However, if your words or actions are ineffective, the outcome probably will not be what you want. So, carefully plan what you say and do in an attempt to receive the response you want. Practice to improve your communication skills, remembering to adjust for individual differences of Alzheimer's patients.

The Alzheimer's Association also offers these suggestions for ways you can help patients understand what you are communicating:

- Identify yourself.
- Call the person by name.
- Use short, simple words and sentences.
- Talk slowly and clearly.
- Give one-step directions.
- Ask one question at a time.
- Patiently wait for a response.
- Repeat information or questions.
- Turn questions into answers.
- Avoid confusing expressions.
- Avoid vague words.
- Emphasize key words.
- Turn negatives into positives.
- Give visual cues.
- Avoid quizzing.
- Give simple explanations.
- Write things down.
- Treat the person with dignity and respect.
- Be aware of your tone of voice.
- Pay special attention to your body language.[4]

ADDITIONAL COMMUNICATION-RELATED ISSUES

Since Alzheimer's disease primarily affects the elderly, many patients have auditory and visual problems that compound the challenge of communicating with them.

Auditory Impairment

For hearing-impaired Alzheimer's patients, the Alzheimer's Association makes the following recommendations:

- Approach the person from the front.
- Stand directly in front of the person when speaking to him or her.
- Get the person's attention by saying his or her name, and give a gentle touch.
- Speak slowly and clearly.
- Use a lower tone of voice.
- Use unspoken communication like pointing, gesturing or touch.

- Write things down, if needed.
- If he or she has a hearing aid, encourage the person to wear it; check the battery often.[5]

Visual Impairment

For visually impaired Alzheimer's patients, the Alzheimer's Association offers the following tips for helping you communicate:

- Avoid startling the person.
- Don't make loud noises or sudden movements.
- Identify yourself as you approach the person.
- Tell the person of your intentions before you begin.
- Use large-print or audiotape materials, if available.
- If he or she has glasses, encourage the person to wear them; keep them clean and have the prescription checked regularly.[6]

For additional information about communicating with Alzheimer's patients, consult the article "Communication Strategies to Promote Spiritual Well-Being Among People with Dementia," by Ellen Ryan, Lori Martin, and Amanda Beaman.

Go ye therefore, and teach all nations, baptizing them in the name of the Father, and of the Son, and of the Holy Ghost: Teaching them to observe all things whatsoever I have commanded you: and lo, I am with you always, even unto the end of the world. Amen.

Matthew 28:19-20

Chapter 8

Alzheimer's Ministry Coordinator

An Alzheimer's ministry program may be meager or quite comprehensive. Much can be done for patients and families with minimal effort and expense. New ministries can be implemented, and existing ones expanded as needed. Ministries will depend on patients' and families' needs as well as resources within the congregation.

Ideally, each congregation will have an Alzheimer's ministry coordinator. Otherwise, the needs of the patients may not be met or may be met haphazardly, at best. Ministerial staff or a volunteer can serve in this capacity.

Preferably, the Alzheimer's ministry coordinator will be someone who had a loved one die *with* the disease:

✧ Anyone who has suffered personally is best equipped to reach out and practice the "art" of Christian love.

To share your congregation's Alzheimer's ministry program with patients and families, you must have an exhaustive understanding of (1) the role, (2) responsibilities, and (3) record-keeping of the Alzheimer's ministry coordinator as well as additional ministry-related issues.

ROLE

Alzheimer's ministry is a team effort. Hopefully, as many congregants as possible will share their gifts, skills, talents, and abilities with patients and families. The size of the congregation and doctrinal beliefs of the denomination partially determine which ministries will be performed by clergy or church members. Administering ordinances of baptism and communion are traditionally assigned to clergy in certain denominations as well as preaching, counseling, and officiating at funerals. Clergy and congregation can be involved in listening, telephoning, praying, pastoral visitation, sharing scriptures, presenting educational seminars, and sending cards.

For the program to function smoothly, one person must organize and coordinate ministries:

⬦ Enlist a volunteer within the church to coordinate help from the congregation.
⬦ Determine how many Alzheimer's patients are in the congregation. Find out what type of help is needed for each patient and family. Seek to provide it, if possible. Otherwise, direct them to appropriate resources.
⬦ Encourage a network of caring individuals who can share in this ministry.

RESPONSIBILITIES

The number of people affected by Alzheimer's within the congregation, needs of patients and families, gifts and abilities of the pastor and pastoral volunteers, and time restraints will influence the responsibilities of the Alzheimer's ministry coordinator, which might include the following:

- Conducting an annual survey of the congregation to find volunteers who are willing to assist with specific ministries, such as visiting in the home or care facility, telephoning, sending cards, cooking and serving meals in the home (monthly), making minor home repairs, providing respite care, mowing the lawn, running errands, and providing transportation.
- Serving as contact person for patients or families to notify when needs arise.
- Organizing visitation and respite programs.
- Arranging weekly contact with caregivers to afford them an opportunity to ventilate.
- Serving as the liaison between pastor and volunteers.
- Serving as the liaison between patients or families and volunteers.

- Assisting the pastor in training volunteers to make pastoral visits.
- Teaching volunteers how to write spiritual assessments, spiritual care goals, and spiritual care plans.
- Maintaining close contact with volunteers to offer suggestions or assistance.
- Making occasional visits with volunteers to lend support and encouragement.
- Tallying volunteers' monthly patient and family ministry reports.
- Notifying pastor of crisis needs and other pertinent information reported by volunteers.
- Activating church committees—benevolence, bereavement, and prayer chain—as needed.
- Conducting quarterly Alzheimer's ministry sessions with the pastor and volunteers.

RECORD-KEEPING

The purpose of maintaining records is to enable the Alzheimer's coordinator, pastor, and pastoral volunteers to know what ministries have been, are being, and will be performed for specific patients and family members. Keeping records should be as effortless as possible, yet serve this purpose.

During the initial visit following diagnosis, the pastor should

- inform the patient and family of the church's Alzheimer's ministry program, including the responsibilities of the coordinator and volunteer services available;
- offer to make arrangements for the coordinator to visit;
- request permission to share pertinent information with the coordinator and pastoral volunteers so ministry may be as comprehensive as possible;
- discuss details regarding information to be shared and, specifically, with whom; and
- obtain the patient's spiritual history.

Initial records may be quite intensive; however, subsequent records will be less involved. The pastor will develop a plan for future ministry including a spiritual history, spiritual assessment, spiritual care goals, and spiritual care plan based on information gained during the visit. Rely on family members to supply facts, if the patient is unable to do so. Additional information will be added as the pastor and volunteers learn more during subsequent visits. Patient's spiritual history will assist in personalized pastoral care as well as provide insight for a meaningful funeral service.

Spiritual assessments are based on the patient's spiritual history and current needs. Assessments, goals, and care plans will change as needs necessitate. After each visit, the pastor or volunteer should make an assessment, list goals, and develop a plan for meeting goals during the next visit. Many spiritual needs are ongoing; however, at times, certain needs are more prominent. Ministers must be intentional in identifying needs before formulating goals and implementing a care plan. More than one goal can be met during a visit. Reports of volunteer visits will be given to the coordinator and shared with the pastor.

Record-keeping helps ensure accountability even though the coordinator will not know of all contacts, particularly those made by persons outside the congregation. Care facility chaplains should maintain similar records.

Records should be kept on each patient who receives ministry from the church or care facility and stored in a locked drawer or cabinet. Since these records may be subpoenaed for court, nothing should be written that would be inappropriate for public documents.

Everyone who provides Alzheimer's ministry must maintain patients' and families' rights to confidentiality and never betray their trust.

See Appendix D for samples of a Pastoral Volunteer Agreement, a monthly Alzheimer's Ministry Report, and a Case Study illustrating the use of a spiritual history, spiritual assessment, spiritual care goals, and spiritual care plan.

ADDITIONAL MINISTRY-RELATED ISSUES

Other issues related to Alzheimer's ministry include (1) expectations of ministry, (2) response to ministry, (3) health care ministry, and (4) spiritual needs.

Expectations of Ministry

Patients, families, and ministers may have unrealistic expectations of what can be accomplished through spiritual care. Patients and families want a cure for the disease. Clergy tend to want to "fix" people or things and make everybody happy. Alzheimer's disease cannot be "fixed." It must be lived with and through. Therefore, the goal of ministers cannot be to restore a patient's memory but rather to be God's representative and an expression of His love.

Response to Ministry

Expect any response to your ministry. Your expressions of kindness, concern, and love may be mistaken or misunderstood. Whatever you say or do may be met with tears, cursing, or gratitude. Some patients and family members will be most appreciative for all that is done for them. Others may be so focused on needs and priorities they fail to acknowledge assistance or express gratitude. They may have no more energy to give anyone. Overlook what appears to be ungratefulness. Understand the situation and continue to minister in Jesus' name and for His sake.

Health Care Ministry

Many churches are recognizing the need, and accepting the responsibility, for providing a health care ministry within the congregation or community. Depending on resources available, such ministry may be as simple as distributing literature about various illnesses or as elaborate as providing a physician, nurse, lab, and pharmacy services. As part of this ministry, invite health care professionals to speak on various aspects of Alzheimer's disease and other topics. Health screenings may be offered periodically for free or at a minimal cost.

For additional information, consult the Congregational Health Care Ministries publications in Chapter 16, "Resources."

Spiritual Needs

Man is created by God, in His image, with a body, mind, and soul. Every person has physical, mental, emotional, financial, social, and spiritual needs. Thomas E. Bollinger provides these insights pertaining to spiritual needs:

> Spiritual needs are the deepest requirements of the self, which, if met, make it possible for the person to function with a meaningful identity and purpose, so that in all stages of life that person may relate to reality with hope. A spiritual need may be met by a religious act, such as praying or receiving Holy Communion, but many spiritual needs are met by warm and sympathetic human relationships.[1]

Although the spirit survives the body, unfortunately, spirituality is often the most neglected aspect of Alzheimer's care. Patients and families have some of the same spiritual needs throughout the disease process (e.g., love, comfort, reassurance, and forgiveness). Yet, needs can be distinctly those of patients *or* family at any time. Ministry during all stages of the illness should be with the patient and family together and each separately. All ministries are to be beneficial rather than a burden.

Spiritual needs must be identified before they can be met through ministry. Ministries such as individual and corporate worship opportunities, Bible reading, visitation, telephone calls, prayer, and sending cards are to be provided throughout the illness for patients and families whether the patient resides at home or in a care facility. Lisa P. Gwyther, in her book *You Are One of Us: Successful Clergy/Church Connections to Alzheimer's Families,* acknowledges the value of sending cards to Alzheimer's patients and families:

> Cards or notes from church members on an occasional basis are the most spontaneous, welcome, least intrusive form of church response.[2]

A respondent also noted the importance of remembering patients and families with written correspondence:

✧ Try to acknowledge birthdays, holidays, and anniversaries. "Thinking of you" cards and other notes of encouragement are always appropriate.

Specific needs of patients and suggestions for ministries are found in Chapter 9, "Implications of Spiritual Care for Patients," and those of families are found in Chapter 10, "Implications of Spiritual Care for Families."

For God is not the author of confusion, but of peace, as in all churches of the saints.

I Corinthians 14:33

Chapter 9

Implications of Spiritual Care for Patients

Since Alzheimer's disease is different from other diseases, meeting the spiritual needs of these patients will, in some ways, be different from meeting the spiritual needs of patients who have other illnesses. For example, Alzheimer's patients can be comforted during every stage of the disease process. However, because of memory impairment, they need to be comforted more frequently than nondemented patients. Also, methods of providing comfort will change from spoken words to touch and other gestures as the ability to understand verbal communication is lost.

Throughout the illness, *always acknowledge an Alzheimer's patient as a person and include the patient in the conversation as much as possible.*

To minister effectively, you must be aware of the (1) spiritual needs of patients, (2) ministry during the different stages of the disease, (3) additional patient-related ministry issues, and (4) creative ministries.

SPIRITUAL NEEDS OF PATIENTS

Many spiritual needs of patients are ongoing; however, some take precedence from time to time, depending on the situation at the moment. Patients may be unaware of and unable to articulate their spiritual needs, which include the following:

- A right relationship and fellowship with God and man
- Reassurance of God's love, presence, and promises

- A sense of belonging—not alienation, isolation, or abandonment
- Expression of grief
- Meaning and purpose in life
- Love of family and friends
- Forgiveness
- Security
- Protection
- Trust in God's provision for all needs
- God's help
- Comfort
- Hope

MINISTRY DURING THE DIFFERENT STAGES OF THE DISEASE

Ministry to Alzheimer's patients is partially determined by the stage of the illness. However, due to individual differences and other variables, ministries cannot follow a distinct delineation because all patients do not have the same needs during the same stage. For example, a diagnosis can be made during any stage. Likewise, care facility placement may be needed at any stage (earlier stages for physical reasons or other extenuating circumstances instead of dementia). Therefore, ministries will be arbitrarily assigned to a stage, with the focus on ministry rather than on the stage.

Early Alzheimer's

Pastors are in a unique position to help parishioners spiritually, emotionally, medically, legally, and financially *ahead of time* for unforeseen catastrophes through classes, programs, seminars, special events, counseling, and sermons. Seminars about various aspects of health care and future planning can be offered periodically utilizing local professionals—physicians, other health care personnel, attorneys, financial planners, social workers, and funeral directors—to educate the congregation. Informed persons are in a better position to make decisions.

The ideal time for parishioners to make health care decisions is while their cognitive abilities are intact. Such a loving act is a gift to family members who may be spared untold future agony. Loved ones and others (physicians, attorneys, and care facility staff, if applicable) should be notified of these decisions. Appropriate forms must be signed. Legal, financial, insurance, and medical documents must always be readily accessible.

For additional information, see the pamphlets *Getting Your Affairs in Order,* by the National Institute on Aging and National Institutes of Health; *Legal Plans: Assisting the Person with Dementia in Planning for the Future,* by the Alzheimer's Association; and *Money Matters: Helping the Person with Dementia Settle Financial Issues,* also by the Alzheimer's Association.

Family, friends, and co-workers are likely to be more cognizant of, and willing to acknowledge, memory deficits than patients are. One respondent shared these suggestions to help ministers deal with patients' forgetfulness:

✧ I want my minister to give Mother the love and respect he would give anyone else. I do not want him to be embarrassed for her, but help when she cannot think of the right words or behaves in a strange manner.

Alzheimer's may be suspected, but the proper time must arrive before a medical consultation is sought. *If* fear of the disease has been shared, you may have an opportunity to encourage the parishioner to obtain an evaluation.

Ministry will be the same as that for other parishioners or nonparishioners.* Patients are able to attend traditional worship services and other events at the church, be involved in ministries, and engage in private devotions at home. Worship opportunities provide comfort, meaning, purpose, peace, socialization, and fellowship.

Mild Alzheimer's

If the diagnosis is Alzheimer's, the physician should inform the patient and provide an opportunity for medical questions to be answered. The pamphlet *Telling the Person, Family and Friends,* by the

---

*For purposes of this book, a nonparishioner includes a person who belongs to another church of the same or a different denomination as well as a person who professes no religious faith.

Alzheimer's Association, is an excellent resource for physicians, family members, and ministers.

Patients may find these Alzheimer's Association pamphlets helpful: *Alzheimer's Disease Statistics; Basics of Alzheimer's Disease: What It Is and What You Can Do; Stages of Alzheimer's Disease;* and *If You Have Alzheimer's Disease: What You Should Know, What You Should Do.*

You should not inform anyone of a patient's diagnosis *unless* specifically requested to do so by the patient or family. Privacy and confidentiality must be respected.

Ideally, ministry will begin prior to diagnosis. This usually happens if the patient or someone in the family is a church member. Even if there is no church affiliation, the crisis can cause patients and families to turn to a clergyperson. It is an honor to be invited into the Alzheimer's pilgrimage at any stage—the earlier, the better. You are trusted if your ministry is sought before, or soon after, diagnosis. Then, there will be no secrets, and you can express genuine concern from the beginning.

Respondents shared the following suggestions for ministry when a patient has been diagnosed with Alzheimer's disease:

✧ Visit the patient and family soon after diagnosis to offer reassurance of God's love and presence.
✧ If patients express frustration regarding memory loss, reassure them the illness is causing it. Let patients talk about their feelings.
✧ Encourage the patient and family to make future plans as soon as possible following the diagnosis because there may not be much time left to do so.
✧ I think life support and feeding tube issues should be discussed then.

Many patients will be able to attend, and even partially participate in, traditional worship services at least through this stage, even if there are evident behavioral changes. However, it may be easier for them to engage in small, informal group worship experiences instead of the congregational setting. Perhaps, an Alzheimer's church service can be held while other family members attend regular church. Larger churches may be able to offer such a service as a community-wide ministry. It must be adequately supervised, preferably with a physician or nurse and several volunteers.

Moderate Alzheimer's

Always speak to patients even if they are unable to verbally communicate. They may understand more than you realize. Therefore, never say anything in their presence that could be upsetting to them.

Ministry will be less structured than it was in previous stages. Worship experiences likely will be in settings other than a church building. Worship is not confined to a place. "For where two or three are gathered together in my name, there am I in the midst of them" (Matthew 18:20).

Informal worship opportunities can be provided whether the patient resides at home or in a care facility. Family or staff can save considerable time, energy, and frustration by quoting a Bible verse, praying, reciting a religious poem, or singing a hymn at various times throughout the day and night. When the patient awakens in the morning, the caregiver can set a pleasant mood for the day by stating, "This is the day which the Lord hath made; we will rejoice and be glad in it" (Psalms 118:24). Before mealtime, a blessing could be offered. Scriptures or songs can be shared spontaneously as the caregiver assists the patient with activities of daily living (bathing, dressing, eating, transferring, walking, and toileting). It takes no longer to perform tasks when moments of inspiration are incorporated, and the caregiver's spirit is nourished along with the patient's!

Family caregivers know their loved ones' religious preferences and beliefs. Care facility staff need to become familiar with each resident's religious background (or lack thereof). Patients' rights must be honored. Direct or indirect participation in worship experiences is not to be imposed on anyone.

When the patient becomes extremely confused, agitated, or disruptive during special Alzheimer's services or traditional worship, alternative worship opportunities should be provided. Clergy can conduct a brief, informal, private worship service in the sanctuary for the patient and family periodically as long as they can attend. Such a setting should trigger spiritual memories and be less stressful for all.

As the patient becomes less mobile, Bible studies can be offered as a homebound ministry. Depending on needs, these can be extremely brief and attended only by the patient and family, or they may include a few compatible couples within the congregation. Responsibilities should be shared so the occasion can be meaningful for everyone without being a burden to anyone. The hostess will provide the place. One guest may bring finger foods, if desired. Children or youth could provide music or other entertainment. A Sunday School teacher or staff member might teach the lesson. One respondent stated:

> ✧ Involve children, youth, men, and musicians. Generally, patients love children and respond to music. Male patients enjoy visiting with other males.

Severe Alzheimer's

Many patients reside in a nursing facility during this stage. For additional information regarding nursing facility placement, please refer to Chapter 11, "Ethical Issues."

It is important for patients to be remembered by their church family, although they likely will be unable to recognize their visitors. One respondent shared:

> ✧ Sometimes patients do not "know" their pastor anymore. Our visitation minister visits my husband regularly in the nursing home even though he receives little, or no, response. However, my husband will join in singing the old hymns.

Develop trusting relationships with staff. Allow them to be your allies. You will need their assistance from time to time. *But, never ask the staff to divulge confidential information about patients or family members.*

Work cooperatively as a team member to reinforce interventions with your parishioners. You, family members, and staff can use Bible therapy to calm patients by quoting favorite verses. Staff and families of other residents may seek your ministry regarding situations in their lives as a result of your rapport and loving interactions with your parishioners.

Patients likely will not remember to tell their families about your visits. One respondent suggested:

> ✧ Notify the family after you visit in the nursing home.

A telephone call provides an opportunity for you to minister to the family as well. Never leave a card because it could be misplaced, lost, thrown away, or even eaten.

Patients may be unable to distinguish edible and inedible items. They might eat toxic plants or swallow rosary beads. So, be careful never to leave items that could result in injury, sickness, or death. Patients must also be closely supervised when objects are brought for worship services.

You might be asked, or volunteer, to conduct worship services in care facilities. Various faiths and cultures may be represented by residents and staff. Respect the beliefs of all participants. Be aware that some residents have had past negative or abusive experiences pertaining to religion. To respect patients' rights, no one should be forced to attend, or participate in, care facility worship services.

Ellor, Stettner, and Spath present these ideas regarding worship: Alzheimer's patients continue to feel and respond to feelings; therefore, ministry should focus on emotional and sensory experiences. Organize worship services around the familiar elements of favorite hymns, favorite Bible verses, liturgical responses, and prayer. Themes of "love," "forgiveness," "reassurance," and "hope" are consistent with pastoral care goals. Ministers have to supply most of the energy and substance of the interaction.[1]

Many Alzheimer's patients enjoy being touched appropriately and respond to it. To avoid frightening them, stand in their line of sight and ask for permission to hold their hand or touch their head when you pray. Such intimacy can be calming and comforting. Touching is an act that conveys your love.

See Appendix D for a sample Care Facility Worship Service.

ADDITIONAL PATIENT-RELATED MINISTRY ISSUES

Other patient-related ministry issues include safety, religious rites, and mutual ministry.

Safety

Because of liability, it might be wise to obtain legal counsel concerning ministries to Alzheimer's patients and families.

Since Alzheimer's affects patients' abilities to think, we must use our brains in their behalf. Anticipate potential hazards and do everything possible to prevent injury and death.

Church facilities should be safety-proofed in the same manner as homes and care facilities. The building and grounds committee should periodically check facilities and properties with an eye open to safety concerns. Issues must be addressed promptly.

While not limited to these matters, a few safety considerations in the church setting include the following:

- Alzheimer's patients should never be left unattended—supervision is always necessary.
- Chemicals and other toxic substances must be kept out of the reach of patients.
- Ensure church structures, equipment, and accessories do not pose a safety risk.
- Inedible and other dangerous objects must be kept out of the reach of patients.
- *Only* trained (certified nursing assistants) and experienced volunteers must be authorized to roll patients in a wheelchair or assist them when walking.
- *Only* trained (certified nursing assistants) and experienced volunteers are to give patients food and drink, to decrease the likelihood of strangling or choking.

Encourage members of the congregation to receive training to become a certified nursing assistant. Such training can be fun with friends and is valuable as an Alzheimer's ministry volunteer or family caregiver.

For more information regarding safety issues, consult the pamphlets *Safety,* by the Alzheimer's Association; *Home Safety for People with Alzheimer's Disease,* by the National Institute on Aging and National Institutes of Health; and *Safety at Home: Adapting the Home to Support the Person with Dementia,* by the Alzheimer's Association; also consult the book *The Complete Guide to Alzheimer's—Proofing Your Home,* by Mark Warner.

A serious safety issue of Alzheimer's patients involves wandering. It is estimated that six out of ten patients will wander at some time during their illness. Wandering is a common problem and one of the greatest challenges of caregivers because serious injury or death can occur.[2]

If you are ever involved in ministering to a family whose loved one becomes lost, your roles might include the following:

- Praying for the patient, family, and those involved in the search
- Reporting the incident to local authorities and Safe Return
- Requesting law officials to broadcast an AMBER Alert or similar alert if available in your area
- Requesting authorities to activate canine search teams if available and appropriate
- Telephoning the family
- Visiting the family
- Suggesting the area be searched thoroughly within close proximity of the location where the patient left
- Participating in the search

For additional information, read the pamphlets *Alzheimer's Association Safe Return®, Safe Return® Wandering Behavior—Preparing for and Preventing It,* and *Safe Return® Wandering: Who's at Risk?* by the Alzheimer's Association.

Religious Rites

Communion (Lord's Supper or Eucharist) and baptism are two ordinances of the Christian faith that have tremendous significance in the life of believers. These rituals can be meaningful to Alzheimer's patients and families. Encourage family members to be present, if possible, when you perform religious rites for their loved ones.

Communion

Communion practices vary among faith traditions. Theological beliefs of some clergy do not allow them to administer this rite to patients who lack the cognitive ability to meet biblical requirements of self-examination and remembrance of Christ's death on the Cross.

Other clergypersons contend it is not their role to determine who should or should not partake and will serve Communion to these patients.

Respondents acknowledged the significance of participating in Communion:

> ✧ We are fortunate to have a caring pastor who visits Mom in the nursing home and gives her Communion when I can be there. Usually, we have lunch with her that day. Because Mom loved to sing, he once sang with her. She relates to music and can remember songs even though she cannot remember having lunch ten minutes earlier.
> ✧ In-home Communion is very meaningful.

If Communion is administered to a patient at home or in a care facility, certain safety precautions must be observed:

- Check to see whether the patient's diet will allow elements of bread and grape juice to be served.
- Remove disposable cups and other objects which the patient might accidentally swallow.
- Unless there is a DNR (do not resuscitate) order, ensure someone will perform CPR if the patient becomes choked or strangled.

Baptism

Baptism may be requested by the patient or a family member on behalf of the patient. While each situation is different, questions arise:

- Is there a risk the patient would be injured or death could result?
- What mode of baptism (sprinkling, pouring, or immersion) would be used?
- Is the patient mentally, physically, and emotionally able to handle this without fear or trauma?
- Where would the patient be baptized—home, church, hospital, or care facility?
- Have you consulted the patient's physician and nursing facility personnel, if applicable?

- Are all family members in agreement?
- Will someone be present who can administer CPR unless there is a DNR order?

If you agree to baptize an Alzheimer's patient, be certain all bases are covered.

If you believe the patient could be injured or die as a result of being baptized, honestly discuss your concern with family members. You may want to remind them that although Jesus gave the example of baptism, there was no opportunity for the dying thief on the Cross to be baptized. Denominations differ theologically regarding the necessity of baptism for salvation.

Caution: *Patients' conditions decline; therefore, a rite that can be safely administered at one time may not be safe at a later time.*

Mutual Ministry

Typically, we think of ministry as flowing from clergy, other family members, friends, health care professionals, and strangers to patients and families. Ironically, families and even patients can minister to other family members, friends, health care professionals, strangers, and clergy as love is given and received. Ministry may be long term or just for a moment. It takes many forms, including smiling, lending a listening ear, speaking an encouraging word, singing a hymn, reciting a familiar Bible verse, marveling at God's creation, and praying.

CREATIVE MINISTRIES

Many ministries can be provided during any, and every, stage of the illness. Personalize them as much as possible. Do not be afraid to create new ones. Creativity is good for patients, families, and ministers. Look for ways to make ministry fun!

Creative ministries include the following:

- Adopting an Alzheimer's patient
- Having educational events during Alzheimer's Disease Awareness Month
- Recording audiotapes

- Reading books
- Viewing pictures
- Sharing potluck meals
- Improving quality of life
- Engaging in religious activities
- Utilizing reminiscence packets
- Viewing scrapbooks
- Sewing projects
- Making worship videos

Adopting an Alzheimer's Patient

Individuals, couples, Sunday school classes, as well as youth and mission groups may adopt a patient. This is an excellent way to meet the patient's needs as well as to foster intimacy within a group. It will be easier if the patient is known to, and by, those ministering. Skills, gifts, and abilities of individuals determine which needs could be met. Hopefully, participants will feel rewarded doing what they would want done for them and their family, if the situation were reversed. Most people want to be remembered, not ignored or forgotten!

Having Educational Events During Alzheimer's Disease Awareness Month

Pastors have numerous educational opportunities during November, which is Alzheimer's Disease Awareness Month and Family Caregiver Month. Suggestions include the following:

- Show videos pertaining to Alzheimer's.
- Conduct special services with prayers for victims.
- Present a program on "Spirituality and Alzheimer's" at a support group meeting.
- Display materials about Alzheimer's and caregivers in the church library.
- Preach sermons on biblical caregivers.
- Write articles highlighting patients and families for the church newsletter.
- Ask family members to speak briefly during a worship service.

- Provide information in newsletters and bulletins for making donations to the Alzheimer's Association.
- Obtain brochures from the Alzheimer's Association for bulletin inserts.
- Communicate needs of patients and families when requested.

Recording Audiotapes

As a mission or choir project, record music, scripture, prayers, and inspirational stories. Tapes provide worship opportunities and have a calming effect. They can be played in the patient's home or care facility with supervision. Family members and staff benefit from them too.

Reading Books

Certain children's books that have a simple and truthful message can be used effectively one-on-one or in a group setting to provide worship experiences for patients. Repetitive phrases and colorful pictures further enhance the suitability of a selection. An excellent book with these qualities is *Love You Forever,* by Robert Munsch.[3]

Viewing Pictures

Pictures of Bible characters can be utilized for worship opportunities. Family pictures afford opportunities to discuss good times and God's blessings.

Inspirational paintings and cross-stitch pictures can be used in like manner. Years ago, I cross-stitched an awesome picture of the words and symbols found in Isaiah 9:6. It adorns the wall behind my computer. How it ministers to my spirit when I gaze on the names of God! Who can say the spirits of Alzheimer's patients are not likewise touched by the beauty of such depictions?

Sharing Potluck Meals

Several purposes are accomplished when Sunday school classes or mission groups share meals with Alzheimer's patients and families— ministry, physical nourishment, fellowship, socialization, and fun.

✧ Once a month or so, plan for the Sunday school class to take a meal to the home.

Since many elderly people have visual difficulty when driving at night, a potluck lunch would probably be preferable to a dinner. Food should be brought in disposable containers so the family will not have the chore of returning dishes. Members of the class can stay for the meal and assist with serving and cleanup. A nice gesture is to leave the leftovers.

After the meal, the patient may need a nap, but Bible Trivia or other games could be played by class members, or a leisure time of adult conversation and companionship can be enjoyed by the caregiver.

As the illness progresses, it may become necessary to limit the number of Sunday school class members to avoid agitation and increased confusion. If this monthly get-together becomes too taxing for the patient, adjustments can be made:

✧ Individuals can take a covered dish periodically. It is nice to have a special treat.

Improving Quality of Living

It is important for patients to live as fully as possible for as long as possible. Seek ways to help them continue to be useful, maintain interests, and share their gifts:

✧ Encourage patients to be involved in ministries. Because my husband was a gardener, our minister asked him to help with flowers at church. He also found someone to take my husband to a prayer breakfast.

Engaging in Religious Activities

A fun way to keep patients' spiritual connections alive is to spend time in religious activities:

✧ Patients may be able to play Bible Trivia, if they learned Bible verses in their younger years.

Due to their inability to recall titles of songs, patients probably will be unable to play "Name That Tune." Consider adapting the game to "Sing That Tune." A leader starts singing a hymn or praise chorus. The object is to finish the song. If played in a group setting, the winner is the person who sings the most of the song. Feel free to play the game spontaneously, even if only one patient is available.

Utilizing Reminiscence Packets

Alzheimer's patients need assistance triggering spiritual associations. Items can be kept nearby for this purpose.

Reminiscence packets are especially useful for chaplains ministering one-on-one to persons of various denominations in care facilities. They can also be used by pastors and family members with parishioners living at home or in a care facility. Ministers collect religious objects of patients' faith traditions—cards with prayers or scriptures, Bible, pictures, cross—to put in the packets. It is hoped these objects will evoke memories.[4]

Packets should be locked in facility cabinets when not in use or kept in a safe place at home. Otherwise, patients may lose, destroy, or eat objects from the packets.

Viewing Scrapbooks

Mission groups, individuals, or family members can make a scrapbook using pictures of people and places recognized by the patient. Looking at these affords a time of sharing memories. Pictures should be explained rather than asking the patient to describe them.

If the patient lives at home, a scrapbook can be given as a gift. However, if the person resides in a care facility, it is wise to carry the scrapbook with you when you visit because it could be misplaced, damaged, or stolen.

A variation of a family scrapbook is a scrapbook of religious symbols. Discussing the symbols with the patient provides an informal worship opportunity.

With supervision, patients in the early stages may be able to help make scrapbooks.

Sewing Projects

For mission projects, ladies or youth groups can devote fellowship time to make stuffed sheep, prayer bears, and clothing for patients.

Stuffed Sheep

Cuddly animals can serve as security objects for patients to hold during the day and to sleep with at night. Use nontoxic paint for eyes, nose, and mouth. Avoid using any moveable parts that could be swallowed.

David P. Wentroble suggests the idea of allowing dementia patients to hold a stuffed sheep when Psalm 23 is read.[5] Such a visual aid reinforces the truth that God loves His sheep—His people.

Patients can also hold the stuffed animal when the pastor, friend, or family member reads other scriptures pertaining to sheep (e.g., "Jesus and the Good Shepherd," "Parable of the Lost Sheep," etc.) or sings hymns on the theme of sheep (e.g., "Savior, Like a Shepherd Lead Us"; "Gentle Shepherd"; "All the Way My Savior Leads Me"; "My Shepherd Will Supply My Need").

Prayer Bears

Individuals, youth groups, or mission groups can make stuffed bears with a voice box of the patient's favorite scripture or recorded prayer. Prayer bears are excellent ministry tools during pastoral visits. Because of the voice box and other potentially dangerous parts, supervision is required.

It is not advisable to give prayer bears or stuffed animals to residents in care facilities because dementia patients often are unable to distinguish their belongings from those of others. Sharing of personal items could easily transmit communicable diseases.

Clothing

Articles of clothing may be made with the needs of Alzheimer's patients in mind. For example, if patients tend to take their clothes off, one-piece garments may be suitable.

Labels of patients' names for identification may be sewn in clothing of care facility residents. There are pros and cons of sewing labels outside of clothes; however, such identification may prove helpful if a patient wanders.

Since some Alzheimer's patients in care facilities do not have any relatives or any who live nearby, minor repairs could be made on these residents' clothing.

Making Worship Videos

You can record personalized worship videos to be played in the privacy of the patient's home. As a by-product, caregivers are provided an excellent time of respite. If the patient has to be admitted to a care facility, such a familiar video could be used to help facilitate adjustment.

See Appendix D for Worship Video Suggestions and a sample Script for Worship Video.

> For God is not unrighteous to forget your work and labor of love, which ye have showed toward his name, in that ye have ministered to the saints, and do minister.
>
> Hebrews 6:10

Chapter 10

Implications of Spiritual Care for Families

Ramifications of dementia and length of a loved one's illness necessitate that ministry to Alzheimer's families be different from that provided to families whose loved ones have other illnesses. One respondent summarized the situation in this manner:

✧ Everyone can be very supportive at first. But, as new crises arise, attention becomes focused elsewhere. Alzheimer's lasts for years and years. People get tired of asking, "How is Mary?" They lose interest in your problems and go on to someone else's more recent needs.

Throughout the long journey, constant expression of that love is needed from the Christian community. The importance of family ministry is illustrated by this fact: As families receive ministry, they minister to their loved ones in ways clergy cannot.

To provide effective ministry, you must have a knowledge of the (1) spiritual needs of families, (2) ministry during the different stages of the illness, (3) additional family-related ministry issues, and (4) creative ministries.

SPIRITUAL NEEDS OF FAMILIES

Respondents acknowledged having the following needs:

✧ Someone to listen
✧ Information about the illness and the caregiver's role
✧ Contact with others in a similar situation

◇ Respite
◇ Knowledge of resources
◇ Financial assistance
◇ Understanding, patience, emotional support, encouragement, love, and comfort
◇ Help in coping with emotions—disappointment, embarrassment, anger, depression, isolation, helplessness, frustration, loneliness, self-pity, hopelessness, fear, and guilt
◇ Reassurance
◇ Physical and spiritual strength and healing
◇ To know "why" this happened
◇ To accept the situation and live with it
◇ Prayer
◇ Others to believe I am telling the truth
◇ Help in making decisions
◇ Counseling for grief issues
◇ To let go and trust God
◇ Increased faith in God
◇ Forgiveness
◇ Assistance with adjustments—no longer able to attend church or going alone, role reversal, and nursing facility placement
◇ Empathy
◇ To minister to others

MINISTRY DURING THE DIFFERENT STAGES OF THE DISEASE

Ministries to families will correspond to the arbitrarily assigned patient ministry stages. Again, the focus is on ministry rather than on the stage.

Early Alzheimer's

One of the greatest needs of families, beginning in this stage and continuing until their loved ones' facility placement, is respite. Virtually all respondents expressed their need to have some time away from the patient. The wife of one patient stated it this way:

◇ Supply sitters so caregivers can have a little time to "recharge their batteries."

Respite should be according to patients' and families' needs as well as available resources. It can be provided in the patient's home, adult day care facility, church, or community building. Some care facilities accept Alzheimer's patients on a temporary basis.

Cost of respite is a concern for many families, as expressed by this respondent:

✧ It should be at a cost all families can afford.

Another respondent shared a creative solution for receiving respite yet avoiding the expense:

✧ If there are willing and qualified people who can work together, a mutual aid type program might benefit caregivers. I read in a newsletter about a church group that had "respite swaps." Mrs. A would stay with Mrs. B's spouse for *x* number of hours so Mrs. B could get away for whatever reason. Mrs. B would give Mrs. A an IOU for *x* number of hours. At a later date, Mrs. B would stay with Mrs. A's spouse and turn in her IOU. Each knew they could exchange services without feeling guilty. The article indicated this worked well and a large number of people were helped.

Churches may be able to offer respite care for free, or at nominal cost, especially if this ministry is subsidized and volunteers assist. Background checks must be conducted on volunteers in a church setting to attempt to ensure the safety of patients.

Respondents offered these suggestions regarding volunteers who are interested in providing respite:

✧ Qualifications should include love, compassion, patience, understanding, kindness, happy disposition, and experience caring for Alzheimer's patients.
✧ Providing respite care requires real dedication, time, and patience. People must be carefully screened. Many individuals might volunteer to "patient sit" not realizing the hazards involved. Not everyone— regardless of good intentions—is suited to care for Alzheimer's patients. These patients are much more difficult to manage than patients having most other illnesses.
✧ Due to the disease process, Alzheimer's patients may wander, hallucinate, strike people, be unable to communicate, need assis-

tance with mobility, and be incontinent. Those willing to stay with patients must be cognizant of the problems. It is protecting the patient—not just sitting and talking.

✧ Those who have lost their loved ones would be good volunteers.

✧ When asked if he thought it would be a good idea for churches to train volunteers to stay in patients' homes for a few hours each week, the desperation of one husband came forth, "Yes, yes, a thousand times yes."

Respondents suggested additional ideas regarding the possibility of churches training volunteers to provide respite care:

✧ With qualifications, I think it is a good idea. Obtain materials from the Alzheimer's Association and seek consultation before undertaking such a project. Proper training should be provided by caregivers, physicians, nurses, and social workers. Include information about the stages of the illness. Situations vary. It would be helpful for volunteers to observe patients prior to providing respite.

✧ A professional would need to start a church respite care program.

✧ Ministers can help procure volunteers to give families a rest from caregiving.

✧ Couples could "sit" together in the patient's home. Both men and women are needed. I think formal respite needs to be done on an interdenominational level. Several churches might sponsor a "Caregiver's Day Out" program similar to "Mother's Day Out."

For more information about respite care, consult the manuals *In-Home Respite Care: Guidelines for Programs Serving Family Caregivers for Memory-Impaired Adults,* by Lisa Gwyther and Edna Ballard, and *In-Home Respite Care: Guidelines for Training Respite Workers Serving Memory-Impaired Adults,* by Edna Ballard and Lisa Gwyther.

Due to the demands of caregiving, I cannot think of a group of people who need worship opportunities more desperately than Alzheimer's families. Attending worship services and participating in other worship experiences (e.g., listening to Christian music, watching Christian videos, reading devotional literature, etc.) can help them cope with the ongoing situation. Respondents acknowledged their need for worship:

✧ Provide the caregiver a chance to attend worship services. We provide a nursery for the children of young married couples. Let us not forget our elderly.
✧ Create a Sunday school class for caregivers.

Members in a class for caregivers would have common interests and needs; however, provisions should also be made for those who prefer to attend a regular Sunday school class.

Ministry will be the same as that performed for other parishioners and nonparishioners.* Families should be able to attend church services, be involved in ministries, and participate in private devotions unless prohibited because of other reasons.

Mild Alzheimer's

From the time Alzheimer's is suspected until a diagnosis is made may be a long process, as shared by this respondent:

✧ Getting a diagnosis was one of our biggest problems. It took two years. We were in a new community and needed guidance. I would have liked a referral to a Christian neurologist or psychiatrist. Ministers can occasionally recommend physicians, attorneys, nurses, and social workers.

Wanting to be helpful and yet not knowing the outcome for a particular person or situation can present a dilemma. Personalities, medical conditions, and other factors vary. You do not want to be blamed or feel guilty, if results are less than favorable. Therefore, in many cases, a better alternative would be to provide information about physician referral services, if available in your area. Likewise, when you are asked to recommend a care facility, you may relate information about all appropriate facilities. Patients or families must make these decisions. Positive *personal* experiences might be shared *with the understanding you are not recommending a certain physician or care facility.*

---

*For purposes of this book, a nonparishioner includes a person who belongs to another church of the same or a different denomination as well as a person who professes no religious faith.

You may have opportunities to encourage patients or families to share the diagnosis as a way of gaining extra support. However, they must decide who will be told, how, and when. Diagnoses can be conveyed in person, by phone, or through written correspondence. One respondent related her unique approach:

> ✧ I shared my husband's diagnosis in a Wednesday night prayer meeting. Although I was extremely emotional, this proved to be the right thing for me to do.

When people are aware of the situation, they can express their love. The pamphlet *Telling the Person, Family and Friends,* by the Alzheimer's Association, provides excellent tips for discussing the diagnosis.

Although the experience following a loved one's diagnosis can be described differently by family members, this quote illustrates the commonality of feelings and needs:

> ✧ Knowing you cannot do anything for your loved one is devastating. Families hurt as well as the patient. We need to talk about problems, decisions, and feelings.

A few respondents shared how they wish their pastor's ministry had been different following the diagnosis:

> ✧ I did not want to hear the Lord never gives us more than we can bear. I wanted good Christian support. I wanted my pastor to tell me it was all right to be angry and he would stand by me. He told me to trust in the Lord—I have done that since I was twelve years old.
>
> ✧ When my husband was diagnosed, I would have liked for my pastor to have told me that we were not being punished and God did not send my mother's disease. I was tempted to become disillusioned with a God Who "allows" this to happen.

Respondents offered these suggestions for ways you can help after a loved one's diagnosis:

> ✧ Pray.
> ✧ Go slowly. Many people do not want help at first.
> ✧ Provide informed and compassionate listening.

✧ Be understanding.
✧ Offer moral, mental, emotional, physical, and spiritual support.
✧ Remind us the patient cannot help it and is frightened also.
✧ Offer reassurance that the church will be there for us.
✧ Support family decisions.
✧ Offer sympathy and consolation.
✧ Provide Alzheimer's support group information.
✧ Assist in putting us in touch with others in the same situation.

For additional practical suggestions to help families, consult the pamphlets *Support Caregiving Families: A Guide for Congregations and Parishes,* by the National Family Caregivers Association, and *Ten Ways to Help a Family Living with Alzheimer's,* by the Alzheimer's Association.

Attending separate church services may better serve the spiritual needs of patients and families. Try to eliminate families' excuses for not attending church by arranging a worship service for patients simultaneously.

Moderate Alzheimer's

Often, the caregiving role is thrust upon family members who may not be prepared for this nor fully comprehend what is required of them. One respondent replied:

✧ I needed a more complete understanding of the caregiver's role.

Another family member made the following suggestion:

✧ Through sermons, clergy can address what it means to be a caregiver.

Since patients become unable to express appreciation to their families, a fitting tribute is an annual worship service to honor caregivers for their selfless and sacrificial contributions. See the booklets *Model Catholic Caregiving Service, Model Interfaith Caregiving Service,* and *Model Protestant Caregiving Service,* by the National Family Caregivers Association.

Visits are valuable and appreciated throughout the illness, as indicated by this respondent:

✧ Ministers' routine home visits offer more help than can be realized.

To avoid embarrassing the patient or family, it is courteous to telephone before visiting in the home. The caregiver may be on a tight schedule, the home may be in disarray, or the patient and family may be getting little, if any, sleep:

✧ I averaged approximately four or five hours of sleep because my husband was pacing the floor, agitated, nervous, and sleepless. He slept in the daytime while I was at work.

Hopefully, families will be able to attend regular church services throughout their loved ones' illness, if respite is provided or the patient resides in a care facility. However, family members may want to supplement these worship experiences by attending services with the patient. Such would be the case when a pastor conducts informal services in the sanctuary. As the illness progresses, in-home Bible studies afford families another opportunity to supplement conventional worship attendance.

Severe Alzheimer's

As the illness takes its toll on patients, families are faced with multiple major adjustments, as indicated by this respondent:

✧ Clergy can learn from other professionals about psychological effects of Alzheimer's on family members. We had just moved thousands of miles to a new community; therefore, I lost my support system. One of my teenage sons dropped out of high school during his senior year and started smoking pot. My husband was put on sick leave, then given early retirement. I went back into the workforce. Most decisions were left to me.

Alzheimer's causes patients to lose the ability to function in their usual role. A wife or husband may have to assume the role normally expected of the other. Since parents become unable to make decisions expected of parents, a son or daughter may have to function in the parental role. Role reversal is difficult for all involved, as evidenced by these comments:

✧ Role reversal was my most difficult hurdle.
✧ Mother, as I knew her, is gone. I am now mother to her. Our relationship is totally different.
✧ Role reversal necessitates the child having to take responsibility for the parent and to make decisions. For us, it included taking over my mother-in-law's financial affairs, taking away her car, and finally moving her out of the house where she lived for forty-five years. This is intense emotional agony. You always question whether you are making the best decision—whether you have adequately explored all options.

Many patients are placed in care facilities during this stage, if not earlier. For additional information regarding nursing facility placement, please refer to Chapter 11, "Ethical Issues."

When families are faced with end-of-life decisions, an important role of the clergy is to assist them in "letting go" of their loved ones. You can help families prepare for this eventually in the following ways:

✧ Pray.
✧ Preach on a personal, tangible basis.
✧ Ensure the understanding and belief of the Good News about Jesus.
✧ Remind us that every day is a gift from God and is to be lived one day at a time.
✧ Offer reassurance of God's promises.
✧ Provide educational seminars on topics of grief and growth through suffering.
✧ Facilitate discussion of the relationship with the patient.
✧ Counsel.
✧ Families need tremendous support due to the difficult decisions that must be made.
✧ Encourage family members to be active in church—especially those who spend their time at a nursing facility or caring for their loved ones at home. Reassure them they are still a vital part of the congregation.

As family members or facility staff provide spontaneous worship opportunities for patients, they are afforded additional worship experiences while searching for suitable scriptures and songs to use. Regular church attendance can be supplemented by attending worship services with the patient in the nursing facility.

ADDITIONAL FAMILY-RELATED ISSUES

Other issues pertinent to Alzheimer's families include the following:

- Grasping at straws
- When families will not ask for help
- Importance of families' communicating with ministers
- Relationship of family member to the patient
- Needs of children and teenagers
- Importance of families' taking care of themselves
- Ministry following the patient's death

Grasping at Straws

Denial of family members to accept a loved one's Alzheimer's diagnosis may cause them to seek a second or third medical opinion. In desperation, they may want to try anything. You can help by listening, providing accurate information, and facilitating acceptance of the situation.

When Families Will Not Ask for Help

Family members are often reluctant, or unwilling, to seek help. They may be unaware of their eligibility for particular services and benefits, or fear of rejection, embarrassment, pride, or independence may keep them from asking for the assistance they need. These family members confessed:

◇ They know our situation. I just cannot ask for help.
◇ Caregivers try too hard to do it alone. We need more than anything to be told to reach out for help.
◇ Clergy can play a vital role in helping families ask for, and accept, help.
◇ Remind us that God works through people.
◇ Encourage the congregation to offer help rather than wait to be asked. Parishioners can volunteer to do specific chores, such as

washing clothes, cooking, cleaning house, running errands, and mowing the lawn.

✧ I wish my father-in-law's pastor and congregation had encouraged him to call on others and accept their help. His background, including active participation in church, led him to become a very self-sufficient man. He was proud of his ability to care for himself. This strong sense of individualism and self-esteem caused a difficult impasse. Only with the breakdown of his health has he been forced to open himself to the care of others.

Importance of Families' Communicating with Ministers

Needs cannot be met unless they are known. This respondent noted the necessity of family members' communicating their needs:

✧ Although it is difficult to do, families should tell clergy their needs rather than expect them to know. Ministers are not mind readers! Communication is vital.

Relationship of Family Member to the Patient

All members of the family are affected when one has Alzheimer's. Generally, the closer the relationship (e.g., spouse, child, or parent), the greater is the involvement in the care of the patient. No one can do everything; yet, everyone can do something.

Needs of Children and Teenagers

Excellent materials are available to help children and teenagers understand Alzheimer's and how it affects patients. When you visit, consider taking a book listed in the section Children and Teens in Chapter 16, "Resources."

Encourage children and teens to talk about their feelings, adjustments, and loved ones. Answer their questions and assist family members in helping them to cope.

Children and teens should be appropriately involved in the care of their loved ones through visits, phone calls, and activities. It is important for them to have good memories.

For additional information, read the pamphlets *Just for Children: Helping You Understand Alzheimer's Disease, Just for Teens: Helping You Understand Alzheimer's Disease,* and *Parents' Guide: Help-*

ing Children and Teens Understand Alzheimer's Disease, by the Alzheimer's Association.

Importance of Families Taking Care of Themselves

A common desire of family members is to outlive the patient. In this way, they hope to see that their loved ones' needs are met. Respondents shared these comments:

✧ I want to ensure my husband remains as well cared for, happy, and comfortable as possible.
✧ I hope God will help me be and do what is necessary to help my husband through this.

It is important for families to take care of themselves by eating a nutritious diet, getting adequate sleep, exercising, and finding appropriate ways to cope with stress. Seminars can be sponsored periodically to encourage a healthier lifestyle and offer suggestions for coping with stress. This respondent described common stressors of caregivers:

✧ Families experience great periods of stress which change as the disease progresses. Initially, we are overwhelmed by physical and mental changes in the patient such as wandering, sundowning, insomnia, and paranoia. Later, stress results from incontinence and the inability to remember how to handle simple bodily needs. Caregivers need help in coping with these problems and the emotions evoked, especially if there is not a good support system. My husband's daughters by his first wife show no interest in him. I am there to do everything and am bitter toward them. I have chosen to keep him at home as long as I am physically able. At times, I experience almost unbearable stress.

One respondent made this suggestion:

✧ Ministers can help us deal with stress by keeping in touch and reassuring us of God's love and that of the church.

Another respondent acknowledged appreciation to God for helping her throughout her husband's illness:

✧ I had faith I could live through my husband's illness. God allowed me to do that.

For additional information, see the pamphlets *Caregiver Stress: Respect Your Well-Being,* by the Alzheimer's Association, and *12 Tips for Caregivers: Caring for Yourself While Helping a Loved One with Alzheimer's,* by the Rosalynn Carter Institute for Caregiving.

Ministry Following the Patient's Death

Families have numerous spiritual needs after a loved one's death. Therefore, ministry includes that performed before, during, and following the funeral.

Before the Funeral

An immediate and constant need is expressed by this respondent:

✧ Pray for our family.

Other immediate needs are comfort and reassurance. Respondents shared these comments:

✧ Comfort us with God's promises.
✧ Help us remember Mother now has her precious memory. She will *know* me when I rejoin her.
✧ Reassure me that I did my best regardless of others' opinions—especially those who were not so closely involved.
✧ Offer reassurance that research is ongoing for the cause and cure of Alzheimer's.

Family members desire different levels of involvement in planning their loved ones' funerals. Some prefer the pastor plan the service. Others want to help plan it themselves or, at least, have a part in planning the service:

✧ Let me plan my husband's memorial service and reception.
✧ I think I would want to help in preparation of readings for the funeral Mass. Perhaps, give a list of possible readings.
✧ At my husband's funeral, I want lots of his favorite songs, scriptures, and a happy mood. It will be a celebration of him going to be with his Savior.

✧ Discuss funeral arrangements with the family to ensure the service reflects their wishes and emphasizes the message they want delivered.

You can offer to go with families to the funeral home to make arrangements. However, some families prefer to handle the business aspects in the privacy of the family only. Other families find it meaningful for the pastor to accompany them:

✧ I think I would want my pastor to go with us to the funeral home when Mother dies.

Many churches have a committee to help with practical needs following the death of a parishioner or family members of parishioners:

✧ My church has a bereavement committee to assist with illness, sorrow, and death.

Food may be taken to the home of the deceased or other family members, or a meal may be served in the fellowship hall of the church before or after the funeral.

During the Funeral

Respondents shared these thoughts regarding the funeral service they want when their loved ones die and the purposes it should serve:

✧ Talk about good memories. Remember my husband before this dreadful disease robbed him of his mind.
✧ When Mother dies, I want my preacher to praise God for her life and thank Him for releasing her from suffering.
✧ When my wife dies, I want our preacher to preach a message on salvation and the reality of heaven. Let doubters know God is triumphant in everything.
✧ The funeral should begin the healing process.

Respondents whose loved ones have died shared these comments about what they found meaningful during the funeral service:

✧ At my husband's funeral, our rabbi mentioned we lost him a long time ago. Family and friends had said good-bye in different ways and at different times. Now was the time to remember the kind of man he was and how much he was loved by his family, friends, and community.

✧ My pastor gave a lovely tribute to Mother reminding us of the days prior to her illness. It was good to remember.

✧ My minister said exactly the right thing. It was a worship service— a celebration of the resurrection.

A few respondents shared comments regarding how they wish the service had been different:

✧ At Mother's funeral, I wish my pastor had emphasized the Word and God's promises to the redeemed.

✧ The clergyman who officiated at my husband's funeral did not know him. I wish he had asked about him and personalized his service.

✧ I wish the pastor had said, "God understands your feelings and loves you."

During times of grief, it is impossible to remember all that is said and done. This respondent shared an excellent way you can enable families to receive ongoing comfort after the funeral:

✧ My pastor conducted a beautiful service for my husband and taped it for me.

An often overlooked, but meaningful, gesture would be for someone to house-sit during the funeral to protect the property and belongings of the family—especially if the location is in a geographical area where people tend to prey on others' tragedies.

After the Funeral

Families need to be remembered during the weeks and months following their loved ones' death. One respondent offered this suggestion to ministers:

✧ Take me out to lunch and let me talk.

Respondents shared appreciation for these meaningful ministry experiences following their loved ones' death:

✧ My preacher was beautifully supportive in the days and weeks following my mother's death.

✧ A few weeks after my husband died, my pastor came to see me. I do not remember *what he said,* but he *came!*

✧ My preacher said it all by being with me. He visited often and prayed for me in the early days and weeks after my husband's death.

✧ After my grandmother died, her pastor contacted us several times.

One respondent expressed a common need of those who lose a spouse by death and shared disappointment regarding her priest's failure to help meet this need:

✧ During those early days and weeks following the death of my husband, I wish my priest had helped me adjust to the loneliness.

See Appendix D for sample funeral sermons for a Christian and a non-Christian.

CREATIVE MINISTRIES

Alzheimer's family ministry presents a challenge in discovering significant, personal, and creative services as needs change throughout the long cycle prior to diagnosis and following death.

Since it is important for families to saturate their minds with uplifting thoughts, ministries should be designed according to Philippians 4:8:

> . . . Whatsoever things are true, whatsoever things are honest, whatsoever things are just, whatsoever things are pure, whatsoever things are lovely, whatsoever things are of good report; if there be any virtue, and if there be any praise, think on these things.

Creative ministries include the following:

- Helping families find meaning and purpose
- Sharing inspirational material via the Internet
- Conducting memorial services in care facilities
- Honoring patients' lives and memories
- Selecting mottoes
- Making a prayer board
- Making scripture card boxes
- Organizing telephone outreach

Helping Families Find Meaning and Purpose

Caregivers have various hobbies, gifts, skills, and abilities. To enjoy these or engage in new interests can be an excellent way to cope with a loved one's illness as well as find meaning in life. Pastors can seek opportunities within the congregation or community for family members to share their knowledge, skills, and abilities:

> ✧ My pastor has shown great interest in, and encouragement for, the small efforts I have made to put my feelings and experiences in writing. To the extent he shows confidence in me as a Christian layman, I am appreciative. Is there more an Alzheimer's caregiver could ask?

Writing is therapeutic, as family members journal God's provisions. Sharing experiences through articles and books is a wonderful way to help others in similar situations. Writing even has potential as a source of income!

Sharing Inspirational Material via the Internet

Inspirational poems, cards, stories, and prayers can be e-mailed to family members who have access to a computer. Information about Alzheimer's can be found on numerous Web sites. Chat rooms can provide additional support.

Conducting Memorial Services in Care Facilities

Facility memorial services enable families to have an opportunity to grieve the loss of loved ones with staff and residents who likely would be unable to attend the funerals or family visitation. Employees need a time to say good-bye to those who were entrusted to their care because in many cases these patients became like family to them. Such services also afford residents a much-needed occasion to express their grief in losing a friend.

Because of ongoing relationships with patients, families, and staff, the ideal person to conduct care facility memorial services is a facility chaplain. Local active or retired clergy, a social worker, a nursing supervisor, or the administrator could officiate, if a chaplain is not available.

Size of the facility would be a determining factor in how frequently services are held. If there are more than a hundred residents, monthly services would be appropriate. Quarterly services in smaller facilities would be suitable since there would be fewer deaths. Deaths of staff and family members during that period should also be acknowledged *unless a resident has not been informed of a loved one's death.*

If the service is held immediately before or after the day shift change, staff might be more willing, and able, to attend. Employees may participate by singing, playing an instrument, sharing memories, or reading scripture.

Flyers could be posted a few days in advance at entrance doors to indicate the date, time, and location within the facility. Try to schedule services at the same time and place each month or quarter to eliminate confusion. Notices could also be placed in local newspapers, if a fee is not charged. The chaplain or social worker would need to contact family members to inform or remind them of the service; however, families should not feel pressured to attend.

Honoring Patients' Lives and Memories

Depending on personal interests of the deceased, memorials can be given to honor their lives. In lieu of flowers, families may request donations to their church, the Alzheimer's Association, other organizations, special funds, or libraries.

✧ Churches need well-stocked libraries.

Gifts such as Bibles, trees, or magazine subscriptions can be presented to the care facility as a way of remembering a loved one and as an expression of appreciation for the care provided. Community service could be performed through organizations that the deceased attended or supported.

Family and friends may wish to make financial contributions to the Alzheimer's Association. You need to have this information readily available and provide it to local funeral homes and libraries.

Selecting Mottoes

Encourage family members to select a motto to be repeated during challenging times. It may be a Bible verse, phrase, or prayer. Gifts can be given utilizing the motto as a source of inspiration. A few respondents shared their mottoes:

✧ I pray day and night, "Lord, give me rest. Lord, give me peace."
✧ I rely on the Lord's Prayer.
✧ When I am overburdened, I plead, "Oh, dear God, give me strength."

Making a Prayer Board

Purchase a map of the United States and a package of gummed stars. Type and paste Bible verses on the subject of prayer outside the outline of the map. Instruct the caregiver to place a star on each state where it is known as least one person is praying for the patient and family. A prayer board is a source of encouragement and a tangible reminder of others' prayers. This can be a youth or adult mission project.

Making Scripture Card Boxes

Friends, Sunday school classes, as well as youth and mission groups could write or type Bible verses on cards and place in boxes as gifts for family members. Verses could be read or memorized at any time for inspiration. This lasting gift serves as a reminder that others care.

Choose verses from appropriate scriptures found in Appendix C.

Organizing Telephone Outreach

Spouses of Alzheimer's patients who live alone can receive a daily call to see whether they are all right or have special needs. This small, but significant, ministry provides an additional opportunity for adult contact and serves as an example of Christian love in action. During the conversation, pray for each other and the patient.

> Blessed be God, even the Father of our Lord Jesus Christ, the Father of mercies, and the God of all comfort; Who comforteth us in all our tribulation, that we may be able to comfort them which are in any trouble, by the comfort wherewith we ourselves are comforted of God.

> II Corinthians 1:3-4

Chapter 11

Ethical Issues

Alzheimer's patients and families are faced with numerous decisions that have ethical (right or wrong) ramifications. Questions come quickly, answers more slowly. These respondents provide insight into some of the common ethical issues family members encounter:

✧ I struggle to be a real Christian and decent company while facing loneliness, celibacy, frustration, and self-pity.
✧ The caregiver is facing physical, emotional, and moral stresses—especially if the spouse is the patient. How does one deal with shattered expectations, anger, guilt, and self-pity? What happens when one no longer feels like a spouse but is not yet widowed? What happens when the child becomes the parent and the parent becomes the child? What does one do when afraid the patient will die and afraid death will not come? I know the questions, but am not sure I have any answers.

Yes, it seems there are more questions than answers when dealing with Alzheimer's. To help patients and families find answers, you must have an understanding of (1) common ethical dilemmas, (2) guidelines for making ethical decisions, (3) additional ethics-related issues, and (4) the role of ministry.

COMMON ETHICAL DILEMMAS

Concerns of Alzheimer's patients and families that have ethical consequences include the following:

• Diagnosis
• Driving

- Nursing facility placement
- Feeding tubes and respirators
- Infidelity

Diagnosis

The question is often asked, "Should the patient be told of an Alzheimer's diagnosis?" Several considerations need to be taken into account:

- How advanced is the illness?
- Would the patient understand the diagnosis and ramifications?
- How would the patient likely react?
- Would the patient become suicidal or homicidal?
- Would the patient be deprived of the opportunity to plan for the future if not told?
- What advantages are there in informing the patient?
- Are there any disadvantages in telling the patient?
- Are there any disadvantages if the patient is not told?

Generally, I believe the patient has a right to know and should be told unless it is likely suicide or murder would result. The patient may wisely use the knowledge to plan for the future or deny the diagnosis. But, at least, telling the truth will avoid guilt, whereas withholding the diagnosis will likely weave a web of untruths and, ultimately, result in guilt.

If it is determined to be in the patient's best interest to know the diagnosis, other questions arise: When is the best time for the physician to tell the patient? How should the patient be told? See the pamphlets *Telling the Person, Family and Friends* and *Ethical Considerations: Issues in Diagnostic Disclosure,* by the Alzheimer's Association.

Another important, but usually unasked, question is this: Because of privacy laws, is it legal and ethical for a physician to disclose a patient's diagnosis to family members?

Driving

For most adults, driving represents independence. Therefore, no one wants to take the car away too soon from an Alzheimer's patient or wait too long. The wife of one patient shared her experience:

◇ To take the car away from my husband was the most difficult decision I had to make.

Due to the nature of Alzheimer's, it is virtually impossible to determine *the day* a patient can safely drive and *the day* it becomes unsafe unless an accident occurs that day. And, just because a wreck does not happen is no guarantee the patient can drive safely. The elusive goal is to intervene by forbidding a patient to drive before someone is injured or killed. Yet, who can know when that time arrives?

Dr. Stephen Sapp summarizes the problem:

An Alzheimer's patient may be capable of performing the necessary *actions* to drive a car but *judgment* needed to do so safely is lost as well as, perhaps, memory of *where* he or she wants to go and *how* to get there.[1]

Failing to intervene is allowing the patient to continue driving. Serious consequences such as injury and death can result from inaction.

When family members intervene, it should be done without confrontation or argument. Patients need to be allowed to maintain their dignity. A family member can gently, but firmly, say, "I want to drive today" or "Let me drive this time." The focus should be on the present rather than the permanence of the situation. Ironically, patients may sooner or later feel relieved by not having the pressure of driving— and, perhaps, sooner than later!

In some localities, taxicabs and public transportation are alternatives that allow patients to maintain a measure of independence. These solutions can be beneficial for a while, especially if family members do not live nearby. Family and friends also may provide transportation.

For additional information, see the pamphlets *Driving,* by the Alzheimer's Association, and *Older Drivers,* by the National Institute on Aging and National Institutes of Health. Although patients will likely be unable to use the book *Driving Decisions Workbook,* by David

Eby, Lisa Molnar, and Jean Shope, it can be useful for family members to assess their loved ones' driving skills as a tool for determining the time for intervention. This publication is available online at www.aota.org/olderdriver/docs/assessumi.pdf.

Nursing Facility Placement

Placing a loved one in a nursing facility is the most difficult decision many family members face:

◇ The most difficult decision of my life was to send my husband of forty-six years to a nursing home. Doctors told me he would be unmanageable at home.

◇ I did not make the decision about my grandfather's nursing home placement. My parents and grandmother did that. They have experienced tremendous guilt and grief because this was one of his fears when he was well. They need lots of support.

◇ Deciding to place a loved one in a care facility is a soul-searching matter for the closest kin, although persons knowledgeable of the progression of Alzheimer's expect it to be inevitable.

◇ Placing a loved one in a nursing home, tube feeding, and life support systems are personal, moral issues. I made my decisions and placed my husband in God's hands—His hands do not falter.

This emotionally laden decision of nursing facility placement is compounded for some family members because of their interpretation of certain scriptures. Some adult children believe they would commit a sin by not honoring their father or mother, if they put a parent in a nursing facility (Exodus 20:12; Deuteronomy 5:16; Matthew 15:4; Matthew 19:19; Mark 7:10; Luke 18:20).

Timing is a crucial factor in placement. Who can know *the day* a patient can safely live alone or *the day* facility care is needed? Again, the elusive goal is for placement to occur before anyone is injured or killed. These respondents shared experiences regarding the timing of their loved ones' placement:

◇ My most difficult decision was *when* to place Mother in a nursing facility.

◇ My daughter, son, and I concurred when it was time to put my wife in the nursing home.

◇ Even though my parents placed their names in our church-related home while they were very much in command, it was difficult to say, "Mom, the time has come."

◇ My most difficult decision was to support Mother when she put Daddy in a nursing home. I felt it was too soon. She had not tried help in the home. But, of course, that was her decision. Living out of state, I am sure I did not realize how difficult it was on her.

Frequently, one or more family members do not recognize, or admit, the need for the patient's placement as readily as other family members do. A real eye-opener, and often quick remedy, is for family members who are "holding out" to relieve the primary caregiver for a week. By providing total patient care, these family members are likely to realize soon that their loved one needs more care than can be provided in the home. It is important for all family members to acknowledge this need, so the whole family can be united and supportive of one another in the decision.

Transition from home to a care facility frequently follows hospitalization. In these situations, families may have no other viable options and, perhaps, little time to choose the right facility. Respondents shared the following comments:

◇ Help family members accept their limitations in caring for the patient at home.

◇ Offer to accompany the family when selecting a nursing facility.

◇ Be with the caregiver on the day of placement, if appropriate. Check on the patient and family frequently during the first couple of weeks.

◇ My minister supported me in putting my husband in a nursing home. A "burned-out" caregiver is no good to anyone.

Several respondents shared positive experiences following the placement of their loved ones in a nursing facility:

◇ I needed to accept the fact I did what was best for my husband and myself by putting him in the nursing home so I could continue caring for him.

◇ My health has improved since Mother has been in the nursing home. She is doing well even though Alzheimer's is robbing her speech now.

◇ Putting my mother in a nursing home was a relief; however, it was still difficult emotionally.

✧ I had to miss church for about six weeks when I could no longer take care of my husband. At present, I am doing better since he is in a nursing home.

It takes time for Alzheimer's patients to adjust to a care facility. They have to get accustomed to a new routine, new surroundings, and new people in their confused state of mind. You can help in these ways following nursing facility placement:

✧ Encourage the caregiver to be patient during the loved one's adjustment.
✧ There is nothing anyone can say or do—just a listening ear is a tremendous help.
✧ Remind us that placement does not indicate decreased love for the patient.

Generally, family members should allow trained staff to perform activities of daily living while the patient is in the nursing facility. That is the purpose of the patient being there! Visits can be more enjoyable, if energy is not devoted to these tasks. Also, it is important for family members to see the staff can, and will, provide appropriate care for their loved one.

Family members experience major adjustments, too, when their loved one is placed in a care facility. For spouses, two common adjustments are being alone and the ensuing loneliness. Another adjustment involves entrusting the care of their loved one to strangers. Through the years, family members developed their way of doing this; therefore, it is natural for them to feel like no one else knows how or can do as well. While it is important for family members to share with the staff what they found effective, they must accept the fact that other ways can work, too.

Feeding Tubes and Respirators

The use of feeding tubes and respirators represents an end-of-life issue. As death approaches, you can help families "let go" of their loved ones. One respondent noted the importance of making health care decisions prior to need:

◇ Decisions pertaining to feeding tubes and respirators should be addressed in advance so they can be made rationally rather than emotionally.

Several family members shared their struggle in making end-of-life decisions for loved ones:

◇ Tube feeding and respirator usage are very important religious and ethical issues. Do I, as a caregiver, have a right to extend someone's life ad infinitum if the patient's quality of life is poor? If the patient cannot move, eat, or talk, and is in a fetal position, what right does anybody have to prolong life through tubes and other technological devices?

◇ This is a personal decision. Mother is a "no code" patient. She would not want her life extended beyond God's will.

◇ My most difficult decision was "to let my husband go"—to accept the fact he was no longer "living" and no longer "my husband."

◇ The most difficult decision I faced was not to prolong my wife's life.

◇ Each time my husband has been admitted to the hospital I have been asked about resuscitation, if he goes into cardiac arrest. I have said, "No." I decided there will be no tubes and have told the doctor I do not want him hospitalized again. There comes a time one must "let go."

If families must make end-of-life decisions for their loved ones, it is helpful when patients have made their wishes known. Respondents shared these experiences:

◇ My husband told me he did not want to be kept alive with tubes.

◇ My most difficult decision was whether or not to have Mother resuscitated. I was told they could possibly bring her back but probably to pain and tubes. I said, "No." Mother and I had discussed this previously. It was her wish.

◇ My mother and father made their own decisions about feeding tubes and respirators. I will try to carry out their wishes.

Families are relieved when they do not have to make ethical decisions for loved ones:

◇ Thank God I did not have to make decisions about a feeding tube or a respirator for Mother. God spared me of that.

For additional information regarding end-of-life decisions, see the pamphlets *Ethical Considerations: Issues in Death and Dying* and *End-of-Life Decisions: Honoring the Wishes of the Person with Alzheimer's Disease,* by the Alzheimer's Association.

Infidelity

Although countless non-Alzheimer's spouses remain faithful to their marital vows, infidelity is, perhaps, more common than realized. It involves not only sexual infidelity but can include mental, emotional, and spiritual infidelity as well.

Loneliness and aloneness cause vulnerability to temptations. Affairs can happen as a result of members of the opposite sex talking and spending time together. One respondent addressed the issue of stress associated with a lack of adult conversation and companionship:

◇ My master's thesis was about loss experienced by caregivers of Alzheimer's patients. The overwhelming response I received from folks over sixty-five years old was the loss of the adult companion. Family, friends, and neighbors may drift away, leaving the caregiver even more isolated from adult conversation. This seemingly small factor, at times, is the final straw. Living with an adult body that responds in a childlike way combined with the loss of adult communication becomes the highest stress factor. It can be therapeutic for clergy and congregation to help fill that void.

Several spouses shared their struggles with loneliness and the accompanying adjustments necessitated by their loved ones' illness:

◇ I have lost the companionship and intimacy of marriage—both the sexual and emotional support of my husband.

◇ I find it hard to live alone after thirty-eight years of marriage. Many facets of our lives have been affected.

◇ The hardest thing to face on Sunday is getting up, going to church alone, and taking Communion without my husband. For forty-six years, we did this together. But, I did not allow myself to miss that first Sunday and have not missed yet.

Another respondent acknowledged additional common needs of non-Alzheimer's spouses:

✧ I need moral support and understanding.

Nursing facility placement and death of loved ones are especially lonely times for families, as evidenced by these quotes:

✧ My father was extremely lonely after Mother was placed in a nursing home.
✧ Since I have been married fifty years, I think I will face terrible loneliness when my husband dies.
✧ My greatest need is to make the adjustment of being alone.

One respondent posed this solution for coping with loneliness:

✧ To feel God's presence can break chains of loneliness.

When the church embraces Alzheimer's spouses with love and fulfills their needs, infidelity will be less likely to occur. Various suggestions of ways clergy and congregations can provide spouses adult conversation and companionship are mentioned throughout the book. Some of these include worship services, Sunday school, Bible studies, visitation, telephone ministry, fellowships, and social events.

For additional information about ethical issues, consult materials in the section Ethical Decision Making in Chapter 16, "Resources."

GUIDELINES FOR MAKING ETHICAL DECISIONS

You can help families make ethical decisions by encouraging them to (1) obtain information, (2) talk to others who have made the same decision, (3) pray, and (4) search the scriptures.

Obtain Information

Before making decisions, family members need to gather accurate medical, legal, financial, ethical, and spiritual information. And, all family members need the same information. Physicians, attorneys, financial planners, social workers, and clergy may grant permission to have conversations recorded for those unable to attend conferences.

With modern technology and terminology, there may be a different understanding of certain words. For example, "life support" may have a different connotation among family members and the concept may be used even differently by physicians. Questions should be asked and answered for clarification. Family members have to live with themselves and their decisions; therefore, it is important they make the right decisions.

Talk to Others Who Have Made the Same Decision

One respondent offered this suggestion for families facing ethical decisions:

> ✧ It would be helpful to discuss the issue with those who have already made the decision for their loved ones.

Experiences of those "who have been there" can be beneficial as an additional source of information, *if* they confirm the teachings in God's Word. Proverbs 11:14 declares, "Where no counsel is, the people fall: but in the multitude of counselors there is safety."

Decisions should not be based solely on experiences and opinions of others.

Pray

Family members need to pray for wisdom as they seek the mind of Christ. One respondent advised thus:

> ✧ Pray that God's will be known and right decisions made.

An important factor in wanting to know or do God's will is obeying His will as He reveals it. Families are faced with solemn questions:

- Do all family members want to know and obey God's will regarding ethical decisions for their loved one?
- Are all family members in agreement about a certain course of action?
- Will there be guilt if this action is followed?
- Will there be guilt if this action is not implemented?
- Is this course of action what they want or what God wants or what they and God want?
- Is God's will confirmed by the accord of all family members?

God can reveal His will through people and scripture. Obeying His will results in peace not guilt.

Search the Scriptures

The Bible is the authority (guide or rule) for Christians. It is the yardstick for determining what God wants us to do.

All ethical matters are not specifically addressed in scripture; however, principles are given that enable God's will to be known. For example, "respirator" and "feeding tube" are not mentioned in the Bible. Yet, what is revealed about God, His nature and attributes, earthly and eternal life, death, hope, comfort, and the resurrection provide guidance for these issues. By knowing principles, specific decisions can be made that honor Christ.

God's will never contradicts His Word—His Word always confirms His will.

ADDITIONAL ETHICS-RELATED ISSUES

Other ethics-related issues include (1) only child syndrome, (2) ill-advised comments, (3) interventions, and (4) agony of the decision-making process.

Only Child Syndrome

From my experience in ministry, it appears there are unique issues when an "only child" confronts parental issues of aging. Sons who are only children seem to have greater difficulty making and implementing decisions for their demented mothers than family members in other relationships.

While an only child may have support from a spouse, children, and others, no one else shared the same family history and dynamics. Therefore, an only child might feel alone when making decisions. Even though siblings may disagree about issues and timing for implementation, at least they can discuss situations with one another.

Interventions such as nursing home placement, taking the car away, or job termination may not be made as quickly by an only child versus involvement by two or more children. Yet, for various reasons, even when a family consists of more than one child, often one assumes major responsibility for the care of a parent.

Ill-Advised Comments

Acquaintances may offer unsolicited, unwanted, and ill-advised comments. They may say, "I would never put my mother in a nursing home" or "I would never have a feeding tube inserted in my husband." No one knows what would be done unless faced with the same situation. Even then all factors are not equal. Family decisions are to be made by the family. Generally, it is not helpful when people give advice about ethical situations they have not experienced.

Interventions

Due to the nature of Alzheimer's, in that behavior is not always consistent, it is difficult to know *when* to intervene. Considerations for determining the timing include the following:

- Is caring for the patient taking a toll on the caregiver? Some caregivers have died before their patients!
- Is the patient dangerous to self or others?
- How would a family member (who had not intervened) feel if the patient or others were injured or killed?

Word of caution: *When interventions are made, the situation may get worse before it gets better.* Families should develop a plan and present a united front, and then be consistent and persistent in the implementation of the plan, remembering, "This too shall pass!"

Several interventions may be necessary throughout the illness. Each intervention requires adjustments and, finally, acceptance.

Often, a particular family member, friend, or professional can persuade the patient to take the necessary course of action. You may want to inquire whether there is such a person when ministering to families faced with interventions.

Family members *should* want to do everything possible to ensure the safety of their loved one and others. However, help, encouragement, reassurance, and even "permission" by clergy may be needed when making interventions:

✧ Understand what it is like, if possible, to put a loved one in a nursing home. Every day Mother asks to go home, and I feel sad. Keep telling me, "You did the right thing."

Agony of the Decision-Making Process

Perhaps the most agonizing aspect of the decision-making process is the indecision before the decision is made. Gathering information can be overwhelming. Frustration may result from not remembering or understanding all of it. Furthermore, families are often mentally, emotionally, and physically exhausted. After the decision is made, a sense of relief can be expected as the plan is implemented, adjustments are made, and acceptance ensues.

ROLE OF MINISTRY

You can help families struggling with difficult decisions in the following ways:

✧ Listen and reflect.
✧ Empathize.
✧ Support family decisions as much as possible.
✧ Remind us we are not alone.
✧ Offer encouragement, reassurance, comfort from God's promises, and moral support.
✧ Through preaching, teaching, and counseling ministries help us live by the Word.
✧ Help us explore options. Discuss pros and cons, but do not give personal opinions, such as, "I think you should . . ."
✧ Avoid being judgmental.
✧ Discuss "death with dignity."
✧ Facilitate discussion among family members.
✧ Research facts to understand why we made the decisions we did.
✧ Affirm us when we have done all that can be done.

If ye love me, keep my commandments.

John 14:15

Chapter 12

Models for Ministry

Whether ministry to Alzheimer's patients and families is performed by clergy or members of the congregation, hopefully, it will be based on a combination of these biblical models: (1) ministering as unto Christ, (2) ministering according to the "Golden Rule," (3) ministering as servant, and (4) ministering as friend.

MINISTERING AS UNTO CHRIST

Matthew 25:34-40 indicates we are ministering to Jesus when we minister to Alzheimer's patients:

Then shall the King say unto them on his right hand, Come, ye blessed of my Father, inherit the kingdom prepared for you from the foundation of the world: For I was an hungered, and ye gave me meat: I was thirsty, and ye gave me drink: I was a stranger, and ye took me in: Naked, and ye clothed me: I was sick, and ye visited me: I was in prison, and ye came unto me. Then shall the righteous answer him, saying, Lord, when saw we thee hungered, and fed thee? or thirsty, and gave thee drink? When saw we thee a stranger, and took thee in? or naked, and clothed thee? Or when saw we thee sick, or in prison, and came unto thee? And the King shall answer and say unto them, Verily I say unto you, Inasmuch as ye have done it unto one of the least of these my brethren, ye have done it unto me.

Questions:

- Can you see an Alzheimer's patient as Christ Himself?
- If you truly saw Jesus in the face of each Alzheimer's patient you visited, would you make any changes in your ministry? Would you visit more often? Would you be more compassionate? Would you dread the visit or eagerly anticipate it?
- How would you prepare for the visit if you were going to see Jesus?

MINISTERING ACCORDING TO THE "GOLDEN RULE"

Ministry can arise out of doing for others what we think we would want done for us if we were in the same situation. Minister to others as you would want to be ministered unto.

> Therefore all things whatsoever ye would that men should do to you, do ye even so to them. . . .

> Matthew 7:12

Questions:

- If you had just been diagnosed with Alzheimer's, what would you want your pastor and church to do for you and your family?
- How can the church express its love and concern for you and your family throughout your Alzheimer's pilgrimage?
- What would you want the church to do for you and your family if you had to be admitted to a nursing facility?
- How could a minister help your family if they had to make decisions regarding life support or a feeding tube for you?
- How could your pastor help you and your family during your dying moments?
- What would you like a minister to say at your funeral to comfort and encourage your family and friends?
- How can the church express its love and concern to your family following your death?

• What ministry would you desire if your spouse, parents, or children were Alzheimer's patients?

MINISTERING AS SERVANT

True greatness is found in being a servant. Jesus set the example for servant ministry: He "came not to be ministered unto, but to minister, and to give his life a ransom of many" (Matthew 20:18; Mark 10:45).

> . . . whosoever will be great among you, let him be your minister; And whosoever will be chief among you, let him be your servant.
>
> Matthew 20:26-27

> If any man desire to be first, the same shall be last of all, and servant of all.
>
> Mark 9:35

> . . . whosoever will be great among you, shall be your minister: And whosoever of you will be chiefest, shall be servant of all.
>
> Mark 10:43-44

Questions:

• How do you think Jesus would minister to Alzheimer's patients?
• How do you think Jesus would minister to Alzheimer's families?

MINISTERING AS FRIEND

Jesus also set the example of ministering as a friend. Being, and having, a friend in the time of need is a blessing. It involves a mutual, voluntary relationship. Openness, honesty, trust, compassion, and sharing are fostered. A friend goes that extra mile and is always there. Although ministering as friend requires considerable time and energy, rapport will be established before a crisis occurs. A number of respondents noted the importance and value of having a minister who is their friend:

✧ Visit and call to give support. Let us know you care and are there for us. Then when something happens, you are not a stranger but a *real friend.*

✧ As much as possible, be there as a constant companion and friend, not always the pastor.

✧ Keep in touch and help meet needs as they arise. Be a Christian friend.

✧ I was very lucky to have such a loving and understanding pastor— he was a friend as well as pastor during my grief.

✧ Our rabbi had always been our friend.

Questions:

- Are you willing to go beyond the "call of duty" when ministering to Alzheimer's patients and families by spending extra time and energy to meet their needs?
- Are you willing to temporarily sacrifice your pleasures or needs to minister to Alzheimer's patients and families?
- Do Alzheimer's patients and families sense that you minister to them out of your desire rather than your duty?

When I was in chaplaincy training, a supervisor once asked me whether I had been a minister or friend to a patient. In my mind, I immediately thought it was a trick question. It seemed that either answer I gave might be wrong in his eyes. I cannot remember what I finally said. But after much reflection upon that question, I realize I do not have to be minister *or* friend. I can be minister *and* friend. In fact, I minister more effectively to Alzheimer's patients and families when I treat them as I would treat Christ, when I do for them what I would want done for me, when I serve them, and when I am their friend!

And I thank Christ Jesus our Lord, who hath enabled me, for that he counted me faithful, putting me into the ministry.

I Timothy 1:12

Chapter 13

Pastoral Potpourri

Rapport, trust, sensitivity, concern, and availability will partially determine the gamut of issues patients and families will discuss with you. Even if parishioners do not ask about specific matters, occasions may arise for you to sensitively bring certain topics into the conversation. Anticipate common concerns and be informed about these issues. Topics that patients or families may want to discuss include the following:

- Advocacy
- Clinical drug trials
- Concern regarding loved ones' salvation
- Holidays
- Hospitalization of the patient
- Humor
- Long-distance caregiving
- Ministry by two or more clergy
- Pets
- Research
- Television
- Transference and countertransference
- When Alzheimer's strikes clergy and their families
- When patients can no longer fulfill church responsibilities
- Working with law enforcement officials and transit operators

ADVOCACY

You can be the voice of patients who can no longer speak for themselves if you assume an active advocacy role at local, state, and federal levels in ways such as these:

- Raise public awareness of patients' and families' needs.
- Become involved with policymaking.
- Support legislation for additional research funding.
- Seek funds for financial assistance for patients and families.
- Provide additional resources.
- Participate in the annual Memory Walk.
- Serve as an Alzheimer's Association board member.

Since some patients and families do not have a clergyperson, you can encourage your Alzheimer's Association chapter to provide a volunteer or paid chaplain to address spiritual needs. The chaplain also could offer pastoral care to those who feel uncomfortable discussing Alzheimer's issues with their own pastor. Even persons who have a minister could benefit from this additional avenue of spiritual support.

An important, but often overlooked, need is for family restrooms in church facilities and other public places so the spouse or adult child of the opposite sex can assist the patient with toileting. Patients and families should not be denied the right to attend worship services, dine out, or attend community events because of inadequate restroom accommodations.

Seek to ensure that patients and their families have the highest possible quality of life at every stage of the illness.

CLINICAL DRUG TRIALS

Families may want their loved ones to participate in a clinical drug trial in an attempt to find a cure for Alzheimer's. For information about current drug trials, encourage them to contact the Alzheimer's Association and the Alzheimer's Disease Education & Referral Center. Also, see the pamphlet *About Clinical Studies and Participating in Research,* by the Alzheimer's Association.

CONCERN REGARDING LOVED ONES' SALVATION

Christians want everyone—especially their loved ones—to have the joy and peace they experience through faith in Christ. This wife's lament underscores the urgency of presenting the gospel while cognitive abilities are intact:

✧ My husband did not believe. That worries my children and me.

If family members share apprehension about their loved one's spiritual condition while the patient is still living, share God's plan of salvation with the patient in the presence of at least one family member. Try to arrange a time when the patient is expected to be as lucid as possible. Family members need to be reminded ahead of time that regardless of the words the patient says, these words may not be what is intended because of the nature of the disease. Alzheimer's patients sometimes say a word meaning the opposite of the intended word.

The son of an Alzheimer's patient expressed concern about his mother's salvation in this way:

✧ Mom was a different person—very mean. Was she saved? I am confident that if she was ever saved she still is regardless of how the disease causes her to change. Some day I will be with her the way she was.

HOLIDAYS

Family members and patients may have different needs regarding holidays. Often, families want everything to be as it used to be. In an attempt to create this impossibility, they may take their loved ones out of the care facility for the holiday. This could prove to be a disaster for everyone. Patients easily become confused, frustrated, agitated, and hostile in a crowd of noisy "strangers" and an unfamiliar environment.

Needs of patients might best be met by remaining in the facility and having one or two family members visit at a time throughout the day in their familiar setting. Then, hopefully, the holiday will be enjoyed by all. Family members will have treasured memories of the occasion rather than nightmares of a disastrous day.

Excellent suggestions for holidays are found in the pamphlet *Holidays,* by the Alzheimer's Association, and in the article "Holiday Visiting Tips: A Message for the Faith Community and Friends of Alzheimer's Families," by Edna Ballard and J. Whitney Little.

HOSPITALIZATION OF THE PATIENT

From time to time, patients may be hospitalized. Confusion, fear, and agitation can be expected when they are among strangers in an unfamiliar setting. Family or facility staff will need to notify hospital personnel of patients' needs and normal status compared to current condition.

Decisions have to be made during each hospitalization, including answering these questions: (1) Is it safe for the patient to stay alone, or is it necessary for someone to be with the patient at all times? (2) What, if any, heroic measures will be utilized?

For additional information, see the pamphlets *Hospitalization,* by the Alzheimer's Association, and *Hospitalization Happens: A Guide to Hospital Visits for Loved Ones with Memory Disorders,* by the National Institute on Aging and National Institutes of Health.

HUMOR

No one should laugh *at* or make fun of Alzheimer's patients; however, you can encourage families to look for humor in situations. Humor is an excellent coping mechanism when dealing with a loved one's illness. Reading humorous books and watching comical television programs and videos may help families relieve their stress. One respondent stated:

✧ Any little laugh helps.

LONG-DISTANCE CAREGIVING

A modern-day reality is that the patient's next-of-kin may live out of town. Therefore, caregiving might have to be provided at a distance, at least during the early stages of the illness.

With permission, nearby family members may find it meaningful for you to contact out-of-town relatives. This supportive ministry can be offered periodically but especially during times of crises:

✧ When my husband was diagnosed, I needed someone to help my children. Since they lived away, it was difficult for them to realize what was happening and to accept the situation. My rabbi called them long distance.

MINISTRY BY TWO OR MORE CLERGY

Since patients can live with Alzheimer's disease for more than twenty years, it is not likely their pastor at the time of diagnosis will be the same pastor when death occurs. This reality can be difficult for clergy, patients, and families:

✧ My priest was very warm and compassionate, but he has moved to another city.
✧ All the priests in our parish knew my husband and our problems during the early stage of his illness. One by one they moved to new parishes, and their replacements did not know us. When my husband died, his service was held in the funeral parlor instead of the church where he had attended for over twenty-five years. A priest was provided who called me aside to get a little information about my husband's background. He gave a very nice eulogy, and everyone was satisfied.

Also, if family members live in different geographical locations or are members of different churches even in the same community, likely more than one pastor will be involved in meeting spiritual needs.

Opportunities—especially in care facilities—may arise for you to minister to people who have faith traditions other than your own. If you are in doubt about the beliefs and practices of another denomination, contact a clergyperson of that denomination or research beliefs in order not to offend. Be supportive of other ministers and work cooperatively for the welfare of patients and families.

PETS

If an Alzheimer's patient has a pet, safety issues may arise for the patient, the pet, or both. The pet could cause the patient to fall or become injured in other ways. As the disease progresses, the patient may unknowingly and unintentionally injure a beloved pet. If the patient lives alone, the pet may not receive adequate food and water. For various reasons, the time may come when a new home will have to be found for the pet. A cuddly stuffed animal may serve as a substitute.

However, if the patient has to enter a care facility, the spouse remaining at home may want to acquire a pet as a source of companionship during the adjustment of living alone. Pets have a way of being like a magnet to draw people to them as well as to their owners; therefore, friendships may develop as a result of having pets.

RESEARCH

Scientists diligently continue their attempts to find links and associations with Alzheimer's disease. Tests have been performed on countless variables. From time to time, breakthroughs occur that seem promising in putting the pieces of the puzzle together.

Two areas in which I hope further research will be conducted are (1) intelligence and (2) grief. From my observation and experience in ministry, many patients were highly intelligent and had suffered major grief. A large number had suffered the death of a spouse, one or more children, or both spouse and child(ren). One dementia resident lost his spouse and six of his seven children before he died.

TELEVISION

Caregivers should not use television as a babysitter for patients. In fact, it is probably best if patients do not watch or hear TV because they easily become confused, agitated, frustrated, and frightened by the images and sounds. Patients may think a character on television is a real person in the room with them. Pictures of violence can be scary. Inspirational videos and DVDs with scenes of God's beautiful creation and tranquil music are a better alternative since these are soothing, relaxing, and worshipful.

If family members want to watch TV, perhaps, it could be done when the patient is asleep or in another room and cannot see or hear it.

TRANSFERENCE AND COUNTERTRANSFERENCE

You may remind a patient of someone previously known (transference) or the patient might remind you of someone you knew from the past (countertransference). If past relationships were favorable, likely there will be instant rapport in the new relationship.

An Alzheimer's patient may actually think you are the person previously known. It may be wise for the patient to continue to believe you are that person, especially if you can minister in this manner. Stating your true identity will probably not satisfy the patient anyway. Arguing and rationalizing will not help the situation or the relationship.

If the patient had a past negative association with the person you resemble and becomes upset when you visit, consider finding someone else to minister. Explain the situation to family members, if they are unaware. You may be able to minister in other ways, such as sending cards and telephoning. The patient may reach a point when there is no longer a negative association, and you can resume visits.

In crisis situations, patients may not be aware of your identity. At that point, you might want to ask the family whether it would be all right for you to visit. Various factors must be taken into consideration regarding these decisions and handled on an individual basis.

WHEN ALZHEIMER'S STRIKES CLERGY
AND THEIR FAMILIES

Although Alzheimer's is a "no respecter of persons" disease, there are unique issues when clergy and their families have the illness. No matter how much you know about Alzheimer's ministry, it is always *different* and *difficult* when you and your family are affected. But, you and your family need help just like everyone else and should not be expected to bear your burdens alone:

> ✧ Mother was a minister's wife for over forty years. Dad died three years prior to her diagnosis. His colleagues did not minister to her

after his death. I found that unbelievable in clergy circles. She must have been expected to deal with this on a different level than others since she was a "minister's wife." Following diagnosis, she moved to live with one of her children. Her support system dwindled almost immediately when siblings, life long friends, and former neighbors drifted away. Good Christian people deserted her. How sad for our Christian ethic! If we cannot minister to our frail and elderly, why are we here?

When a family member of a clergyperson is affected, likely there will be more interest in the disease and understanding of others in the same situation because of the empathy involved:

✧ My minister's wife was also an Alzheimer's patient. He was, therefore, most understanding and helpful.

It appears many people who serve in helping professions (clergy, physicians, attorneys, etc.) have an extraordinarily difficult time dealing with the situation when someone in their family has Alzheimer's. It is one thing to tell others what they need to do, but it is quite different and difficult when professionals feel helpless and unable to help their loved ones and themselves.

At times, it is not easy to talk about a loved one and the situation:

✧ I am a pastor but did not tell the congregation of my wife's diagnosis until five years later. It was difficult for me to talk about it because of her privacy.

WHEN PATIENTS CAN NO LONGER FULFILL CHURCH RESPONSIBILITIES

A patient will have lost many abilities and functions when unable to perform delegated church roles. Factors that determine how a situation is handled include the role performed and the patient's condition. For example, singing in the choir might be "covered up" easily and not require action. However, mental deficits when teaching or serving as a deacon may necessitate action because inappropriate behavior would probably be more noticeable, embarrassing, and disruptive.

Patients often can function longer in their positions, if others provide the required assistance.

When a patient acknowledges the inability to perform a designated role and relinquishes the position, the matter is readily resolved. But, in some situations, patients fight to maintain control over whatever they have left—including positions and assets. If you are involved in removing a patient from a church office, extreme sensitivity must be exerted to avoid hurting the feelings of the patient, family, and friends. Patients must be treated with dignity and allowed to maintain their self-esteem. Generally, the less said and done regarding the removal of a patient from a church position, the better. Involve no more people than necessary. Understanding family members may be able to offer suggestions for handling this unpleasant task. In an attempt to prevent these situations from occurring, congregations may consider by-laws that limit terms of leadership positions to, perhaps, one year with possible extensions voted upon annually.

When the patient is a clergyperson who can no longer fulfill pastoral responsibilities, the situation is reversed in that it will be church leaders who must delicately handle the dilemma. Again, supportive family members need to assist with decisions that must be made.

Even when patients do not hold an official church position, difficult situations can arise. Patients may make false accusations and speak negatively about the pastor or others in the congregation. Each situation must be dealt with on a case-by-case basis.

WORKING WITH LAW ENFORCEMENT OFFICIALS AND TRANSIT OPERATORS

Occasions may arise when you have opportunities to work with officers and bus drivers to assist Alzheimer's patients and families. Patients might wander and become lost, attempt to board the wrong bus, take items from stores without paying for them, cause disturbances, unintentionally make statements that are not truthful, drive when it is not safe to do so, and exhibit inappropriate sexual behavior.

The wife of an Alzheimer's patient shared her humiliation regarding an incident when her husband took a candy bar at a store without paying for it. The police were called, and she felt like he was treated as a criminal. Yet, in reality, can Alzheimer's patients commit a crime if they have no control over their behavior and no cognition of "breaking the law"?*

In some localities, training is available from the Alzheimer's Association to help police officers understand the nature of Alzheimer's and how to help patients. The pamphlet *Safe Return®: Guide for Law Enforcement,* by the Alzheimer's Association, is an excellent publication. It provides an overview of the illness, warning signs of the disease, communication tips, common behaviors exhibited by patients, and suggestions for finding patients who are lost.

If any of you lack wisdom, let him ask of God, that giveth to all men liberally, and upbraideth not; and it shall be given him.

James 1:5

---

*As a theological aside, I believe God regards the behavior of Alzheimer's patients (who are Christians but have no awareness of what they are saying and doing) as He does the behavior of young children who have not reached the age of accountability. In other words, I do not think He holds such patients "responsible" for actions and attitudes that otherwise would be sinful, if committed by people who do know right from wrong. While God is a just God, He is also a God of love and mercy.

Chapter 14

Faith, Hope, and Love

Virtues of faith, hope, and love are vital for patients and families while enduring the trials that Alzheimer's disease inflicts upon their lives.

To minister effectively to these people, you must have the ability to create, encourage, facilitate, and sustain faith, hope, and love in their lives as well as an understanding of the role of ministry.

FAITH

Alzheimer's family members have varying theological beliefs, interpretations of their loved ones' illness, and perspectives on the role of faith, as evidenced by these quotes:

✧ I never asked, "Why us?" Our family did not blame God for this misfortune.
✧ How could God let this cruel thing happen? How could this be His will? Initially, everything seemed hopeless. I constantly asked, "Why?" "Why him?" But, as time passed, I accepted a situation I could not change. I prayed for patience, courage, and strength. I learned to live one day at a time and came to the conclusion my husband had Alzheimer's because of genetics or something in his physical makeup. I realize it is not God's will and am doing okay.
✧ How could this happen to my grandfather? He is such a good Christian.
✧ Many families feel God has abandoned them and their loved ones.
✧ My faith has sustained me, but there have been many lonely, hard times. I never asked, "Why?" but rather prayed for guidance and strength.
✧ It is hard not to ask, "Why?"

Many family members experience a faith crisis as a result of a loved one's Alzheimer's diagnosis. Respondents shared these comments:

✧ My faith is, at times, being sorely tested.
✧ Why us? What have I done to deserve this? How can I care for my husband and still be a Christian? I experienced a crisis of faith as a result of his illness.
✧ My faith in God has been through a testing period.

A crisis of faith can be beneficial because it is an opportunity for one to determine the source, security, and foundation of that faith. If faith is in anyone or anything other than Christ alone, it will not weather the storms and uncertainties of Alzheimer's. One respondent stated thus:

✧ Ministers can reiterate to family members their need for faith in God no matter what happens.

Family members acknowledged their need for faith in God, as revealed in these quotes:

✧ My greatest spiritual need is to keep the faith that God's plan for allowing my grandfather's illness will soon be revealed. I believe my faith will help me through this.
✧ My greatest need is spiritual strength and faith.

Numerous respondents shared the significance of their faith and how it helped them in the Alzheimer's expedition:

✧ Faith kindles endurance.
✧ My faith gives me strength.
✧ My faith is that God is sufficient for my needs and will turn what has happened into something good.
✧ I have faith God will help me through this and not give me more than I can handle.
✧ My faith assures me that I am not dealing with this alone.
✧ Mother has been a faithful Christian. I know God has not forgotten her.

At times, the faith of one person strengthens or sustains that of another person. Family members shared these examples:

✧ I have witnessed my husband's faith, and it has strengthened me.
✧ When my wife was diagnosed, our pastor helped me to keep my faith in the Lord.

HOPE

Biblical hope looks to the future in expectation of a better time or condition. Alzheimer's families need hope to cope with their situation in life and in death.

In the Alzheimer's experience, initial hope is that the diagnosis will not be Alzheimer's. But, if it is, the focus of earthly hope can be momentary or remain constant throughout the illness. Respondents shared these comments regarding ongoing hope:

✧ I hope God will be merciful to my husband.
✧ I hope I can cope with all the stress.

A scientific and medical hope we all have is that a cure for Alzheimer's disease will soon be found. Diligent research has been conducted toward this end. For additional information about the progress that has been made, see the pamphlet *What's Being Done About Alzheimer's,* by the Alzheimer's Association.

Many respondents focused on hope in reference to healing. One respondent stated:

✧ My hope is for my wife's healing.

Other comments indicate a lack of hope for their loved ones' healing:

✧ I am a retired minister. As a result of my wife's illness, I have encountered the issue of the validity of spiritual healing. It has been eleven years since she was diagnosed. Although I have lost hope that she will be healed, I thank God for making our paths relatively "easy."
✧ I have no hope for my mother's recovery or improvement—but faith she will be set free to a better life after death.
✧ Since there is no cure, I hoped our life together would be as full as possible and that my wife's death would be painless. I hoped and prayed for a quick death.

Several respondents expressed hope that their loved ones' death would come quickly:

⬦ My hope is for my mother's release. My faith says she will live in eternal peace hereafter.

⬦ My hope and daily prayer is that God will not let my husband suffer many years.

⬦ I had faith and hope it would be over quickly, but my wife is lasting a long time.

⬦ I hope for a brighter future and a speedy death for my husband.

⬦ I hope God will take my husband home before he becomes totally mindless.

Even when medical hope has been exhausted for individual patients, spiritual hope remains for them and their families. A number of family members shared the significance of their hope and how it has helped them:

⬦ My hope and faith give me "confidence unshaken."

⬦ I have hope God will give me strength to carry on during this difficult time in my life.

⬦ My wife's illness has caused me to seek to deepen my faith in Christ, the source of my hope. I pray daily for strength and wisdom.

⬦ I have a strong faith and know there is always hope as long as there is life.

LOVE

Expressions of love by clergy and the church family for Alzheimer's patients and families need not be costly but should be frequent. Gifts of your presence are often more meaningful than your presents. These comments express the importance of love:

⬦ Love is my greatest need.

⬦ The most meaningful thing a minister can do to help in our pilgrimage is to love us.

⬦ The church can be supportive by showing love for the patient and family.

⬦ We need lots of love from our pastor and the church.

✧ Although patients will never be like they were, love is still needed. Love, in its purest form, is the only way. Alzheimer's patients respond to love.

ROLE OF MINISTRY

Clergy can help patients and families with issues of faith, hope, and love in the following ways:

✧ Love us.
✧ Encourage us to have faith and hope in God.
✧ Help us keep our faith as strong as possible.
✧ Offer hope and reassurance.
✧ Pray for and with us—prayer reinforces hope.
✧ Help dispel the ever-present hopelessness.
✧ Offer courage, hope, and love through preaching, teaching, and counseling ministries.
✧ Recount the hope found in God's Word.

The triad of faith, hope, and love enables Alzheimer's patients and families to see light at the end of the tunnel while awaiting the return of Christ and the resurrection of the dead.

And now abideth faith, hope, charity, these three; but the greatest of these is charity.

I Corinthians 13:13

Chapter 15

Remembering Blessings
During Difficult Times

Patients and families affected by Alzheimer's disease may be so caught up in the tragedy and its impact they do not readily recognize God's blessings in their midst. You have opportunities to offer encouragement as God reflects and reveals His love even during the darkest days.

Blessings that may result from Alzheimer's disease include being a(n)

- catalyst to draw patients and families closer to God,
- instrument of spiritual growth,
- opportunity to develop new friendships,
- illness without indication of physical pain,
- opportunity to love,
- illness with an inability to remember,
- catalyst to cause families to make personal health care decisions,
- opportunity for families to find meaning in the experience,
- instrument God uses to teach lessons,
- avenue of release when death occurs for Christians, and
- channel of blessing.

CATALYST TO DRAW PATIENTS
AND FAMILIES CLOSER TO GOD

Alzheimer's disease is a crisis experience. When this illness intrudes upon the entire family, those affected have an opportunity to move away from God or closer to Him. Many people admit their inability to handle this situation alone and depend on God to meet their needs. Respondents shared the following comments:

✧ I do not believe God put this illness on us. God's will is entirely good. I am not sure I understand why He permitted it, but I am seeking to turn what Satan intended as a curse into a blessing.

✧ As a result of Mother's illness, I have developed a closer relationship with God. I talk to Him more.

✧ I look forward to the "good" that will come from my grandfather's illness. God has blessed me, and I have become stronger through every hardship. I constantly pray his illness would bring my parents back to God.

INSTRUMENT OF SPIRITUAL GROWTH

God can use Alzheimer's to help family members develop spiritual maturity. Respondents shared experiences of spiritual growth as a result of their loved ones' illness:

✧ I am growing because of the experience. I pray for a way of escape when I have feelings of resentment, frustration, and hate. Often, peace returns within the hour. My greatest need is to forgive and walk in love. I know the Lord is with me.

✧ This has been a time of great growth—a time of soul-searching and finding out who I am. To do this, I needed a support group and spiritual counseling. My husband's greatest gift to me has been that I have discovered myself.

OPPORTUNITY TO DEVELOP NEW FRIENDSHIPS

God can use Alzheimer's disease to bring people together who otherwise may never have met. Through these associations and the commonality of the illness, friendships can develop and deepen as people bond together to cope with their loved ones' illness:

✧ Friends prayed for me during Mother's illness and following her death. God gave me a peace I cannot explain.

ILLNESS WITHOUT INDICATION
OF PHYSICAL PAIN

Patients who have Alzheimer's disease usually do not appear to be in physical pain and often seem oblivious to their situation. One respondent stated:

✧ I consider the blessing of my husband's illness. He is not in pain and lives in his own little world unaware of what has happened to him.

OPPORTUNITY TO LOVE

Alzheimer's has the capability of drawing family members closer to one another. Grayce Bonhan Confer shares the experience of a deeper relationship with her husband in her book, *Alzheimer's: Another Opportunity to Love.*[1]

These respondents related examples of improved family relationships due to their loved ones' illness:

✧ Prayer has opened our communication with each other as well as with God.
✧ It was the saddest day of my life that Thanksgiving I was totally responsible for making the dressing. I did not know how. It was Mother's job. I now make it a point to share things with my daughter which we normally take for granted "Mother will always be there to do."

ILLNESS WITH AN INABILITY TO REMEMBER

The bane of forgetfulness can also be a blessing. Patients become disoriented and do not know where they are. This makes the situation easier on families, if patients have to be placed in a nursing facility.

✧ Most of the time, my husband does not know where he is.

CATALYST TO CAUSE FAMILIES
TO MAKE PERSONAL HEALTH CARE DECISIONS

When loved ones have Alzheimer's, families and friends may decide to make their own health care decisions. Respondents shared these experiences:

✧ Because of my father-in-law's illness, my wife and I have thought more seriously about our own futures—what kind of medical care and prolongation of life we would want.

✧ My parents saw the agony we experienced with my mother-in-law. They did not want me to be guilt-ridden, so they made sure I knew their wishes.

OPPORTUNITY FOR FAMILIES TO FIND MEANING
IN THE EXPERIENCE

It is common for families to be bewildered—especially soon after diagnosis. One respondent stated:

✧ I do not understand why I must go through this valley. No one can walk it for me. While I would never choose this way, I do not consider it punishment. I know God could heal my husband instantly. However, I do not have the whole picture and can only walk with the insight I do have.

Many people write articles or books to share insights gained from their interpretation of a tragedy. Teresa Strecker, in her book *Alzheimer's: Making Sense of Suffering,* recounts the meaning she found in the experience of her father's illness.[2]

Several respondents indicated their desire to help others as a result of their loved ones' illness:

✧ Because of my mother-in-law's illness, we hope we have been placed in circumstances where the Lord can use us to minister to others.

✧ My greatest need is to tell others about my experiences and hope they help someone else.

✧ I hope I learn from this experience and can help others in similar situations.

✧ I hope what I have learned will help someone else and will be an honor to my Lord and Mother.

INSTRUMENT GOD USES TO TEACH LESSONS

In the eyes of some people, it may seem life has no significance for an Alzheimer's patient, as evidenced by these comments:

✧ My husband is only a shell of the man I married.
✧ In some cases, the patient lies there seemingly less than human. The spark that made my husband unique is gone.

However, as long as God gives a person breath, He has a purpose for that life regardless of how it appears to others. He can accomplish His will in ways we cannot fathom. God uses Alzheimer's patients to teach families, friends, and staff lessons He would have learned, such as patience, strength in weakness, dependence upon Him to provide for every need, comfort in trials, sharing faith in times of crises, and life priorities.

AVENUE OF RELEASE WHEN DEATH OCCURS FOR CHRISTIANS

Alzheimer's disease may be the means God uses to bring a person into His presence. Numerous respondents shared the comfort they experience regarding their loved ones' death:

✧ Death, after all, is going home to God. Life for a Christian goes on.
✧ I know my husband is with God and is better off now.
✧ We have trusted that Mother is now well in heaven. This is a source of comfort to the family.
✧ I believe death is the greatest celebration a Christian will have. There is a time to die. God's will has been served, and Mother's battle has been won. She is no longer bound to the thief that stole her mind and dignity.
✧ I know I will see my father again.
✧ Death can be a positive time, if the patient and family have trusted Christ as their Savior.

CHANNEL OF BLESSING

When care facility staff lovingly and faithfully serve God by ministering to the physical, medical, emotional, and spiritual needs of Alzheimer's patients, it is natural for family members to want them to receive God's blessings:

✧ I want God to bless the staff in the nursing home who care for Mother.

The following poignant story by Hester Tetreault[3] beautifully attests to blessings that come to those who minister to Alzheimer's patients and their families.

The Passerby

I saw him most mornings when I looked out of the living room window. He became part of my day. Slightly bent, he dragged one leg a little, the foot twisted so that he walked more on the side of his foot than the sole. I guessed he was in his eighties. He wore only a flannel shirt. When I could see his breath against the air on a frosty morning, I wondered if he was cold.

While working in the garden one morning, I saw the old man smile and tousle the hair of a small boy who passed by him on his way into school.

"It's now or never," I decided, emboldened to cross the street and introduce myself.

His pale blue eyes enlivened and his face wrinkled in another smile. This time for me. "My wife and I are from Switzerland. We came first to Canada and then to America, many years ago," he told me. "We work very hard. In time we save enough to buy our own farm. I do not speak English so good, so I pick up children's first readers and secretly I study until I learn," he laughed. He gazed toward the elementary school beyond the wire fence, and his face grew solemn. "We never had any children."

I pondered the conversation in the quiet of the day, touched deeply by the loneliness in his voice as he spoke of the few remaining relatives in his native homeland, distanced not only by miles, but by lives lived worlds apart.

"My wife is not so good," he told me when I asked about her.

I wanted to jump in, offer help, be a friend, but I had already pushed myself upon this stranger. Reserve ruled the moment. I pointed to my house. "Please," I said, leaving the next overture to his discretion, "stop in and have a cup of coffee with me sometime when you are out walking."

I didn't see him after that, but I thought about him often. Was he housebound or sick? Had his wife's health deteriorated suddenly? If only I knew his name, or where he lived. My invitation mocked me with its ineptitude. I had so wanted to be a friend. Months went by before I saw him again. On an errand, and only fifteen minutes' walk from home, I saw the familiar limp and swing. He moved slowly, shoulders slumped, and one foot twisted so that the heel did not stay in his shoe. His pale face was thinner than I remembered, but his eyes still twinkled, and he smiled in recognition as I reintroduced myself. I learned his name was Paul.

"I don't walk as far as I used to," he explained, "my wife, I cannot leave her very long. Her mind is going," he grimaced with a touch to his forehead, "she forgets things." He gestured toward a green and white wood-framed house across the street and said, "Would you like to come in and see my drawings?"

"I'm on my way to pick up my car from the garage," I said regretfully, "but I'd love to see them another time."

"You come this evening then?" He looked hopeful.

"Oh, yes," I said, "I'll come this evening."

The pungent smell of damp fir needles permeated the chilly, sulky evening air. Paul stood expectantly by the window. When he opened the door, he was groomed for company.

His wife, slender and frail, came from the kitchen, tucking wisps of white hair back into a tidy bun. "Come in, come in," she bid, with a smile full of the grace of her generation. She reached out a worn, soft hand.

"This," Paul said, "is my wife, Bertha." He straightened and grew in stature. "We've been married fifty-six years."

That evening I was introduced to Paul's pen and ink sketches. We went from room to room. Pictures hung in modest frames, pages were tucked in drawers. There were sketches of celebrities, scenes, anything that took his fancy. Each had a story. But the compelling story was the harsh reality of talent ignored for people like him of that generation. "It won't put bread on the table," his father told him. "If you sit around drawing like that you'll never amount to anything."

His mother died when he was nine. He remembered the gentle tap of her stick against his head whenever she found him with pad and pencil in hand. "Make yourself useful. Don't waste your time," she chided.

When we returned to the kitchen, Bertha searched for some tangible expression of her hospitality. "I wish I had cookies to offer you. I can't cook like I used to."

"I couldn't eat a thing, I just finished dinner," I said.

Their dinner was "Meals on Wheels," three days a week. "We cannot eat so much. We have plenty for the next day. Except Mondays. Mondays we try to cook for ourselves."

They wanted me to stay awhile. We sat and talked. Dignity filled their house.

Paul answered the door the following Monday. His eyes fell on the tray I carried.

He was glad I'd come, but his pinched and agitated face told me I'd stumbled upon an outburst of anger.

Bertha, pale and flustered, gathered herself. "We're not feeling so good today, and I'm having trouble with my head and remembering." She threw her hands up. "I don't know what it is . . . old age!"

They led me into the kitchen. Canned soup dripped where it spilled over the stove. Paul's hands shook as he showed me the hole scorched in his shirtsleeve as he tried to cope with a meal. The flare-up, cut short by my arrival, had taken its toll. He put his hand to his forehead and sighed, gaining equilibrium. "It's just that she upsets me sometimes," he said, arranging the knives and forks on the table as I set out the lunch I had cooked. Bertha still fretted to know where she had put the wooden spoon he no longer needed, and my heart ached for her.

Frailty of age, its irritability, frustrations, limitations and fears had been too much for them both that morning. Impassioned by their need, I reached for Bertha's trembling hand. "Could we sit down and pray?" I asked.

"Oh," Bertha exclaimed, "that's what we need more of."

Paul joined us in a chair beside the couch.

After I prayed for them I looked up. Gratitude and relief flooded their faces. All tension was gone. I hugged them both and delighted in the hugs I received in return.

"You are too good to us," Paul said, making his way to the dining room table and pulling out a chair for his wife.

No, I thought, *God is too good to me. He allowed me to share this moment as He touched two people He loves very much.* How blessed I was in the process. I wanted to be their friend, and He had given me the desire of my heart."

Bless the Lord, O my soul, and forget not all his benefits.

Psalms 103:2

Chapter 16

Resources

Medical, legal, financial, emotional, social, and spiritual needs change throughout the course of the illness, as do programs and services. Laws, policies, and materials are subject to change as well. Therefore, verify information in this book and other references at time of need before purchasing or recommending these items, programs, and services. Resources listed are *representative* not *inclusive.*

ORGANIZATIONS

Information about the following organizations was obtained from their Web sites and home pages. Check sites periodically for new publications.

Ageless Design
3197 Trout Place Road
Cumming, GA 30041
1-800-752-3238
Home page: www.agelessdesign.org
E-mail: e@agelessdesign.org

Resource for caregivers and professionals. Products, including some spiritual resources, are available for purchase through the Alzheimer's Store to improve patients' and caregivers' quality of life. Alzheimer's Daily News is a feature that enables caregivers to receive e-mails on topics of interest. Articles can be read online.

Alzheimer's Association
225 North Michigan Avenue, Floor 17
Chicago, IL 60601-7633
(312) 335-8700
1-800-272-3900
Fax: (866) 699-1246
Home page: www.alz.org
E-mail: info@alz.org

Seeks to eliminate Alzheimer's, provide care and support for patients and families, and reduce risk of dementia. Variety of services include

* a 24/7 Helpline,
* online educational and support forums,
* Safe Return® program to help locate patients who become lost,
* Green-Field Library,
* online CareFinder™ to assist with care options,
* training assisted living and nursing facility personnel,
* disseminating information about clinical drug trials, and
* advocacy for research and funding.

Organizational framework includes national headquarters, regional chapters, and local support groups.

Wealth of information (online and in print form) on issues pertinent to patients, families, and professionals. Some publications are available in various languages.

Alzheimer's Association Green-Field Library
225 North Michigan Avenue, Floor 17
Chicago, IL 60601-7633
(312) 335-9602
1-800-272-3900
Fax: (866) 699-1238
E-mail: greenfield@alz.org

Online catalog includes a "Spirituality and Dementia" resource list. Materials are not loaned directly to the public but may be used in the facility or borrowed through Alzheimer's chapters and interlibrary loan. Fees may be charged.

Alzheimer's Disease Education & Referral Center (ADEAR)
P.O. Box 8250
Silver Spring, MD 20907-8250
1-800-438-4380
Fax: (301) 495-3334
Home page: www.alzheimers.org
E-mail: adear@nia.nih.gov

Service of the National Institute on Aging. Provides information about Alzheimer's, caregiving, clinical drug trials, and related topics. On-line publications include *Connections* newsletter. Some materials are available in Spanish and English.

Alzheimer's Disease International (ADI)
64 Great Suffolk Street
London
SE1 OBL
UK
+44 20 79810880
Fax: +44 20 79282357
Home page: www.alz.co.uk
E-mail: info@alz.co.uk

Composed of worldwide Alzheimer's Associations. Online publications are available in various languages.

American Association of Retired Persons (AARP)
601 E. Street, NW
Washington, DC 20049
1-888-687-2277
Home page: www.aarp.org

Addresses issues of persons fifty years of age and older. Provides information, services, and advocacy. Publications include *The AARP Magazine.*

Duke Family Support Program
P.O. Box 3600 DUMC
Durham, NC 27710
(919) 660-7510

Fax: (919) 684-8569
NC: 1-800-672-4213
Outside NC: 1-800-646-2028
Home page: www.dukefamilysupport.org

Online publications include "FAQ's on Caring for Others" that contains suggestions for coping with difficult situations. Resources related to Alzheimer's and caregiving are available for purchase.

Family Caregiver Alliance (FCA)
180 Montgomery Street, Suite 1100
San Francisco, CA 94104
(415) 434-3388
1-800-445-8106
Fax: (415) 434-3508
Home page: www.caregiver.org
E-mail: info@caregiver.org

Provides information, education, services, research, and advocacy to support families caring for a loved one who has a chronic, disabling health condition. Online publications and discussion group are available.

Georgia Division of Aging Services
Georgia Department of Human Services
2 Peachtree Street, NW, Suite 9-398
Atlanta, GA 30303-3142
(404) 657-5336
Fax: (404) 818-6600
Home page: www.aging.dhr.georgia.gov

Developed an innovative concept of a "Mobile Day Care Program" (online video) whereby rural communities provide respite for caregivers and a day care program for patients.

MayoClinic.com
Home page: www.mayoclinic.com

Online site contains articles about Alzheimer's disease and caregiving issues, including "Alzheimer's: Spirituality Can Be Comforting."

Alzheimer's Research Forum
Home page: www.alzforum.org

Provides information about scientific findings, research, and clinical trials. Discussion forums available on various topics.

National Family Caregivers Association (NFCA)
10400 Connecticut Avenue, Suite 500
Kensington, MD 20895-3944
(301) 942-6430
1-800-896-3650
Fax: (301) 942-2302
Home page: www.nfcacares.org
E-mail: info@thefamilycaregiver.org

Seeks to improve caregivers' quality of life. Excellent resources for honoring caregivers can be downloaded: Model Interfaith Caregiving Service, a Protestant Caregiving Service, and a Catholic Service Celebrating National Caregivers Month. "Supporting Caregiving Families: A Guide for Congregations and Parishes" is available online and can be purchased for bulletin inserts and health care ministry.

Rosalynn Carter Institute for Caregiving (RCI)
800 GSW Drive
Georgia Southwestern State University
Americus, GA 31709-4379
(229) 928-1234
Fax: (229) 931-2663
Home page: www.RosalynnCarter.org

Offers education and training for caregivers. Online publications include "12 Tips for Caregivers: Caring for Yourself While Helping a Loved One with Alzheimer's Disease."

Safe Return
225 North Michigan Avenue, Floor 18
Chicago, IL 60601
1-800-272-3900
Registration: 1-888-572-8566
Incident Line: 1-800-572-1122
Web site: www.alz.org/safereturn

National identification and support program of Alzheimer's Association that works at local level to assist in finding patients who become lost. Enrollment and annual fees. Patient identification items available for purchase.

Stephen Ministries
2045 Innerbelt Business Center Drive
St. Louis, MO 63114-5765
(314) 428-2600
Fax: (314) 428-7888
Home page: www.stephenministries.org

Materials can be purchased for training laypersons to provide a caring, practical, Christian ministry to those within the congregation and community.

WebMD
Home page: www.webmd.com

Online site contains information about various aspects of Alzheimer's and other diseases.

PUBLICATIONS

A significant ministry will be to give or lend articles, books, audiocassettes, and videos to families since they may not have time, energy, or money to buy or borrow these. Family members will more likely utilize such resources if taken to their home than if they had to search for them. Leaving pertinent materials is a reminder of the church's love.

Medical, financial, legal, and organizational information as well as governmental policies and eligibility requirements can quickly become dated. Some information contained in the following sources is obsolete; however, I will indicate portions within the sources that you might find valuable.

Autobiographies or Biographies Pertaining to Alzheimer's
and Spirituality (for Clergy and Families)

Bell, Sherry M. (2000). *Visiting mom: An unexpected gift* (Second edition). Sedona, AZ: ELDER Press. Skills and lessons learned from visiting mother, faith issues, barriers to good visits, great habits, and guides for visitors.

Bresnahan, Rita (2003). *Walking one another home: Moments of grace and possibility in the midst of Alzheimer's.* Liguori, MO: Liguori/Triumph. Sacred journey of daughter and mother, nursing home placement and adjustment, blessings, patient's ministry in nursing home, family mementos reflecting on healing grace, and gifts to share.

Bryden, Christine (2005). *Dancing with dementia: My story of living positively with dementia.* Philadelphia, PA: Jessica Kingsley Publishers. Christian fronto-temporal dementia patient's experience and involvement in the Australian Alzheimer's Association, Alzheimer's Disease International, and Dementia Advocacy and Support Network International; ways to help; hope; communication tips; patient's and family's adaptation and change; environment; patient's reality; spirituality; patient's true self; spirit-to-spirit connection; and physical, emotional, and spiritual healing.

Burchett, Harold (2002). *Last light: Staying true through the darkness of Alzheimer's.* Colorado Springs, CO: NavPress. Lessons God taught former pastor "in the College of Dementia Caregiving," God's provisions and grace, practical help for giving and receiving care, sharing diagnosis with congregation, wife's ministry as a patient, love, humor, positive and realistic hints for caregivers, communication, and importance of prayer.

Childress, Ellen, as told to Paulette ErkenBrack (2001). *Shattered lives: Finding hope in the midst of Alzheimer's and other related dementia.* Pittsburgh, PA: Dorrance Publishing Company. Husband's experience with dementia, couple's spiritual journey, advice to family members for coping, expectations of family members when loved one is in care facility, guilt, let go and let God, acceptance, end-of-life issues, inspirational reflections, and scriptures.

Confer, Grayce Bonham (1992). *Alzheimer's: Another opportunity to love.* Kansas City, MO: Beacon Hill Press. Husband's illness and practical suggestions for common problems.

Davis, Patti (2004). *The long goodbye.* New York: Alfred A. Knopf. President Ronald Reagan's daughter's memoir of his life, illness, and death.

Davis, Robert (1989). *My journey into Alzheimer's disease: A story of hope.* Wheaton, IL: Tyndale House Publishers. Personal spiritual journey of former pastor before and after his illness, forced retirement at fifty-three years of age, effects of Alzheimer's, struggles and victories with faith, spiritual changes, and suggestions for patient ministry.

DeHaan, Robert F. (2003). *Into the shadows: A journey of faith and love into Alzheimer's*. Grand Haven, MI: FaithWalk Publishing. Wife's illness and encouragement for caregivers through God's love and grace.

Fish, Sharon (1996). *Alzheimer's: Caring for your loved one, caring for yourself*. Wheaton, IL: Harold Shaw Publishers. Mother's illness; informative and practical sharing; hope; reasons to face a loved one's diagnosis; avoiding catastrophic reactions; spiritual support; common behavioral problems; safety; support groups, relatives, and friends; caregivers' emotions; difficult decisions; and guide for evaluating a nursing home.

Hall, Elizabeth T. (2000). *Caring for a loved one with Alzheimer's disease: A Christian perspective*. Binghamton, NY: The Haworth Pastoral Press. Diagnosis, glory to God through mother's illness, legal affairs, guilt, anger, forgiveness, communication problems, role reversal, caring for yourself, pets, support groups, survival tips, and moral issues.

McQuilkin, Robertson (1998). *A promise kept*. Wheaton, IL: Tyndale House Publishers. Inspiring and beautiful testimony of a man's sacrificial love in caring for wife.

Miller, Sue (2003). *The story of my father*. New York: Alfred A. Knopf. Memoir of father's illness, ethical issues, grief, finding meaning and purpose in father's illness, gifts father gave her, and consolation in writing his story.

Simpson, Robert, and Anne Simpson (1999). *Through the wilderness: A guide in two voices*. Minneapolis, MN: Augsburg Fortress. Patient and wife journal experiences as a guide for caregivers.

Strecker, Teresa R. (1997). *Alzheimer's: Making sense of suffering*. Lafayette, LA: Vital Issues Press. Overview of illness, diagnosis, caregiver as victim, call to love, trust God, respond with mercy, role of family and friends, searching for answers, help, nursing facility, saying good-bye, establishing new life, life and death decisions, Alzheimer's and the future, and scripture readings.

Upton, Rosemary J. (1990). *Glimpses of grace: A family struggles with Alzheimer's*. Grand Rapids, MI: Baker Book House. God's grace in caring for her mother (Grace), ethical considerations of nursing home placement, guilt, patient and family adjustments, grief, and conflict of letting go and dreading mother's death.

Wall, Frank A. (1996). *Where did Mary go? A loving husband's struggle with Alzheimer's*. Amherst, NY: Prometheus Books. Struggles and lessons learned while caring for wife (Parkinson's, multi-infarct dementia, and Alzheimer's patient); how diseases affected family; value of humor, support groups, and religion; care for caregiver; and roadmap for families.

Children and Teens

Altman, Linda Jacobs (2002). *Singing with Momma Lou.* New York: Lee & Low Books. African-American girl's weekly visits with grandmother in nursing facility and sharing memories through scrapbook and singing. Fiction.

Alzheimer's Association (n.d.). *Helping children and teens understand Alzheimer's disease.* Chicago, IL: Alzheimer's Association. Changes, adjustments, feelings; coping; activities to do with patient; and sources of help.

———— (1998). *Just for children: Helping you understand Alzheimer's disease* [fact sheet]. Chicago, IL: Alzheimer's Disease and Related Disorders Association. Worksheet to help children understand effects of Alzheimer's and how to help loved ones.

———— (1997). *Just for teens: Helping you understand Alzheimer's disease* [fact sheet]. Chicago, IL: Alzheimer's Disease and Related Disorders Association. Worksheet to help teens understand Alzheimer's and how to help loved ones.

Brill, Marlene Targ (2005). *Alzheimer's disease.* Tarrytown, NY: Benchmark Books. Story of boy and his grandmother, explanation of Alzheimer's, what it is like to have the illness, and how to deal with it. Fiction for teens.

Cargill, Kristi (1997). *Nana's new home: A comforting story explaining Alzheimer's disease to children.* Abilene, TX: KrisPer Publications. Understanding and accepting impact of Alzheimer's on patient and family, nursing facility adjustment, and importance of love. Fiction.

Glass, Sue (2003). *Remember me? Alzheimer's through the eyes of a child.* Green Bay, WI: Raven Tree Press LLC. Girl mistakenly blames herself for grandfather's memory loss and mother's sadness about it, importance of honestly discussing problems, and helping children cope. Written in English and Spanish. Fiction.

Guthrie, Donna (1986). *Grandpa doesn't know it's me.* New York: Human Sciences. Answers common children's questions when a loved one has Alzheimer's.

Kibbey, Marsha (1988). *My grammy.* Minneapolis, MN: Carolrhoda Books. Explanation of Alzheimer's, adjustments for patient and family, children's common emotions, involvement of children, and acceptance of loved one's illness. Fiction.

Leighton, Audrey O. (1995). *A window of time*. Lake Forest, CA: NADJA Publishing. Boy accepts grandfather's illness. Fiction.

Shriver, Maria (2004). *What's happening to grandpa?* New York: Little, Brown and Company. Focuses on love, support, and involvement of whole family and answers children's questions about Alzheimer's. Fiction.

Weitzman, Elizabeth (1996). *Let's talk about when someone you love has Alzheimer's disease*. New York: Rosen Publishing Group's PowerKids Press. Overview of Alzheimer's and how it affects patients, care of patient at home and in nursing facility, feelings of children, and what children can do to help. Fiction.

White, Debra (2007). *She touched my heart*. Mustang, OK: Tate Publishing & Enterprises. Uplifting and poignant story by a daughter of her mother's illness written from a Christian perspective, reminiscences, adjustments necessitated, struggles with ethical decisions, suggestions for making the "best" of situations, family involvement in care, value of humor in coping, and hope in life and death.

Wilkinson, Beth (1992). *Coping when a grandparent has Alzheimer's disease*. New York: Rosen Publishing Group. Denial of children to face loved one's diagnosis, progression of illness, behavioral problems and solutions, sharing home with patient, nursing facilities, holidays, grief, death, guilt, and memories.

Willett, Edward (2002). *Alzheimer's disease*. Berkeley Heights, NJ: Enslow Publishers. Overview of illness, history, diagnosis, treatment, social implications, prevention, and research. Juvenile nonfiction.

Communication with Alzheimer's Patients

Feil, Naomi (1993). *The validation breakthrough: Simple techniques for communicating with people with "Alzheimer's-type dementia."* Baltimore, MD: Health Professions Press. Concept and techniques of validation, using validation with early onset Alzheimer's patients, and examples and benefits of validation.

Goldsmith, Malcolm (1996). *Hearing the voice of people with dementia*. London, England, and Bristol, PA: Jessica Kingsley Publishers Ltd. Insights for optimal communication with dementia patients, effects of environment; nonverbal communication, services, individual differences, life story; informing of diagnosis, and challenging behavior.

Healing Arts Communications (2001). *Home care companion video collection*, Volume 3: *Communication: How to communicate with someone who has Alzheimer's disease.* Progression of language problems, feelings rather than thinking, repetitive questions, aggressive behavior, forms of communication, impaired language skills, tone of language and body posture, cues, and answering difficult questions. Written and directed by Marion Karpinski. Suitable for clergy, families, support groups, and care facility staff. Approximately thirty minutes in length. 1911 United Way, Medford, OR 97504; 1-888-846-7008.

Ryan, Ellen B., Lori Schindel Martin, and Amanda Beaman (2005). Communication strategies to promote spiritual well-being among people with dementia, *Journal of Pastoral Care & Counseling, 59*(1/2):43-55. Person-centered approach, verbal and nonverbal communication, environment, life stories, remembering boxes, and assisting patients to participate in religious experiences.

Congregational Health Care Ministries

Carson, Verna Benner, and Harold G. Koenig (2004). *Spiritual caregiving: Health care as a ministry.* Philadelphia, PA: Templeton Foundation Press. Examines state of health care system and its impact on spiritual well-being on those who work in it, overview of preparation for spiritual caregiving, providing spiritual care, spiritual care for special populations (including Alzheimer's patients and caregivers), nurturing the spirit, reflective questions, and suggestions to help health care professionals renew spiritual focus. Appendixes include beliefs and practices of various religions and resources for spiritual assessment and support.

Chapin, Shelley (1992). *Counselors, comforters, and friends: Establishing a caregiving ministry in your church.* Wheaton, IL: SP Publications, Inc. Suffering, grief, and death; needs of sufferers; church's role in ministry of comfort; example of Jesus' ministry of comfort; depression; establishing a ministry of care and concern within the church; qualifications of volunteers; recruiting volunteers; sample training program; minister's role; support groups and the church.

Ellor, James W., John Stettner, and Helen Spath (1987). Ministry with the confused elderly, *Journal of Religion & Aging 4*(2):22, 28-30. Listening, ministry of presence, role of congregation, support, nursing facility placement, feelings, elements of worship, and suggested order of worship.

Gwyther, Lisa P. (1995). *You are one of us: Successful clergy/church connections to Alzheimer's families.* Durham, NC: Duke University Medical

Center. Overview of illness, communication, effects on families, nurturing spiritual self, church and Alzheimer's, visiting patients at home and nursing facilities, beyond visits, church's response, requests from patients, and family caregiver affirmations.

Hale, W. Daniel, and Richard G. Bennett (2000). *Building healthy communities through medical-religious partnerships.* Baltimore, MD: Johns Hopkins University Press. Chapter on "Dementia." Explanation of dementia, how it affects patients and families, suggestions for and examples of congregational programs, and resources.

Hale, W. Daniel, and Harold G. Koenig (2003). *Healing bodies and souls: A practical guide for congregations.* Minneapolis, MN: Fortress Press. Chapter on "Sharing One Another's Burdens." Description of adult day care center at St. Mary Magdalen Catholic Church, community-wide "Share the Care" program, overview of Alzheimer's, and suggestions for congregations.

Haugk, Kenneth C. (2004). *Don't sing songs to a heavy heart: How to relate to those who are suffering.* St. Louis, MO: Stephen Ministries. Caring for people, fellowship of suffering, entering another's pain, who you bring to the relationship, and suggestions for what to do and say when people are hurting.

Hellen, Carly R. (1998). Spirituality: Compassionate connectedness and well-being, in *Alzheimer's disease: Activity-focused care* (Second edition). Boston, MA: Butterworth-Heinemann, pp. 339-352. Spiritual needs, support from clergy and congregation, uniting an Alzheimer's care center and a congregation, guidelines for worship service, service of remembrance, and staff involvement in meeting spiritual needs.

Justice, William G. (2005). *Training guide for visiting the sick: More than a social call.* Binghamton, NY: The Haworth Pastoral Press. Personal ministry preparation, hospital visitation, care facility visitation, ministry to the dying, and ministry to Alzheimer's patients.

Miller, Joan E. (1998). *Circle of hope resource manual: A guide for congregations assisting dementia families.* Charlotte, NC: Carolina Piedmont Chapter, Alzheimer's Association. Five stages of family adjustment to diagnosis, needs of families, care teams, tips for providing one-to-one support, respite care, companionship with patient, communication, activities, coping with challenging behavior, and support groups.

O'Neill Foundation for Community Health (2004). *Alzheimer's disease.* W. Daniel Hale interviews Peter V. Rabins in this video. Alzheimer's versus normal aging, dementia, diagnosis, progression and stages, treatment, planning for future, challenges families face, facility placement, coping with stress, support network, heredity, and contributions of congregation to patients and families. Suitable for congregations, ministerial meetings, support groups, and care facility staff. Approximately twenty-five minutes in length. P.O. Box 1529, DeLand, FL 32721-1529; (386) 748-3775.

Richards, Marty (1999). *Caregiving: Church and family together.* Louisville, KY: Westminster John Knox Press. Family systems and dynamics, feelings, elder abuse, ethical and spiritual concerns, worksheet for making decisions, long-distance caregiving, self-care for caregivers, resources, hope, and how the church can help.

Ronch, Judah L. (1989). *Alzheimer's disease: A practical guide for those who help others.* New York: Continuum Publishing Company. Impact of Alzheimer's on patient and family; communication; counseling older adults; counselors' feelings; dealing with problem behaviors; assessing needs, finding resources, and making referrals; and care facility placement.

Shelp, Earl E., and Ronald H. Sunderland (2000). *Sustaining presence: A model of caring by people of faith.* Nashville, TN: Abingdon Press. Chapter on "Alzheimer's Care Teams." Lay care team concept and model for pastoral ministry.

Strauss, Claudia J. (2001). *Talking to Alzheimer's: Simple ways to connect when you visit with a family member or friend.* Oakland, CA: New Harbinger Publications. Suggestions for making meaningful visits, interacting with staff and management, anticipate questions and concerns of patients, practical answers, take care of yourself, and helping children visit.

Stuckey, Jon C. (1998). The church's response to Alzheimer's disease, *Journal of Applied Gerontology 17*(1):25-37. Study examined nineteen spousal caregivers and their clergy. Church's response to families, losses of caregivers, visitation programs, difference in clergy and family perspectives regarding dilemmas of family caregivers, families' expectations of clergy and dissatisfaction with performance, church participation, caregiver-clergy relationship, church-sponsored programs, and guidelines for responding to caregivers' needs.

Taylor, Sarah (1989). Clergy and church/synagogue: Special support for Alzheimer's caregivers, *Caregiver: Newsletter of the Duke Family Support Program* (October):11-12. Educational strategies for helping clergy and congregation.

Coping Day by Day (for Families)

Ballard, Edna L., and Cornelia M. Poer (1993). *Sexuality and the Alzheimer's patient.* Durham, NC: Duke University Medical Center. Affection and self-esteem needs of patient, value of touch, effects of Alzheimer's on marital intimacy, common behaviors that appear to be sexual, explicit sexual behaviors and how to deal with them, how to meet patient's sexual needs, what to tell children who may be frightened by patient's behavior, medications, effective coping, sexuality and the nursing home, and professional help. Includes "Dementia and Sexuality: A Clergy Perspective" by Patricia K. Suggs.

Ballard, Edna L., Cornelia M. Poer, and participants of Duke University Alzheimer Support Groups (1999). *Lessons learned: Shared experiences in coping.* Durham, NC: Duke Family Support Program, Duke University Medical Center. Support group participants share what they learned in an attempt to help others in similar situations.

Bell, Virginia, and David Troxel (2002). *A dignified life: The best friends approach to Alzheimer's care.* Deerfield Beach, FL: Health Communications. Characteristics of "best friends" philosophy, emotions of patients, overview of dementia and Alzheimer's, treatments, dealing with diagnosis, decision making, honoring patient's life through life story, principles of dementia care, suggestions for coping with problem behaviors, communication, spiritual journeying and religion, care facility placement, self-care for caregivers, and resources.

Canfield, Jack, Mark Victor Hansen, and LeAnn Thieman (2004). *Chicken soup for the caregiver's soul.* Deerfield Beach, FL: Health Communications. Uplifting stories, quotations, and cartoons to encourage caregivers.

Carter, Rosalynn, with Susan K. Golant (1994). *Helping yourself help others: A book for caregivers.* New York: Crown Publishing Group. Personal stories, caregiving research, emotional dilemmas, family harmony, isolation, avoiding burnout, dealing with physicians, institutionalization, and fulfillment in caregiving.

Farran, Carol J., and Eleanora Keane-Hagerty (1989). Twelve steps for caregivers, *American Journal of Alzheimer's Care and Related Disorders & Research* (November/December):38-41. Alcoholics Anonymous's Twelve Steps adapted for caregivers and provides ways caregivers can take care of themselves.

Gray-Davidson, Frena (1999). *The Alzheimer's sourcebook for caregivers: A practical guide for getting through the day* (Newly revised third edition). Chicago, IL: Lowell House. Spiritual and emotional journey for caregiver, hope, finding meaning and purpose in caregiving, problem solving, how to avoid trap of overachieving caregiver, family council and dynamics, safety, sexuality, activities for patients, caring for caregiver, letting go, end-of-life issues, and death.

Gruetzner, Howard (2001). *Alzheimer's: A caregiver's guide and source-book* (Third edition). New York: John Wiley & Sons. Symptoms; phases; dementia; depression; myths; coping; caregiving; understanding behavioral changes; stages of family adjustment; family responses to care; caregiver's bill of rights; values, beliefs, and caregiver experience; responding positively to Alzheimer's behaviors; problem behaviors: common responses, Alzheimer's interpretation, helpful responses; stress; spiritual focus; resources; and treatment.

Hendershott, Anne (2000). *The reluctant caregivers: Learning to care for a loved one with Alzheimer's.* Westport, CT: Bergin & Garvey. Personal experience in caring for mother-in-law; "super caregivers," "martyr caregivers," and "reality based caregivers"; dangers and accomplices in denial; ways to avoid conflict in making family decisions; granny dumping; practical suggestions for home safety; effects of caregiving on children and teens; heredity and genetics; and reluctant caregivers.

Lawson, Judy, ed. (2002). *Male caregivers' guidebook: Caring for your loved one with Alzheimer's at home* (Revised edition). Des Moines, IA: Greater Iowa Chapter, Alzheimer's Association. Focuses on issues unique to male caregivers.

Lovette, Katie (1999). *Loving care for Alzheimer's patients: Practical solutions for caregivers and their families.* Los Angeles, CA: Health Information Press. Tips on hygiene, feeding, giving medications, incontinence, equipment and services, lifting patient, traveling, getting through holidays, how to care for patient in all stages of illness, and solving day-to-day problems. Includes photos of devices and equipment.

Mayo, Mary Ann (2003). *Twilight travels with Mother: How I found strength, hope, and a sense of humor living with Alzheimer's.* Grand Rapids, MI: Fleming H. Revell. Daughter's story of happy and humorous times during her mother's illness; living between "diagnosis" and death; empowerment through education and choices; treatments and care options; family members' fear of developing Alzheimer's; planning for the future; role of genetics and stress; preventive measures; medications; caregiving; research; end-of-life decisions; value of faith and religion.

Parrent, Joanne (2001). *Courage to care: A caregiver's guide through each stage of Alzheimer's.* Indianapolis, IN: Alpha Books. Diagnosis, planning for future, what to expect and how to survive each stage, dealing with difficult behaviors, medical interventions, letting go and moving on, home safety, mealtime, hygiene, getting help from family and friends, choosing a nursing facility and making the transition, issues for spouse and children, meaningful visits, and hope.

Piepenbrink, Linda, ed. (2002). *Caring for aging loved ones*. Wheaton, IL: Tyndale House Publishers. Spiritual perspective, biblical basics for honoring aged loved ones, family dynamics in caregiving, caring for yourself, physical and emotional changes in elderly, memory loss and dementia, getting help, encouraging and supporting patient's faith, elder abuse, assisting patient at home, when patient must move from home, nursing facility care, end-of-life issues, and coping with grief.

Samples, Pat, Diane Larsen, and Marvin Larsen (2000). *Self-care for caregivers: A twelve step approach*. Center City, MN: Hazelden Foundation. Based on Twelve Steps of Alcoholics Anonymous. Hope, ways to assist caregivers in caring for themselves, emotions, guilt, grief, spirituality, let go and let God, finding strength, and forgiveness.

Sapp, Stephen (2002). *When Alzheimer's strikes!* (Fifth edition). Palm Beach, FL: Desert Ministries. Statistics; overview of illness; symptoms; diagnostic process; treatment; effects of patient's illness on family—role changes, grief, guilt, anger, helplessness, loss of hope, embarrassment, isolation, depression, and fear; and rewards of caregiving.

Smith, Patricia B., Mary Mitchell Kenan, and Mark Edwin Kunik (2004). *Alzheimer's for dummies*. Hoboken, NJ: Wiley Publishing. Reference on Alzheimer's facts; symptoms; causes; risk factors; diagnosis; identifying fears; stages; drug therapies; avoiding ineffective treatments; clinical drug trials; alternative therapies; providing patient care—making medical decisions, legal and financial issues, care options; respite care for caregiver—coping, balancing work and family responsibilities, and finding support.

Warner, Mark L. (2000). *The complete guide to Alzheimer's-proofing your home* (Revised and updated edition). West Lafayette, IN: Purdue University Press. Suggestions for home safety; issues and fears of dementia patients; behavioral problems, interpretations, and possible solutions; making activities of daily living more manageable; wandering; incontinence; products and manufacturers; mobility; and access denial. Helpful for ministers as well.

Devotional Reading (for Families and Other Caregivers)

American Bible Society (1992). *God's love for us is sure and strong: Comfort from God's Word for caregivers of persons with Alzheimer's disease*. New York: American Bible Society. Excellent booklet for caregivers; scriptures can also be shared with patients; helps caregivers face their feelings, day-to-day care, difficult decisions, loss and death.

Bagnull, Marlene, ed. and comp. (1994). *My turn to care: Affirmations for caregivers of aging parents.* Nashville, TN: Thomas Nelson Publishers. Brief devotionals on themes of growing older; needing more support; live-in parents; nursing facility decision; watching, waiting, and praying; and going home.

Cain, Danny, and Bob Russell (1995). *Blessed are the caregivers: A practical and spiritual guide for caregivers of Alzheimer's patients.* Prospect, KY: NB Publishing & Marketing. Brief devotionals and practical solutions for issues pertaining to Alzheimer's.

Murphey, Cecil (2000). *My parents, my children: Spiritual help for caregivers.* Louisville, KY: Westminster John Knox Press. Brief stories related to various aspects of care—learning to care, practical caring, caring between generations; caring and feeling; and caring until the end. Biblical passage and prayer included with each meditation.

——— (2004). *When Someone you love has Alzheimer's: Daily encouragement.* Kansas City, MO: Beacon Hill Press. Vignettes on various aspects of Alzheimer's and caregiving, initial reactions to diagnosis, facing the illness, adjustments, self-caring, latter stages, and end-of-life decisions. Prayer included with each meditation.

Roche, Lyn (1996). *Coping with caring: Daily reflections for Alzheimer's caregivers.* Forest Knolls, CA: Elder Books. Three hundred and sixty-five brief reflections pertinent to caregivers' concerns, feelings, and challenges followed by a tip for the day.

Syverson, Betty Groth (1987). *Bible readings for caregivers.* Minneapolis, MN: Augsburg Publishing House. Brief devotions consisting of scripture, meditation, and prayer.

Ethical Decision Making (for Ministers, Other Professionals, and Families)

Dunn, Hank (2001). *Hard choices for loving people: CPR, artificial feeding, comfort care, and the patients with a life-threatening illness* (Fourth edition). Herndon, VA: A&A Publishers. Considerations for dementia patients, decision making, end-of-life issues, and letting go.

Nelson, James Lindemann, and Hilde Lindemann Nelson (1996). *Alzheimer's: Answers to hard questions for families.* New York: Doubleday. Uses stories of fictional characters to consider real ethical dilemmas, family relationships and conflicts, and planning for the future.

Post, Stephen G. (2000). *The moral challenge of Alzheimer's disease: Ethical issues from diagnosis to dying* (Second edition). Baltimore, MD: Johns Hopkins University Press. Explores ethical issues of Alzheimer's from diagnosis to death, including truth in diagnosis, driving, competency and autonomy, behavior control, dying with dignity, quality of life, medications, genetics, and enhancing the well-being of dementia patients; artificial nutrition and hydration; respect for spirituality in coping; and caregiver spirituality.

Price, David M. (2001). Hard decisions in hard times: Helping families make ethical choices during prolonged illness, in *Caregiving and loss: Family needs, professional responses,* Kenneth J. Doka and Joyce D. Davidson, eds. Washington, DC: Hospice Foundation of America, pp. 271-286. Shared and sound decision making, do-not-resuscitate and do-not-hospitalize orders, and tube feeding.

Purtilo, Ruth B., and Henk A.M.J. ten Have, eds. (2004). *Ethical foundations of palliative care for Alzheimer's disease.* Baltimore, MD: Johns Hopkins University Press. Includes "Darkness Cometh: Personal, Social, and Economic Burdens of Alzheimer's Disease" by Richard L. O'Brien; "Elderly Persons with Advanced Dementia: An Opportunity for a Palliative Culture in Medicine" by Pierre Boitte; "The Moral Self As Patient" by Judith Lee Kissell; "Advance Directives and End-of-Life Decision Making in Alzheimer's Disease: Practical Challenges" by Winifred J. Ellenchild Pinch; and "Ethical Dimensions of Alzheimer's Disease Decision Making: The Need for Early Patient and Family Education" by Linda S. Scheirton.

General Information About Alzheimer's Disease (for Ministers, Care Facility Staff, and Families)

Aronson, Miriam K., ed. (1988). *Understanding Alzheimer's disease.* New York: Charles Scribner's Sons. Handling embarrassing situations, younger patients, guidelines for caregivers, driving, sexual issues, wandering, incontinence, caring for caregiver, emergency situations, emotional turmoil, helping children and young adults cope, support groups, care facility placement, and visiting loved one in a facility.

Coughlan, Patricia Brown (1993). *Facing Alzheimer's: Family caregivers speak.* New York: Ballantine Books. Stories of patients and caregivers, initial changes in patients, adjustments, crisis situations, managing day by day, nursing facility placement and transition, love and obligation, death, coping, and support groups.

Dash, Paul, and Nicole Villemarette-Pittman (2005). *Alzheimer's disease.* New York: Demos Medical Publishing and St. Paul, MN: American Academy of Neurology. Dementia, normal aging versus Alzheimer's, diagnosis, stages, depression, medications, treatments, preventing Alzheimer's, practical issues, transition of care, care for caregiver, and research.

Kuhn, Daniel (2003). *Alzheimer's early stage: First steps for family, friends and caregivers* (Second edition). Alameda, CA: Hunter House Publishers. Overview of Alzheimer's; symptoms; sharing diagnosis; risk factors; providing care; how relationships, roles, and responsibilities change; making practical decisions; improving communication; planning for future; spiritual and religious practices; caring for yourself; getting help; lessons learned; and advocacy.

Mace, Nancy L., and Peter V. Rabins (2006/1981). *The 36-hour day: A family guide to caring for persons with Alzheimer's disease, related dementing illnesses, and memory loss in later life.* New York and Boston, MA: Warner Books. Originally published, Baltimore, MD: Johns Hopkins University Press. Dementia; getting help; problems of dementia, independent living, daily care, behavior, and mood; when caregiver dies; family unit; how caregivers are affected; caring for caregiver; legal and financial issues; living options; causes of dementia; and research.

Petersen, Ronald (2002). *Mayo clinic on Alzheimer's disease: Practical answers on memory loss, aging, research, treatment and caregiving.* Rochester, MN: Mayo Clinic Health Information. Normal aging versus Alzheimer's, diagnosis, treatments, research, quick guide for caregivers, becoming a caregiver, day-to-day care, and long-term care planning.

Powell, Lenore S., with Katie Courtice (2002). *Alzheimer's disease: A guide for families and caregivers* (Third edition). Cambridge, MA: Perseus Publishing. Overview of Alzheimer's, possible causes, phases, diagnosis, research, denial, anger, depression, guilt, fears, physical challenges, psychological toll of memory loss, coping day to day, nursing home dilemma, care options, visiting, legal matters, death and bereavement, take care of yourself, help for troubled caregivers, family issues, support groups, and psychotherapy.

Shimer, Porter (2002). *New hope for people with Alzheimer's and their caregivers.* Roseville, CA: Prima Publishing. Importance of family unity, ethics of diagnosis, overview of Alzheimer's, treatments, care for caregiver, knowing when facility care is needed and deciding where, anti-Alzheimer's lifestyle, and racing for a cure.

Grief (for Clergy, Other Professionals, and Families)

Ballard, Edna L. (2006). *"Hit pause": Helping dementia families deal with anger.* Durham, NC: Duke Family Support Program and Bryan Alzheimer's Disease Research Center, Duke University Medical Center. Uses scenarios to help professionals understand common situations involving anger and offers suggested responses to help families cope.

Ballard, Edna L., Lisa P. Gwyther, and T. Patrick Toal (2001). *Pressure points: Alzheimer's and anger.* Durham, NC: Duke University Medical Center. Definition of anger, risk factors for anger in Alzheimer's care, nonnegotiables, tips for maintaining control, children and anger toward patient, patient's anger and options, when professionals lose control—risk factors and guidelines, and abuse.

Canfield, Jack, and Mark Victor Hansen (2003). *Chicken soup for the grieving soul: Stories about life, death and overcoming the loss of a loved one.* Deerfield Beach, FL: Health Communications. Inspirational stories, quotations, poems, and cartoons about life, death, and grief.

Cohen, Donna, and Carl Eisdorfer (2001). *The loss of self: A family resource for the care of Alzheimer's disease and related disorders* (Revised and updated edition). New York: W.W. Norton and Company. Diagnosis, patients' reactions to diagnosis, setting goals, ways of caring, coping with stress, depression, guidelines for choosing a nursing home, and death and dying.

Dempsey, Marge, and Sylvia Baago (1998). Latent grief: The unique and hidden grief of carers of loved ones with dementia, *American Journal of Alzheimer's Disease* (March/April):84-91. Dimensions of loss and model of latent grief.

Doka, Kenneth J. (2001). Grief, loss, and caregiving, in *Caregiving and loss: Family needs, professional responses,* Kenneth J. Doka and Joyce D. Davidson, eds. Washington, DC: Hospice Foundation of America, pp. 215-230. Intervention strategies to help caregivers cope with loss, dying patients' needs, grief and caregiving after death, and professional caregivers' grief.

Holder, Jennifer Sutton, and Jann Aldredge-Clanton (2004). *Parting.* Chapel Hill, NC: University of North Carolina Press. Suggestions for those who serve as a spiritual companion to the dying.

Manning, Doug (1999). *Share my lonesome valley: The slow grief of long-term care.* Oklahoma City, OK: In-Sight Books. Help caregivers cope, "unblessed child" and "caregiver" syndromes, losses during long-term care, role reversal, grief process, repressed emotions, significance and understanding for patients and caregivers, support groups, "Primary Caregiver's Bill of Rights," end-of-life decisions, and value of recording memories.

McCall, Junietta Baker (1999). *Grief education for caregivers of the elderly.* Binghamton, NY: The Haworth Pastoral Press. Designing a grief education workshop, clergy as caregivers, future eldercare, and material for conducting seven workshops on various aspects of grief.

Ronch, Judah L. (1996). Mourning and grief in late life Alzheimer's dementia: Revisiting the vanishing self, *American Journal of Alzheimer's Disease* (July/ August):25-28. Uses case studies to describe patients' losses.

Ministry to Patients and Families (for Clergy)

Alzheimer's Association (n.d.). Cedar Rapids, IA: East Central Iowa Chapter, Alzheimer's Association. *Helping individuals and families face Alzheimer's disease through spirituality: A guide for clergy.* Importance of listening, communication, ways religious leaders and congregations can help families, tips for worship in care centers, and ministry to patients. Includes some fact sheets from the Alzheimer's Association.

——— (2006). Chicago, IL: Alzheimer's Association. *Lighting the path for people affected by Alzheimer's: African-American clergy guide.* Statistics and risks for African Americans, warning signs of Alzheimer's, stages, changes in memory and behavior, best ways to communicate, spirituality, ways to be a healthy caregiver, symptoms of caregiver stress, suggestions for congregation, and Safe Return®. 23 pp.

Alzheimer's Disease and Related Disorders Association (2000). *Alzheimer's disease: A guide for clergy.* Chicago, IL: Alzheimer's Association. Description of the illness and associated problems, communication tips, comfort and care for patient and caregiver, how the congregation can help patient and caregiver, and Safe Return®. 13 pp.

Alzheimer's Outreach Center, Alzheimer's Disease Research Center, and Alzheimer's Association Greater Pittsburgh Chapter (1995). *"Even these may forget, but God remembers": A resource guide for the clergy.* Pittsburgh, PA: Greater Pittsburgh Chapter Alzheimer's Association. Overview of disease, pastoral care challenge, spiritual support resources, pastoral care member/family profile form, empowering caregivers, and various association publications.

Barrett, John J. (1993). Counseling those who care for a relative with Alzheimer's disease, *Pastoral Psychology* 42(1):3-9. Impact of Alzheimer's on caregiver, caregivers' responses to stressors, possible predictors of adaptation, and implications for pastoral care.

Bell, Virginia, and David Troxel (2001). Spirituality and the person with dementia—A view from the field, *Alzheimer's Care Quarterly* 2(2):31-45. Spirituality versus religion, spiritual needs of dementia patients, ways to fulfill spiritual needs, prayers and sacred readings from many faith traditions, and training staff on issues of spirituality.

Blackwell, George, and Harold Stern (2001). Providing spiritual support to family caregivers, in *Caregiving and loss: Family needs, professional responses,* Kenneth J. Doka and Joyce D. Davidson, eds. Washington, DC: Hospice Foundation of America, pp. 233-246. Supporting others when their expression of spirituality is different from yours, ministry of presence, value of prayer, and SPIRIT acronym to assess spiritual needs after listening to patients' and caregivers' stories.

Clayton, Jean (1991). Let there be life: An approach to worship with Alzheimer's patients and their families, *Journal of Pastoral Care 45*(2):177-179. Suggestions for ecumenical worship services in care facilities with emphasis on familiar scripture, music, and prayers rather than sermon.

Elliott, Hazel (1997). Religion, spirituality and dementia: Pastoring to sufferers of Alzheimer's disease and other associated forms of dementia, *Disability and Rehabilitation 19*(10):435-441. Pastoral visits at home, hospital, and nursing home; examples of patients' responses to ministry; conducting religious services for dementia patients; and unique issues when clergy have Alzheimer's.

Everett, Deborah (1996). *Forget me not: The spiritual care of people with Alzheimer's.* Edmonton, Canada: Inkwell Press. Nature of dementia; image of "The Church" having spiritual dementia; theological reflection of dementia; spiritual assessment; grief; role of reminiscence; alternate approaches to spiritual care—music, play, humor, nature, symbols, rituals, scripture, prayer, touch, aroma, and color; empowering caregivers through spirituality; impact of spiritual care; and paradox of caring—the one who gives, receives.

Fitchett, George (1993). *Assessing spiritual needs: A guide for caregivers.* Minneapolis, MN: Augsburg Fortress. Assessment in pastoral care, 7 x 7 spiritual assessment model, guidelines for evaluating spiritual assessment models, review of three spiritual assessment models, and spirit of assessment.

Hellen, Carly R. (1994). The confused worshipper with dementia, the clergy and the caring congregation, *Aging & Spirituality: Newsletter of ASA's Forum on Religion, Spirituality & Aging* (Spring):1, 4, 8. How to give and receive love, role of caregivers as partners in worship, support patients' abilities in worship, shared love and respect, clergy can model comfort and acceptance of patients in worship services when behavior is abnormal, and participation of congregants.

Keck, David (1996). *Forgetting whose we are: Alzheimer's disease and the love of; God.* Nashville, TN: Abingdon Press. Etiology and teleology of the disease; theological questions raised by Alzheimer's; God's memory—foundation of our hope, theological appreciation of memory, personal experience and pastoral needs, theological convictions, passive-voice soul, deactivation of active-voice soul, caregiving and resurrection, an Alzheimer's hermeneutic and the love of God, death and dying, what the church can learn, and burden of guilt.

Kimble, Melvin A., and Susan H. McFadden, eds. (2003). *Aging, spirituality, and religion: A handbook,* Volume 2. Minneapolis, MN: Fortress Press. Includes "Spiritual Counseling of Persons with Dementia" by Jane M. Thibault; "The Divine Is Not Absent in Alzheimer's Disease" by Jon C. Stuckey; "The Role of Spiritual Assessment in Counseling Older Adults" by James W. Ellor; "Making Decisions at the End of Life: An Approach from Sacred Jewish Texts" by Richard Address; "Ethics and Dementia: Dilemmas Encountered by Clergy and Chaplains" by Stephen Sapp; and "Ethical Issues in Care of Individuals with Alzheimer's Disease" by Ladislav Volicer and Paul R. Brenner.

Lapsley, James N. (2002). The clergy as advocates for the severely demented, *Journal of Pastoral Care & Counseling* (Winter):317-325. Nature of pain, advocacy issues for ministers related to patients' pain, and ethical issues.

McKim, Donald K., ed. (1997). *God never forgets: Faith, hope, and Alzheimer's disease.* Louisville, KY: Westminster John Knox Press. Presentations at "Memory and Hope: Alzheimer's Disease in Biblical and Theological Perspectives" conference held at Memphis Theological Seminary on October 10-12, 1994. Includes "Celebrating the Human Spirit" by James W. Ellor; "Failing Brain, Faithful God" by Denise Dombkowski Hopkins; "Memory: The Community Looks Backward" by Stephen Sapp; "Love, Wisdom, and Justice: Transcendent Caring" by James W. Ellor; "Failing Brain, Faithful Community" by Denise Dombkowski Hopkins; and "Hope: The Community Looks Forward" by Stephen Sapp.

Meiburg, Albert L. (1983). Pastoral communication with the confused, *Pastoral Psychology* (Summer):271-281. Patient's attention, orientation, and meaning.

National Family Caregivers Association (n.d.). *Model Catholic caregiving service.* Booklet based on Interfaith Family Caregiving Service held November 16, 1998, at St. John's Episcopal Church in Washington, DC, to celebrate National Family Caregivers Month. Suggestions for parish liturgy committee.

——— (n.d.). *Model interfaith caregiving service.* Used at first National Family Caregiving Association Interfaith Family Caregiving Service held November 16, 1998, at St. John's Episcopal Church in Washington, DC. Service bulletin, detailed planning guide, and time line.

———— (n.d.). *Model Protestant caregiving service.* Based on National Family Caregiving Association Interfaith Family Caregiving Service held November 16, 1998, at St. John's Episcopal Church in Washington, DC. Service bulletin, detailed planning guide, and time line.

———— (2000-2005). *Supporting caregiving families: A guide for congregations and parishes.* Practical suggestions of ways congregations can help caregivers.

Richards, Marty (1990). Meeting the spiritual needs of the cognitively impaired, *Generations* (Fall):63-64. Rituals and symbols; spiritual well-being; importance of "being with" patients, spiritual history; grief; validate the moment; feelings; and communication.

Roberts, Joan D. (1991). *Caring for those with Alzheimer's: A pastoral approach.* New York: Alba House. Description of caring for an Alzheimer's patient; overview of illness; emotional, spiritual, and psychological needs of caregivers; sample homily; and scriptures.

Ruffcorn, Kevin (1993). Caring for the confused, *Leadership* (Winter):91-93. Personal reflection regarding Alzheimer's ministry, examples of visits, lessons learned, and transformation in self and Alzheimer's ministry.

Shamy, Eileen (2003). *A guide to the spiritual dimension of care for people with Alzheimer's disease and related dementia: More than body, brain and breath.* London, England: Jessica Kingsley Publishers. Spiritual dimension of care, worship ideas for patients, Lord's Supper, being present to dementia patients, factors influencing spiritual health, tools for pastoral encounters, use of symbols, power of touch, humor, pastoral care of dying patients, caring for caregivers, implications for ministry, guilt, ceremony to acknowledge patient's transition from home to care facility, ministering to professional caregivers, children, hope, sample worship services, and guide for pastors.

Shelly, Judith Allen (2000). *Spiritual care: A guide for caregivers.* Downers Grove, IL: InterVarsity Press. Definition of spiritual care; spiritual needs assessment; barriers to providing spiritual care; assess congregation's resources; proper use of prayer, Bible reading, and touch; organize and train others to minister; and find a spiritual mentor.

Sligar, Sam J. (1987). A funeral that never ends: Alzheimer's disease and pastoral care, *Journal of Pastoral Care 41*(4):343-351. Overview of disease; stages and characteristics; families' disintegration of social, emotional, and spiritual lives; feelings; denial; anger; guilt of nursing home placement; hope; and role of pastoral care.

University of Alabama Center for Public Television (1995 and 1997). *Pastoral care for the Alzheimer's victim and family caregiver,* Part I and Part II. Tuscaloosa, AL: University of Alabama Center for Public Television. Videos. Part I: What to expect, providing dignity and respect, and ways to help. Approximately eighteen minutes in length. Part II: Symptoms and causes of dementia, affects brain but not soul, worth and dignity, importance of knowledge, medical explanation of patients' inability to recognize family, usage of profanity, accusations of stealing and other untrue beliefs, heredity, dignity and respect, care but no cure, and love. Suitable for ministerial meetings and clergy seminars. Approximately thirty-six minutes in length. Box 870150, Tuscaloosa, AL 35487; (205) 348-6210.

University of Pittsburgh Alzheimer's Disease Center (1991). *Even these may forget (A pastoral care challenge: Training program for clergy).* Video. Pittsburgh, PA: University of Pittsburgh Alzheimer's Disease Center. Symptoms, tests for diagnosis, treatment, statistics, empathy, whole congregation is affected, and support services. Suitable for ministerial meetings and Alzheimer's Clergy Seminars. Approximately eighteen minutes in length.

VandeCreek, Larry, ed. (1999). *Spiritual care for persons with dementia: Fundamentals for pastoral practice.* Binghamton, NY: The Haworth Pastoral Press. Pastoral care to dementia patients and theological reflections; spirituality, religion, and Alzheimer's; pastoral care of problematic dementia patients in nursing facility; assuring professional pastoral care for nursing facility residents; and helping staff provide memorial services in nursing facilities.

Weaver, Glenn D. (1986). Senile dementia and a resurrection theology, *Theology Today* 42(4):444-456. Biblical based theology to understand journeys of patients, hope of Christ's resurrection, psalms of lament, stages of Alzheimer's, identity, struggle of patients to stay connected to God, triumph of God's grace, power of Holy Spirit, and church's mission.

Wiser Now Newsletter (1995). Using spirituality to cope with Alzheimer's, *Wiser Now Newsletter* 4(3):2-5. Importance of spirituality when brain deteriorates, reasons for spiritual activities, guidelines for making spiritual activities, cautions, flexibility in worship, suggestions for a memorial service, and ideas to incorporate worship activities.

Woodman, Charles E. (2005). Seeking meaning in late stage dementia, *Journal of Pastoral Care & Counseling* 59(4):335-343. Techniques ministers can use to teach caregivers how to prolong meaningful connection with patients utilizing case study illustrations.

Wright, Scott D., Clara C. Pratt, and Vicki L. Schmall (1985). Spiritual support for caregivers of dementia patients, *Journal of Religion and Health* 24(1):31-38. Overview of dementia, role of family, spiritual support as coping strategy for caregivers, emotional and spiritual support during nursing facility placement, and implications for pastoral community.

Yearwood, Mary Margaret Britton (2002). *In their hearts: Inspirational Alzheimer's stories.* Victoria, Canada: Trafford Publishing. Stories of patients and lessons learned while author served as chaplain on an Alzheimer's unit.

Nursing Facility Ministry (for Clergy)

Carlson, Dosia, and Sam Seicol (1990). Adapting worship to changing needs, *Generations* (Fall):65-66. Essence of worship; adaptation of worship through hearing, sight, mobility, and cognitive changes; and settings.

Kirkland, Kevin, and Howard McIlveen (1999). *Full circle: Spiritual therapy for the elderly.* Binghamton, NY: The Haworth Press. Planning worship services in care facilities based on themes (feelings, life review, sensory, special occasions, and spiritual) to assist dementia residents to come *full circle* in their faith and suggestions for hymns, secular songs, story(ies), quotations, discussion, sensory cue, and prayer on each theme.

Manning, Doug (2006). *When love gets tough: The nursing home decision.* Oklahoma City, OK: In-Sight Books. Experience of placing mother-in-law in nursing home—making, implementing, adjusting, and living with the decision.

O'Connor, Thomas St. James (1992). Ministry without a future: A pastoral care approach to patients with senile dementia, *Journal of Pastoral Care* (Spring):5-12. Dementia; different way of thinking, relating, and use of traditional religious symbols; and case studies.

Pohlmann, Elizabeth, and Gloria Bloom, comp. (n.d.). *Worship services for people with Alzheimer's disease and their families: A handbook.* Troy, NY: Eddy Alzheimer's Services. Guidelines for interfaith and Jewish worship services, suggested format, liturgical resources, music, and excerpts from Marion Roach Smith's and Jonathan Currier's presentations at the annual meeting of the American Association of Homes for the Aging in San Diego, CA, October 1993.

Richards, Marty, and Sam Seicol (1991). The challenge of maintaining spiritual connectedness for persons institutionalized with dementia, *Journal of Religious Gerontology* 7(3):27-40. Importance and difficulty of ministering to spiritual needs, spiritual well-being, problem of memory, grief, role of caregivers, symbols and rituals, verbal and nonverbal communication, and spiritual retreat for staff.

Simmons, Henry C., and Mark A. Peters (1996). *With God's oldest friends: Pastoral visiting in the nursing home.* Mahwah, NJ: Paulist Press. Helping ministers feel comfortable in the nursing facility "world"; home setting; history of nursing homes; intentionality; pastoral care versus pastoral counseling; needs and capabilities of residents, ministers' strengths and gifts; work done by staff; practicalities; physical limitations of residents and what can be done to enhance visits; basic pattern of pastoral visit; Alzheimer's units and ministry; ministry in special cases—person is asleep, sick, or unresponsive; death of resident; sacraments and rituals; transition from home to nursing facility; and prayer.

Respite Care (for Ministers)

Alzheimer's Association (n.d.). *Respite guide: How to find what's right for you.* Chicago, IL: Alzheimer's Association. Definition of respite care, concerns of using respite services, types of respite services, assessment of needs, and choosing respite service.

Ballard, Edna L., and Lisa P. Gwyther (1988). *In-home respite care: Guidelines for training respite workers serving memory-impaired adults.* Durham, NC: Duke University Center for the Study of Aging Family Support Program. Understanding Alzheimer's, sensitivity to the disease and related issues, and managing challenging behavior.

Gwyther, Lisa P., and Edna L. Ballard (1988). *In-home respite care: Guidelines for programs serving family caregivers for memory-impaired adults.* Durham, NC: Duke University Center for the Study of Aging Family Support Program. Respite care, what families want from services, and liability issues.

Murphy, Judith K. (1986). *Sharing care: The Christian ministry of respite care.* New York: United Church Press. Definition of respite, why we are called to provide respite care, organizing respite care in the church, finding families and volunteers, training volunteers, matching family and volunteers, respite models, and sample forms.

Ver Hoef, Judi, and Diana Findley (1993). *Building a volunteer respite program.* Des Moines, IA: Alzheimer's Association, Des Moines Chapter. Guidelines for planning, preparation, and implementation of volunteer respite programs; overview of Alzheimer's; stages; symptoms; behavior management; communication; nursing facility placement; types of respite care; recruiting and training volunteers; activities for patients; nutrition; and forms. [Out of print.]

Support Group Ministry (for Ministers)

Otwell, Patricia Anne (1986). *A chaplain-led ministry to families of Alzheimer's disease patients through the development and utilization of a support group.* Fort Worth, TX: Southwestern Baptist Theological Seminary. Doctor of Ministry Project Report. Development, organization, and facilitation of support group in Paris, Texas; perspective and process of ministry; measuring response to ministry; and implications of ministry.

Schmall, Vicki L. (1984). It doesn't just happen: What makes a support group good? *Generations* (Winter):64-67. Models, leadership, confidentiality, structure, logistics, physical setting, and agenda.

Training (for Professionals and Families)

Barton, Julie, Marita Grudzen, and Ron Zielske (2003). *Vital connections in long-term care: Spiritual resources for staff and residents.* Baltimore, MD: Health Professions Press. Understanding and touching the "spirit" in others, discussion questions, hope, rituals that give meaning to life, guidelines for good communication, importance of self-care, letting go, end-of-life decisions, spiritual legacy, spiritual assessment form, and forty-nine ways to provide spiritual care when there is no chaplain.

Bell, Virginia, and David Troxel (2001). *The Best Friends staff: Building a culture of care in Alzheimer's programs.* Baltimore, MD: Health Professions Press. Best friends model, recruiting and training staff, facts and experience of Alzheimer's, assessment and expectations, friendship, life story, communication, activities, caregivers as Best Friends team members, and training tool kits.

Coste, Joanne Koenig (2003). *Learning to speak Alzheimer's: A groundbreaking approach for everyone dealing with the disease.* New York: Houghton Mifflin Company. Positive approach developed through caring for husband; making early decisions; five tenets of habilitation—physical environment, communication, focus on remaining skills, live in patient's world, enrich patient's life; care for caregiver; home care and care outside home; and inspiration.

Fazio, Sam, Dorothy Seman, and Jane Stansell (1999). *Rethinking Alzheimer's care.* Baltimore, MD: Health Professions Press. Philosophy of care, caring behaviors and approaches, rediscovering the soul, home environment, and working with families.

Gwyther, Lisa P. (2001 and 1985). *Caring for people with Alzheimer's disease: A manual for facility staff* (Second edition). Washington, DC:

American Health Care Association and Chicago, IL: Alzheimer's Association. Overview of Alzheimer's disease; person-centered approach to patient care by focusing on communication, activity, and environment in dealing with challenging behaviors; helping families adjust to loved one's care facility placement; and tips to assist staff in coping with their difficult times.

Hoffman, Stephanie B., and Constance A. Platt (2000). *Comforting the confused: Strategies for managing dementia.* New York: Springer Publishing Company. Objectives, pretests, and posttests; overview of dementia; communication; diagnosing Alzheimer's; stages; coping; depression and suicidal behavior; solving behavior problems; feeding; wandering; feelings of residents and staff; stages of family caregiving; guilt; support groups; special care units; and dying and grieving.

Jones, Moyra (1999). *Gentlecare: Changing the experience of Alzheimer's disease in a positive way.* Point Roberts, WA: Hartley & Marks. System for dementia care that includes body, mind, and soul; understanding Alzheimer's; assessment; new approach to programs; nutrition; design for living; and impact of people on care. Primarily valuable for care facility staff, although many tips can be useful for families.

McFadden, Susan H., and Maryellen Hanusa (1998). Nourishing the spirit in long term care: Perspectives of residents and nursing assistants on sources of meaning in residents' lives, *Journal of Religious Gerontology* *10*(4):9-24. Study of nineteen female nursing assistants at three long-term care facilities. Spirituality and religion; connections with self, others, world, and God; reflections on meaning; and implications for training.

Shelly, Judith Allen, and Sharon Fish (1988). *Spiritual care: The nurse's role* (Third edition). Downers Grove, IL: InterVarsity Press. Case studies to examine spiritual needs; definition of spiritual needs; spiritual needs and the nursing process; use of self, prayer, scripture; clergy referral; nurse's personal spiritual resources; ideas for meeting spiritual needs; and spiritual care workbook.

. . . of making many books there is no end.

Ecclesiastes 12:12

Conclusion

Guide to Ministering to Alzheimer's Patients and Their Families ends although it is never finished. Chapters remain to be written on our hearts, if not on paper, as we continue to minister to, and learn from, these dear souls. In the future, it is my hope we will become more adept at learning all they teach.

Out of the mouth of a dying dementia patient came the essence of life, death, and Alzheimer's ministry. In his book *The Cure for a Troubled Heart,* Ron Mehl relates the story of an elderly saint whose memory was failing.[1] Throughout her life, she had depended on God's Word and had memorized many scriptures, including her favorite verse, ". . . for I know whom I have believed, and am persuaded that he is able to keep that which I have committed unto him against that day" (II Timothy 1:12). As time passed, she could no longer remember all of the words. "I know whom I have believed . . . he is able to keep . . . what I have committed . . . to him." Then it became, "What I have committed . . . to him." Finally, she could only say one word of her life verse, "Him." In her dying moments, she whispered, "Him . . . Him . . . Him."

Appendix A

Questionnaire

Name: _____

Address: _____

Telephone Number: _____

Church Denomination: _____

Relationship of patient to you: _____

1. Please put an X in the space below beside the most appropriate answer regarding your current situation.

    _____a. Patient has recently been diagnosed with Alzheimer's Disease (AD).

    _____b. I'm coping with my loved one's illness day by day; death does not seem imminent.

    _____c. Patient has already died; date of death

2. Did you tell your minister of your loved one's diagnosis of AD? ☐ Yes ☐ No

    Did someone else inform your minister of the illness? ☐ Yes ☐ No

    If so, who told your minister? _____

    How soon after the diagnosis was your minister informed?

    Was it difficult for you to talk about the situation? ☐ Yes ☐ No

    If yes, what made it difficult? _____

    _____

    What could your minister have said and/or done during this time to make it easier for you to talk about the situation? _____

    _____

3. Did you help your minister learn more about AD? ☐ Yes ☐ No

If yes, how did you do this? _____

_____

What suggestions would you offer concerning how ministers could learn more about AD? _____

_____

How can ministers learn more about ministering to AD patients and family members? _____

_____

What books and other resources related to AD would you recommend to your minister? _____

_____

4. What needs did you have at the time of your loved one's diagnosis?

_____

What would you have liked for your minister to have done and/or said at the time of diagnosis? _____

_____

5. What spiritual issues have you encountered as a result of your loved one's illness?_____

_____

What is your greatest need at this time?

_____

6. "Hope" is one of the great tenets of the Christian faith. Please discuss your "faith" and "hope" as related to your situation in coping with a loved one who has AD. _____

_____

7. Have you found prayer to be meaningful to you?   ☐ Yes   ☐ No

If yes, how has it been helpful to you? _____

_____

8. Family members of AD patients experience many losses (grief experiences) from the time of diagnosis to the time of death of their loved one. How can your minister help you better understand the grief process and how it is affecting you?_____

_____

How can you help your minister better understand the grief process and how it is affecting you? _____

9. What suggestions would you offer to ministers regarding ministry to AD patients? _____

What suggestions would you offer to ministers regarding ministry to AD families?_____

10. What Bible verses strengthened you following the diagnosis of your loved one?_____

11. What is the most meaningful thing a minister can do to help AD family members in their pilgrimage? _____

12. Can ministers help you in your situation through the sermons they preach?   ☐ Yes ☐ No

If yes, how? _____

Can ministers help you in your situation through their teaching ministry?   ☐ Yes ☐ No

If yes, how? _____

Can ministers help you in your situation through their counseling ministry?   ☐ Yes ☐ No

If yes, how? _____

13. What special programs and/or ministries would you like for your church to implement for AD patients and families?_____

How can the church be supportive of AD family members soon after diagnosis? _____

How can the church be supportive of AD family members during the course of the illness? _____

_____

Do you think it would be a good idea for churches to
sponsor a support group for AD family members?   ☐ Yes   ☐ No

If so, what suggestions do you have for this? _____

_____

Do you think it is a good idea for churches to train volunteers to stay
in AD patients' homes for a few hours each week?   ☐ Yes   ☐ No

If so, what suggestions would you offer regarding this? _____

_____

Do you think it would be a good idea for churches
to offer respite care?   ☐ Yes   ☐ No

If so, what suggestions would you offer concerning this? _____

_____

Please complete the following if your loved one is still living.

1. Living with an AD patient at home, or having your loved one in a nursing home can be extremely stressful. How could a minister help family members during this time? _____

_____

2. What do you think you would like for your minister to say and/or do at the time of your loved one's death? _____

_____

    How can ministers be helpful to families before and during the funeral service?_____

_____

    What would you want your minister to say and/or do for you and your family in the early days and weeks following your loved one's death?

_____

3. What Bible verses do you think would be meaningful to you following the death of your loved one? _____

_____

4. How can ministers help prepare family members for the death of their loved one?_____

_____

5. Has your loved one had to be placed in a nursing home? ☐ Yes ☐ No

What can ministers say and/or do during this process to make the situation easier for the family? _____

_____

6. Have you had to make a decision to have or/not to have a feeding tube for your loved one? ☐ Yes ☐ No

What can ministers say and/or do to help families during this time? ___

_____

7. Have you had to decide whether or not to have your loved one placed on a respirator? ☐ Yes ☐ No

What can ministers say and/or do to help families during this time? ___

_____

8. What is the most difficult decision you have had to make regarding your loved one?_____

_____

How can ministers help in such a time? _____

Please complete the following if your loved one has already died.

1. What would you have liked for your minister to have said and/or done at the time of your loved one's death? _____

_____

2. What would you have liked for your minister to have said and/or done during the funeral service? _____

_____

3. What would have liked for your minister to have said and/or done during the early days and weeks following the death of your loved one?___

_____

4. How can ministers help prepare family members for the death of their loved one?_____

_____

5. What Bible verses helped to sustain you during the course of the illness? _____

What Bible verses have you found helpful following the death of your loved one? _____

Before the death of your loved one, did he or she have to go to a nursing home?   ☐ Yes   ☐ No

What can ministers say and/or do during this process to make the situation easier for the family? _____

_____

6. Did you have to make a decision to have/or not to have a feeding tube for your loved one?   ☐ Yes   ☐ No

What can ministers say and/or do to help families during this time?

_____

7. Were you ever faced with having to decide whether or not to have your loved one placed on a respirator? ☐ Yes   ☐ No

What can ministers say and/or do to help families during this time?

_____

8. What is the most difficult decision you have had to make regarding your loved one? _____

_____

How can ministers help in such a time? _____

_____

Appendix B

Statistical Information

Of approximately 600 questionnaires distributed, sixty-seven were returned. Sixty-six respondents were family members. One respondent was a professional who works with Alzheimer's patients and families but did not have a family member diagnosed with the illness. Sixty-seven Alzheimer's patients were represented in this study (daughter and husband of same patient responded; one respondent gave a composite of her mother, cousin, and friend). One patient who has Pick's disease (a similar illness) is also included. Some respondents did not answer all questions. The following results provide insight for the answers recorded.

State Representation

State	Number of Respondents
Alabama	1
Arkansas	1
California	2
Colorado	1
Florida	1
Georgia	1
Idaho	1
Illinois	1
Indiana	2
Iowa	1
Kentucky	2
Louisiana	4
Missouri	6

Montana	2
Nebraska	2
New York	1
Ohio	4
Oklahoma	1
Pennsylvania	4
Tennessee	1
Texas	23
Wisconsin	2

Church Denomination

In a few instances, the denomination of the patient and family member was not the same. For clarity, the family member's denomination is recorded.

Denomination	Number of Respondents
Assembly of God	1
Baptist	13
Catholic	10
Church of Christ	3
Church of God	1
Disciples of Christ	4
Jewish	1
Independent, fundamental	1
Lutheran	6
Methodist	11
Nondenominational	1
None	1
Presbyterian	7
Salvation Army	2
Quaker	1
Unknown	3

Sex of Patients

Sex	Number of Patients
Male	32
Female	32

Relationship of Patient to Family Member

Relationship	Number of Respondents
Aunt	1
Father	3
Husband or ex-husband	27
Grandfather	1
Grandmother	1
Mother	16
Mother-in-law	3
Wife	9
Composite of mother, cousin, friend	1
No relative	1
Unknown	10

Patients Living or Deceased

Status	Number of Patients
Living	44
Deceased	20

Informing Clergy of Alzheimer's Diagnosis

	Number of Respondents
Informed clergy	48
Did not inform clergy	8

The length of time following diagnosis until clergy was notified ranged from "immediately" to "six years." One minister, whose wife is an Alzheimer's patient, told his congregation of her diagnosis "five years later."

Discussing Diagnosis with Minister

	Number of Respondents
Difficult to discuss with clergy	16
Not difficult to discuss with clergy	43

Helping Ministers Learn More About Alzheimer's Disease

	Number of Respondents
Did not help minister learn more	29
Helped minister learn more	21
Some	3
Maybe	2
Not really	1
A little	1
I try	1

Books and Other Resources

Respondents listed approximately twenty-seven books that they would recommend to their minister.

Prayer

	Number of Respondents
Meaningful	57
Somewhat	4
Not meaningful	3
Yes and no	1

Are Preaching, Teaching, and Counseling Ministries Helpful?

Preaching Ministry	Number of Respondents
Yes	38
No	6
Unsure	6

<u>Teaching Ministry</u>

Yes	38
No	3
Unsure	5

<u>Counseling Ministry</u>

Yes	41
No	2
Unsure	4

Should Churches Sponsor Alzheimer's Family Support Groups?

	Number of Respondents
Yes	43
No	9
Possibly	3
Unsure	1

Should Churches Train Volunteers to Stay in Patients' Homes a Few Hours Each Week?

	Number of Respondents
Yes	51
No	4
Unsure	4

Should Churches Offer Respite Care?

	Number of Respondents
Yes	41
No	9
Unsure	7

Nursing Facility Placement

	Deceased Patients
Yes	15
No	4
	Patients Still Living
Yes	26
No	10

Feeding Tubes

	Deceased Patients
Yes	5
No	13
	Patients Still Living
Yes	10
No	26

Respirators

	Deceased Patients
Yes	3
No	15
	Patients Still Living
Yes	9
No	27

Families' Most Difficult Decision

	Number of Respondents
Placing loved one in care facility or family's home	23
When to place loved one in care facility	4
Acceptance of fact that there was no cure and seemed to be no treatment	2

Support family in nursing home decision	1
Autopsy	1
End-of-life issues	6
Take loved one to my home from nursing home	1
How to cope with loneliness	1
Dispose of loved one's belongings	1
To make decisions for loved one	5
Have loved one committed for neurological exam	1
Family disagreement over loved one's ability	1
Forcing loved one to quit working	2
Ensure loved one is comfortable and receives quality care	1
Applying for paper divorce to protect assets	1
To forbid loved one to drive	1
How to live with loved one	1

Appendix C

Strength from the Scriptures

Have not I commanded thee? Be strong and of a good courage; be not afraid, neither be thou dismayed: for the Lord thy God is with thee whithersoever thou goest. (Joshua 1:9)

***

For I know that my redeemer liveth, and that he shall stand at the latter day upon the earth: And though after my skin worms destroy this body, yet in my flesh shall I see God. (Job 19:25-26)

***

Hear me when I call, O God of my righteousness: thou hast enlarged me when I was in distress; have mercy upon me, and hear my prayer. (Psalm 4:1)

***

The Lord is my shepherd; I shall not want. He maketh me to lie down in green pastures: he leadeth me beside the still waters. He restoreth my soul: he leadeth me in the paths of righteousness for his name's sake. Yea, though I walk through the valley of the shadow of death, I will fear no evil: for thou art with me; thy rod and thy staff they comfort me. Thou preparest a table before me in the presence of mine enemies: thou anointest my head with oil; my cup runneth over. Surely goodness and mercy shall follow me all the days of my life: and I will dwell in the house of the Lord forever. (Psalm 23)

***

The angel of the Lord encampeth round about them that fear him, and delivereth them. . . . Many are the afflictions of the righteous: but the Lord delivereth him out of them all. (Psalm 34:7, 19)

***

God is our refuge and strength, a very present help in trouble. . . . Be still, and know that I am God: I will be exalted among the heathen, I will be exalted in the earth. The Lord of hosts is with us; the God of Jacob is our refuge. Selah. (Psalm 46: 1, 10-11)

***

God be merciful unto us, and bless us; and cause his face to shine upon us; Selah. That thy way may be known upon earth, thy saving health among all nations. Let the people praise thee, O God; let all the people praise thee. . . . God shall bless us; and all the ends of the earth shall fear him. (Psalm 67:1-3, 7)

***

Save me, O God; for the waters are come in unto my soul. . . . I am weary of my crying: my throat is dried: mine eyes fail while I wait for my God. . . . I am become a stranger unto my brethren, and an alien unto my mother's children. . . . But as for me, my prayer is unto thee, O Lord, in an acceptable time: O God, in the multitude of thy mercy hear me, in the truth of thy salvation. . . . Hear me, O Lord; for thy loving-kindness is good: turn unto me according to the multitude of thy tender mercies. And hide not thy face from thy servant; for I am in trouble: hear me speedily. . . . Reproach hath broken my heart; and I am full of heaviness: and I looked for some to take pity, but there was none: and for comforters, but I found none. (Psalm 69:1, 3, 8, 13, 16-17, 20)

***

In thee, O Lord, do I put my trust: let me never be put to confusion. Deliver me in thy righteousness, and cause me to escape: incline thine ear unto me, and save me. . . . For thou art my hope, O Lord God: thou art my trust from my youth. . . . I am as a wonder unto many; but thou art my strong refuge. . . . Cast me not off in the time of old age; forsake me not when my strength faileth. . . . O God, be not far from me: O my God, make haste for my help. . . . But I will hope continually, and will yet praise thee more and more. . . . I will go in the strength of the Lord God: I will make mention of thy righteousness, even of thine only. . . . Now also when I am old and grayheaded, O God, forsake me not; until I have showed thy strength unto this generation, and thy power to everyone that is to come. (Psalm 71:1-2, 5, 7, 9, 12, 14, 16, 18)

***

Unto thee, O God, do we give thanks, unto thee do we give thanks: for that thy name is near thy wondrous works declare. (Psalm 75:1)

***

I cried unto God with my voice, even unto God with my voice; and he gave ear unto me. In the day of my trouble I sought the Lord: my sore ran in the night, and ceased not: my soul refused to be comforted. I remembered God, and was troubled: I complained, and my spirit was overwhelmed. Selah. Thou holdest mine eyes waking: I am so troubled that I cannot speak. I have considered the days of old, the years of ancient times. I call to remembrance my song in the night: I commune with mine own heart: and my spirit made diligent search. Will the Lord cast off forever? and will he be favorable no more? Is his mercy clean gone forever? doth his promise fail for evermore? Hath God forgotten to be gracious? hath he in anger shut up his tender mercies? Selah. And I said, This is my infirmity: but I will remember the years of the right hand of the most High. I will remember the works of the Lord: surely I will remember thy wonders of old. I will meditate also of all thy work, and talk of thy doings. Thy way, O God, is in the sanctuary: who is so great a God as our God? Thou art the God that doest wonders: thou hast declared thy strength among the people. (Psalm 77:1-14)

***

He that dwelleth in the secret place of the most High shall abide under the shadow of the Almighty. I will say of the Lord, He is my refuge and my fortress: my God; in him will I trust. . . . A thousand shall fall at thy side, and ten thousand at thy right hand; but it shall not come nigh thee. . . . Because thou hast made the Lord, which is my refuge, even the most High, thy habitation; There shall no evil befall thee, neither shall any plague come nigh thy dwelling. For he shall give his angels charge over thee, to keep thee in all thy ways. . . . He shall call upon me, and I will answer him: I will be with him in trouble; I will deliver him, and honor him. With long life will I satisfy him, and show him my salvation. (Psalm 91:1-2, 7, 9-11, 15-16)

***

Unless the Lord had been my help, my soul had almost dwelt in silence. When I said, My foot slippeth; thy mercy, O Lord, held me up. In the multitude of my thoughts within me thy comforts delight my soul. (Psalm 94:17-19)

***

Mine eyes shall be upon the faithful of the land, that they may dwell with me: he that walketh in a perfect way, he shall serve me. He that worketh deceit shall not dwell within my house: he that telleth lies shall not tarry in my sight. (Psalm 101:6-7)

***

Bless the Lord, O my soul: and all that is within me, bless his holy name. Bless the Lord, O my soul, and forget not all his benefits: Who forgiveth all thine iniquities; who healeth all thy diseases; Who redeemeth thy life from destruction; who crowneth thee with loving-kindness and tender mercies; Who satisfieth thy mouth with good things; so that thy youth is renewed like the eagle's. . . . The Lord is merciful and gracious, slow to anger, and plenteous in mercy. . . . As far as the east is from the west, so far hath he removed our transgressions from us. Like as a father pitieth his children, so the Lord pitieth them that fear him. For he knoweth our frame; he remembereth that we are dust. As for man, his days are as grass: as a flower of the field, so he flourisheth. For the wind passeth over it, and it is gone; and the place thereof shall know it no more. But the mercy of the Lord is from everlasting to everlasting upon them that fear him, and his righteousness unto children's children; To such as keep his covenant, and to those that remember his commandments to do them. (Psalm 103:1-5, 8, 12-18)

***

Precious in the sight of the Lord is the death of his saints. (Psalm 116:15)

***

With my whole heart have I sought thee: O let me not wander from thy commandments. Thy word have I hid in mine heart, that I might not sin against thee. . . . My soul melteth for heaviness: strengthen thou me according unto thy word. . . . Remember the word unto thy servant, upon which thou hast caused me to hope. This is my comfort in my affliction: for thy word hath quickened me. . . . Before I was afflicted I went astray: but now have I kept thy word. . . . The proud have forged a lie against me: but I will keep thy precepts with my whole heart. . . . It is good for me that I have been afflicted; that I might learn thy statutes. . . . Thy hands have made me and fashioned me; give me understanding, that I may learn thy commandments.

. . . I know, O Lord, that thy judgments are right, and that thou in faithfulness hast afflicted me. Let, I pray thee, thy merciful kindness be for my comfort, according to thy word unto thy servant. . . . Trouble and anguish have taken hold on me: yet thy commandments are my delights. . . . Let my cry come near before thee, O Lord: give me understanding according to thy word. Let my supplication come before thee: deliver me according to thy word. (Psalm 119:10-11, 28, 49-50, 67, 69, 71, 73, 75-76, 143, 169-170)

***

I will lift up mine eyes unto the hills, from whence cometh my help. My help cometh from the Lord, which made heaven and earth. He will not suffer thy foot to be moved: he that keepeth thee will not slumber. Behold, he that keepeth Israel shall neither slumber not sleep. (Psalm 121:1-4)

***

Trust in the Lord with all thine heart; and lean not unto thine own understanding. In all thy ways acknowledge him, and he shall direct thy paths. (Proverbs 3:5-6)

***

Man's goings are of the Lord; how can a man then understand his own way? (Proverbs 20:24)

***

To everything there is a season, and a time to every purpose under the heaven: A time to be born, and a time to die; a time to plant, and a time to pluck up that which is planted; A time to kill, and a time to heal; a time to break down, and a time to build up; A time to weep, and a time to laugh; a time to mourn, and a time to dance; A time to cast away stones, and a time to gather stones together; a time to embrace, and a time to refrain from embracing; A time to get, and a time to lose; a time to keep, and a time to cast away; A time to rend, and a time to sew; a time to keep silence, and a time to speak; A time to love, and a time to hate; a time of war, and a time of peace. What profit hath he that worketh in that wherein he laboreth? I have seen the travail, which God hath given to the sons of men to be exercised in it. He hath made everything beautiful in his time: also he hath set the world in their heart, so that no man can find out the work that God maketh from the beginning to the end. I know that there is no good in them, but for a man to rejoice, and to do good in his life. And also that every man should eat and drink, and enjoy the good of all his labor, it is the gift of God. I know that, whatsoever God doeth, it shall be forever: nothing can be put to it, nor anything taken from it: and God doeth it, that men should fear before him. (Ecclesiastes 3:1-14)

***

Hast thou not known? Hast thou not heard, that the everlasting God, the Lord, the Creator of the ends of the earth, fainteth not, neither is weary? there is no searching of his understanding. He giveth power to the faint; and to them that have no might he increaseth strength. Even the youths shall faint and be weary, and the young men shall utterly fall: But they that wait upon the Lord shall renew their strength; they shall mount up with wings as eagles; they shall run, and not be weary; and they shall walk, and not faint. (Isaiah 40:28-31)

***

Fear thou not; for I am with thee: be not dismayed; for I am thy God: I will strengthen thee; yea, I will help thee; yea, I will uphold thee with the right hand of my righteousness. (Isaiah 41:10)

***

Seek ye the Lord while he may be found, call ye upon him while he is near: Let the wicked forsake his way, and the unrighteous man his thoughts: and let him return unto the Lord, and he will have mercy upon him; and to our God, for he will abundantly pardon. For my thoughts are not your thoughts, neither are your ways my ways, saith the Lord. For as the heavens are higher than the earth, so are my ways higher than your ways, and my thoughts than your thoughts. (Isaiah 55:6-9)

***

He hath shewed thee, O man, what is good; and what doth the Lord require of thee, but to do justly, and to love mercy, and to walk humbly with thy God? (Micah 6:8)

***

After this manner therefore pray ye: Our Father which art in heaven, Hallowed by thy name. Thy kingdom come. Thy will be done in earth, as it is in heaven. Give us this day our daily bread. And forgive us our debts, as we forgive our debtors. And lead us not into temptation, but deliver us from evil: For thine is the kingdom, and the power, and the glory, forever. Amen. (Matthew 6:9-13)

***

Therefore I say unto you, Take no thought for your life, what ye shall eat, or what ye shall drink; nor yet for your body, what ye shall put on. Is not the life more than meat, and the body than raiment? Behold the fowls of the air: for they sow not, neither do they reap, nor gather into barns; yet your heavenly Father feedeth them. Are ye not much better than they? Which of you by taking thought can add one cubit unto his stature? And why take ye thought for raiment? Consider the lilies of the field, how they grow; they toil not, neither do they spin: And yet I say unto you, That even Solomon in all his glory was not arrayed like one of these. Wherefore, if God so clothe the grass of the field, which today is, and tomorrow is cast into the oven, shall he not much more clothe you, O ye of little faith? Therefore take no thought, saying, What shall we eat? or, What shall we drink? or, Wherewithal shall we be clothed? (For after all these things do the Gentiles seek:) for your heavenly Father knoweth that ye have need of all these things. But seek ye first the kingdom of God, and his righteousness; and all these things shall be added unto you. Take therefore no thought for the morrow: for the morrow shall take thought for the things of itself, Sufficient unto the day is the evil thereof. (Matthew 6:25-34)

***

Ask, and it shall be given you; seek, and ye shall find; knock, and it shall be opened unto you: For everyone that asketh receiveth; and he that seeketh findeth; and to him that knocketh it shall be opened. Or what man is there of you, whom if his son ask bread, will he give him a stone? Or if he ask a fish, will he give him a serpent? If ye then, being evil, know how to give good gifts unto your children, how much more shall your Father which is in heaven give good things to them that ask him? Therefore all things whatsoever ye would that men should do to you, do ye even so to them: for this is the law and the prophets. (Matthew 7:7-12)

***

Come unto me, all ye that labor and are heavy laden, and I will give you rest. Take my yoke upon you, and learn of me; for I am meek and lowly in heart: and ye shall find rest unto your souls. For my yoke is easy, and my burden is light. (Matthew 11:28-30)

***

Teaching them to observe all things whatsoever I have commanded you: and, lo, I am with you always, even unto the end of the world. Amen. (Matthew 28:20)

***

Blessed are ye that hunger now: for ye shall be filled. Blessed are ye that weep now: for ye shall laugh. (Luke 6:21)

***

For God so loved the world, that he gave his only begotten Son, that whosoever believeth in him should not perish, but have everlasting life. (John 3:16)

***

Verily, verily, I say unto you, He that heareth my word, and believeth on him that sent me, hath everlasting life, and shall not come into condemnation; but is passed from death unto life. (John 5:24)

***

I am the good shepherd, and know my sheep, and am known of mine. As the Father knoweth me, even so know I the Father: and I lay down my life for the sheep. And other sheep I have, which are not of this fold: them also I must bring, and they shall hear my voice; and there shall be one fold, and one shepherd. Therefore doth my Father love me, because I lay down my life, that I might take it again. No man taketh it from me, but I lay it down of myself. I have power to lay it down, and I have power to take it again. This commandment have I received of my Father. (John 10:14-18)

***

Jesus said unto her, I am the resurrection, and the life: he that believeth in me, though he were dead, yet shall he live: And whosoever liveth and believeth in me shall never die. Believest thou this? (John 11:25-26)

***

Let not your heart be troubled: ye believe in God, believe also in me. In my Father's house are many mansions: if it were not so, I would have told you. I go to prepare a place for you. And if I go and prepare a place for you, I will come again, and receive you unto myself; that where I am, there ye may be also. And whither I go ye know, and the way ye know. Thomas saith unto him, Lord, we know not whither thou goest; and how can we know the way? Jesus saith unto him, I am the way, the truth, and the life: no man cometh unto the Father, but by me. . . . And whatsoever ye shall ask in my name, that will I do, that the Father may be glorified in the Son. . . . And I will pray the Father, and he shall give you another Comforter, that he may abide with you forever; Even the Spirit of truth; whom the world cannot receive, because it seeth him not, neither knoweth him: but ye know him; for he dwelleth with you, and shall be in you. I will not leave you comfortless: I will come to you. Yet a little while, and the world seeth me no more; but ye see me: because I live, ye shall live also. . . . But the Comforter, which is the Holy Ghost, whom the Father will send in my name, he shall teach you all things, and bring all things to your remembrance, whatsoever I have said unto you. Peace I leave with you, my peace I give unto you: not as the world giveth, give I unto you. Let not your heart be troubled, neither let it be afraid. (John 14:1-6, 13, 16-19, 26-27)

***

So when they had dined, Jesus saith to Simon Peter, Simon, son of Jonah, lovest thou me more than these? He saith unto him, Yea, Lord; thou knowest that I love thee. He saith unto him, Feed my lambs. He saith to him again the second time, Simon, son of Jonah, lovest thou me? He saith unto him, Yea, Lord; thou knowest that I love thee. He saith unto him, Feed my sheep. He saith unto him the third time, Simon, son of Jonah, lovest thou me? Peter was grieved because he said unto him the third time, Lovest thou me? And he said unto him, Lord, thou knowest all things; thou knowest that I love thee. Jesus saith unto him, Feed my sheep. Verily, verily, I say unto thee, When thou wast young, thou girdest thyself, and walkedst whither thou wouldest: but when thou shalt be old, thou shalt stretch forth thy hands, and another shall gird thee, and carry thee whither thou wouldest not. This spake he, signifying by what death he should glorify God. And when he had spoken this, he saith unto him, Follow me. (John 21:15-19)

***

And not only so, but we glory in tribulations also: knowing that tribulation worketh patience; And patience, experience; and experience, hope: And hope maketh not ashamed; because the love of God is shed abroad in our hearts by the Holy Ghost which is given unto us. For when we were yet without strength, in due time Christ died for the ungodly. For scarcely for a righteous man will one die: yet peradventure for a good man some would even dare to die. But God commendeth his love toward us, in that, while we were yet sinners, Christ died for us. Much more then, being now justified by his blood, we shall be saved from the wrath through him. (Romans 5:3-9)

***

And we know that all things work together for good to them that love God, to them who are the called according to his purpose. For whom he did foreknow, he also did predestinate to be conformed to the image of his Son, that he might be the firstborn among many brethren. Moreover whom he did predestinate, them he also called: and whom he called, them he also justified: and whom he justified, them he also glorified. What shall we then say to these things? If God be for us, who can be against us? He that spared not his own Son, but delivered him up for us all, how shall he not with him also freely give us all things? Who shall lay anything to the charge of God's elect? It is God that justifieth. Who is he that condemneth? It is Christ that died, yea rather, that is risen again, who is even at the right hand of God, who also maketh intercession for us. Who shall separate us from the love of Christ? shall tribulation, or distress, or persecution, or famine, or nakedness, or peril, or sword? As it is written, For thy sake we are killed all the day long; we are accounted as sheep for the slaughter. Nay, in all these things we are more than conquerors through him that loved us. For I am persuaded, that neither death, nor life, nor angels, nor principalities, nor powers, nor things present, nor things to come, Nor height, nor depth, nor any other creature, shall be able to separate us from the love of God, which is in Christ Jesus our Lord. (Romans 8:28-39)

***

There hath no temptation taken you but such as is common to man: but God is faithful, who will not suffer you to be tempted above that ye are able;

but will with the temptation also make a way to escape, that ye may be able to bear it. (I Corinthians 10:13)

***

Though I speak with the tongues of men and of angels, and have not charity, I am become as sounding brass, or a tinkling cymbal. And though I have the gift of prophecy, and understand all mysteries, and all knowledge; and though I have all faith, so that I could remove mountains, and have not charity, I am nothing. And though I bestow all my goods to feed the poor, and though I give my body to be burned, and have not charity, it profiteth me nothing. Charity suffereth long, and is kind; charity envieth not; charity vaunteth not itself, is not puffed up, Doth not behave itself unseemly, seeketh not her own, is not easily provoked, thinketh no evil; Rejoiceth not in iniquity, but rejoiceth in the truth; Beareth all things, believeth all things, endureth all things. Charity never faileth: but whether there be prophecies, they shall fail; whether there be tongues, they shall cease; whether there be knowledge, it shall vanish away. For we know in part, and we prophesy in part. But when that which is perfect is come, then that which is in part shall be done away. When I was a child, I spake as a child, I understood as a child, I thought as a child: but when I became a man, I put away childish things. For now we see through a glass, darkly; but then face to face: now I know in part; but then shall I know even as also I am known. And now abideth faith, hope, charity, these three; but the greatest of these is charity. (I Corinthians 13)

***

If in this life only we have hope in Christ, we are of all men most miserable. . . . For as in Adam all die, even so in Christ shall all be made alive. . . . The last enemy that shall be destroyed is death. . . . Now this I say, brethren, that flesh and blood cannot inherit the kingdom of God; neither doth corruption inherit incorruption. Behold, I show you a mystery; We shall not all sleep, but we shall all be changed, In a moment, in the twinkling of an eye, at the last trump: for the trumpet shall sound, and the dead shall be raised incorruptible, and we shall be changed. For this corruptible must put on incorruption, and this mortal must put on immortality. So when this corruptible shall have put on incorruption, and this mortal shall have put on immortality, then shall be brought to pass the saying that is written, Death is swallowed up in victory. O death, where is thy sting? O grave, where is thy victory? The sting of death is sin; and the strength of sin is the law. But thanks be to God, which giveth us the victory through our Lord Jesus

Christ. Therefore, my beloved brethren, be ye steadfast unmovable, always abounding in the work of the Lord, forasmuch as ye know that your labor is not in vain in the Lord. (I Corinthians 15:19, 22, 26, 50-58)

***

Blessed be God, even the Father of our Lord Jesus Christ, the Father of mercies, and the God of all comfort; Who comforteth us in all our tribulation, that we may be able to comfort them which are in any trouble, by the comfort wherewith we ourselves are comforted of God. . . . Who delivered us from so great a death, and doth deliver: in whom we trust that he will yet deliver us; . . . For which cause we faint not; but though our outward man perish, yet the inward man is renewed day by day. For our light affliction, which is but for a moment, worketh for us a far more exceeding and eternal weight of glory; While we look not at the things which are seen, but at the things which are not seen: for the things which are seen are temporal; but the things which are not seen are eternal. (II Corinthians 1:3-4, 10; 4:16-18)

***

But we all, with open face beholding as in a glass the glory of the Lord, are changed into the same image from glory to glory, even as by the Spirit of the Lord. (II Corinthians 3:18)

***

For we know that if our earthly house of this tabernacle were dissolved, we have a building of God, an house not made with hands, eternal in the heavens. . . . We are confident, I say, and willing rather to be absent from the body, and to be present with the Lord. (II Corinthians 5:1, 8)

***

And he said unto me, My grace is sufficient for thee: for my strength is made perfect in weakness. Most gladly therefore will I rather glory in my infirmities, that the power of Christ may rest upon me. (II Corinthians 12:9)

***

I am crucified with Christ: nevertheless I live; yet not I, but Christ liveth in me: and the life which I now live in the flesh I live by the faith of the Son of God, who loved me, and gave himself for me. (Galatians 2:20)

***

But the fruit of the Spirit is love, joy, peace, long-suffering, gentleness, goodness, faith, meekness, temperance: against such there is no law. (Galatians 5:22-23)

***

For this cause I bow my knees unto the Father of our Lord Jesus Christ, Of whom the whole family in heaven and earth is named, That he would grant you, according to the riches of his glory, to be strengthened with might by his Spirit in the inner man; That Christ may dwell in your hearts by faith; that ye, being rooted and grounded in love, May be able to comprehend with all saints what is the breadth, and length, and depth, and height; And to know the love of Christ, which passeth knowledge, that ye might be filled with all the fullness of God. Now unto him that is able to do exceeding abundantly above all that we ask or think, according to the power that worketh in us, Unto him be glory in the church by Christ Jesus throughout all ages, world without end. Amen. (Ephesians 3:14-21)

***

Giving thanks always for all things unto God and the Father in the name of our Lord Jesus Christ. (Ephesians 5:20)

***

But if I live in the flesh, this is the fruit of my labor: yet what I shall choose I wot not. For I am in a strait betwixt two, having a desire to depart, and to be with Christ; which is far better: Nevertheless to abide in the flesh is more needful for you. (Philippians 1:22-24)

***

Rejoice in the Lord always: and again I say, Rejoice. Let your moderation be known unto all men. The Lord is at hand. Be careful for nothing; but in everything by prayer and supplication with thanksgiving let your requests be made known unto God. And the peace of God, which passeth all understanding, shall keep your hearts and minds through Christ Jesus. (Philippians 4:4-7)

***

I can do all things through Christ which strengtheneth me. (Philippians 4:13)

***

But my God shall supply all your need according to his riches in glory by Christ Jesus. (Philippians 4:19)

***

Put on therefore, as the elect of God, holy and beloved, bowels of mercies, kindness, humbleness of mind, meekness, long-suffering; Forbearing one another, and forgiving one another, if any man have a quarrel against any: even as Christ forgave you, so also do ye. And above all these things put on charity, which is the bond of perfectness. And let the peace of God rule in your hearts, to the which also ye are called in one body; and be ye thankful. Let the word of Christ dwell in you richly in all wisdom; teaching and admonishing one another in psalms and hymns and spiritual songs, singing with grace in your hearts to the Lord. And whatsoever ye do in word or deed, do all in the name of the Lord Jesus, giving thanks to God and the Father by him. (Colossians 3:12-17)

***

Wherefore comfort yourselves together, and edify one another, even as also ye do. (I Thessalonians 5:11)

***

And the very God of peace sanctify you wholly; and I pray God your whole spirit and soul and body be preserved blameless unto the coming of our Lord Jesus Christ. (I Thessalonians 5:23)

***

For I am now ready to be offered, and the time of my departure is at hand. I have fought a good fight, I have finished my course, I have kept the faith: Henceforth there is laid up for me a crown of righteousness, which the Lord, the righteous judge, shall give me at that day: and not to me only, but unto all them also that love his appearing. (II Timothy 4:6-8)

***

For ye have need of patience, that, after ye had done the will of God, ye might receive the promise. (Hebrews 10:36)

***

Wherefore seeing we also are compassed about with so great a cloud of witnesses, let us lay aside every weight, and the sin which doth so easily beset us, and let us run with patience the race that is set before us, . . . And ye have forgotten the exhortation which speaketh unto you as unto children, My son, despise not thou the chastening of the Lord, nor faint when thou art rebuked of him: For whom the Lord loveth he chasteneth, and scourgeth every son whom he receiveth. . . . Now no chastening for the present seemeth to be joyous, but grievous: nevertheless afterward it yieldeth the peaceable fruit of righteousness unto which are exercised thereby. (Hebrews 12:1, 5-6, 11)

***

Let brotherly love continue. Be not forgetful to entertain strangers: for thereby some have entertained angels unawares. Remember them that are in bonds, as bound with them; and them which suffer adversity, as being yourselves also in the body. (Hebrews 13:1-3)

***

Let your conversation be without covetousness; and be content with such things as ye have: for he hath said, I will never leave thee, nor forsake thee. So that we may boldly say, The Lord is my helper, and I will not fear what man shall do unto me. (Hebrews 13:5-6)

***

If any of you lack wisdom, let him ask of God, that giveth to all men liberally, and upbraideth not; and it shall be given him. (James 1:5)

***

Casting all your care upon him; for he careth for you. (I Peter 5:7)

***

Appendix D

Sample Programs, Services, Forms

ALZHEIMER'S CLERGY SEMINAR AGENDA

Want to Minister to Alzheimer's Patients and Families
***but* Don't Know How?**

8:30-9:00 a.m.	Registration and Continental Breakfast
9:00 a.m.	Welcome
9:05 a.m.	Invocation
9:10-9:30 a.m.	Essentials for Effective Ministry to Alzheimer's Patients and Families
9:30-9:50 a.m.	Overview of Alzheimer's Disease (physician, nurse, or Alzheimer's Association representative)
9:50-10:15 a.m.	Techniques for Communicating with Alzheimer's Patients
10:15-10:30 a.m.	Break
10:30-11:30 a.m.	Spiritual Care for Alzheimer's Patients
11:30 a.m.-1:00 p.m.	Lunch
1:00-1:45 p.m.	Spiritual Care for Alzheimer's Family Members
1:45-2:45 p.m.	Role-Play or Video*
2:45-3:00 p.m.	Resources
3:00-3:30 p.m.	Panel Discussion of Family Members Sharing Meaningful Ministry Experiences
3:30-4:00 p.m.	Questions and Comments
4:00 p.m.	Benediction

---

*Suggested videos: *Alzheimer's Disease: A Pastoral Challenge* (Pittsburgh, PA: University of Pittsburgh Medical Center, 1991) or *Pastoral Care,* Part I and Part II (Tuscaloosa, AL: University of Alabama Center for Public Television, 1995 and 1997).

ROLE-PLAY SCENARIOS FOR CLERGY SEMINARS
AND OTHER MINISTERIAL PEER GROUPS

Discuss what might be helpful for ministers to say or do if the following situations are encountered (safety considerations are indicted within brackets). What would you say to patients (name italicized for clarity)? Family members? Others, if necessary?

Jim curses and yells when you are visiting in his home. His wife is extremely embarrassed.

Sally cries when you read Psalm 23 to her.

Billy accuses his wife, Jane, of having an affair.

A patient of the opposite sex tries to kiss you.

When visiting *Arthur* at the nursing facility, he asks you to drive him home. [Report the incident to the charge nurse.]

Lillie is crying. She tells you her son died this morning. You know his death occurred twenty years ago.

Richard asks you every few minutes what time it is.

Paul quotes a Bible verse incorrectly.

Ed, an only child, discusses his guilt for having placed his mother in a nursing facility.

Delores tells you she feels guilty for getting angry at her husband, *Gene.*

Rick is concerned about the salvation of his wife, *Sue.*

Mae urinates in the lobby of the nursing facility when you are conducting a worship service. [Immediately get an employee to assist her.]

You are alone with *Tom* in his room at the nursing facility, and he pulls your hair. [Try to remain calm. Do not scold him. Leave the room and report the incident to the charge nurse.]

You are visiting *Bob* in his room at the nursing facility when suddenly you hear someone screaming in the next room when an employee is bathing the resident. [Report the incident immediately to the administrator and charge nurse.]

Elsie thinks you are her ex-husband whom she detests.

One of your parishioners asks you whether *Mr. Nix* has Alzheimer's. You have been told by his daughter that he does. How will you answer, maintaining his right to confidentiality and your integrity?

Cheryl tells you she just does not understand why God will not let her husband, *Vic,* die.

John's family is struggling about placing him in a nursing facility so they tell him he is going to another hospital rather than telling him the truth.

Jacob is heartbroken because *Jan,* his wife of fifty-five years, does not
know him.

Ted starts yelling in his room at the nursing facility. An employee thinks
you are upsetting him and asks you to come back another day.

Mary says her family never comes to see her, but you are aware that they
do.

A nursing facility employee asks you to visit *Irene,* an Alzheimer's
patient you do not know.

Alan resides in a nursing facility and says he is going to kill himself. [Re-
port this immediately to the administrator and charge nurse.]

Mildred says she has not eaten in three days but you know she ate lunch
ten minutes ago.

Sam removes his clothes while you are conducting a worship service in
the nursing facility.

Ann lives in a nursing facility and asks you to give her some water. [Do
not give water or food. Her diet may not allow what is requested. She
could also choke or strangle and you would not know what to do.
Never do anything for residents that could result in injury or death.
Tell her you will find an employee to help.]

CARE FACILITY MEMORIAL SERVICE*

SOLOIST OR PARTICIPANTS: "Precious Memories."

WORSHIP LEADER: We are gathered here today to honor the lives and memories of our family at Cherry Hill Manor who died during the month [or quarter]. For our comfort and encouragement, as I read each name and pause, you will have an opportunity to share any memories you wish.

PARTICIPANTS: Share memories.

SOLOIST OR CONGREGATION: "The Unclouded Day" or "How Beautiful Heaven Must Be."

WORSHIP LEADER: For all who confess their sins, repent, seek forgiveness, and put their faith in Jesus for salvation, a home awaits in heaven. This home is far better than anything we can imagine. The Bible says . . .

PARTICIPANTS: "Let not your heart be troubled: ye believe in God, believe also in me. In my Father's house are many mansions: if it were not so, I would have told you. I go to prepare a place for you. And if I go and prepare a place for you, I will come again, and receive you unto myself; that where I am, there ye may be also. . . . Jesus saith unto him, I am the way, the truth, and the life: no man cometh unto the Father, but by me." [John 14:1-3, 6]

SOLOIST OR PARTICIPANTS: "When We All Get to Heaven."

WORSHIP LEADER: The home God has prepared for His own is eternal.

PARTICIPANTS: "The Lord is my shepherd; I shall not want. He maketh me to lie down in green pastures: he leadeth me beside the still waters. He restoreth my soul: he leadeth me in the paths of righteousness for his name's sake. Yea, though I walk through the valley of the shadow of death, I will fear no evil: for thou art with me; thy rod and thy staff they comfort me. Thou preparest a table before me in the presence of mine enemies: thou anointed my head with oil; my cup runneth over. Surely goodness and mercy shall follow me all the days of my life: and I will dwell in the house of the Lord forever." [Psalms 23]

WORSHIP LEADER: That eternal home in heaven will be a place where . . .

---

*An Order of Service could be printed for use during the service and as a source of comfort for families afterward. Refreshments may be provided to encourage a time of socialization following the service.

PARTICIPANTS: "God shall wipe away all tears from their eyes; and there shall be no more death, neither sorrow, nor crying, neither shall there be any more pain: for the former things are passed away." [Revelation 21:4]

SOLOIST: "Finally Home."

WORSHIP LEADER: Friends, take comfort and courage now and in the days ahead from your precious memories, songs of faith, and promises in God's Word knowing that . . .

SOLOIST: "God Will Take Care of You."

WORSHIP LEADER: Let us join our hearts in prayer.

PRAYER: Most gracious, loving, Heavenly Father: We thank You for Your wonderful provisions on earth and in heaven. We are just pilgrims passing through this world on our way to our eternal home, if we are Christians. You have done all You can to enable us to spend eternity with You in heaven. We must do our part by confessing our sins, repenting, seeking forgiveness, and putting our faith in Jesus to save us. Christ paid the penalty for our sins by dying on the cross in our place. Let us eagerly anticipate that day when we see Jesus face to face and are reunited with our loved ones in Christ who have gone before. In Jesus' name, Amen.

SOLOIST: "When the Roll Is Called Up Yonder."

PASTORAL VOLUNTEER AGREEMENT

It is my desire to minister to Alzheimer's patients and families. Therefore, I promise with God's help and to the best of my ability:

(1) To visit _____ (name of patient and/or family member[s]) and/or provide other specific ministries including

_____

on _____ (dates) and at _____ (time).

(2) To maintain patients' and families' rights to confidentiality by not discussing their situation with others except to report significant information on reports given to Alzheimer's ministry coordinator.

(3) To write spiritual assessment, spiritual goals, and spiritual care plan following each visit and submit to Alzheimer's ministry coordinator.

(4) To complete monthly ministry report and submit to the Alzheimer's ministry coordinator.

(5) To attend Alzheimer's ministry training sessions periodically.

(6) To attend quarterly Alzheimer's ministry sessions with pastor and the Alzheimer's ministry coordinator.

Name _____

Date _____

MINISTRY REPORT*

Name of volunteer _____

Date _____

Patient Ministry

Number of contacts

_____ Visits

_____ Cards

_____ Telephone calls

_____ Correspondence

_____ Transportation provided

_____ Meals provided

_____ Tape ministry (audiotapes, videotapes, or DVDs of worship service taken to home)

_____ Other

Family Ministry

Number of contacts

_____ Visits

_____ Cards

_____ Telephone calls

_____ Correspondence

_____ Transportation provided

_____ Meals provided

_____ Minor home maintenance or repairs

_____ Respite

_____ Errands

_____ Tape ministry (audiotapes, videotapes, or DVDs of worship service taken to home)

_____ Other

---

*Some contacts will be with patient and family; report these accordingly.

CASE STUDY

To illustrate the use of a spiritual history, spiritual assessment, spiritual care goals, and spiritual care plan, I would like to share a fabricated case study of a fictitious patient, Ted Adams.

Background

Ted is a seventy-nine-year-old white male. He has been married to Sue for fifty-five years. They have one deceased son (John), one living son (Tim), and a daughter-in-law (Becky). About five years ago, Ted began showing signs of forgetfulness. Initially, the family just laughed it off, but his forgetfulness became so frequent they had to acknowledge it. Even though he balked at the idea, Ted reluctantly agreed to have some medical tests performed and was diagnosed with Alzheimer's disease. His family learned to live with his forgetfulness as well as other behaviors that surfaced—asking the same question repeatedly, agitation, confusion, and frustration. Gradually, they had to take over his business affairs. His mild-mannered demeanor turned to hostility—especially toward those he loves the most.

These changes have been extremely hard for his loving family to accept. He just does not seem like the same person anymore.

Ted's physical condition is very good; however, he recently had several falls. His appetite fluctuates from being ravenous to hardly eating at all.

Although his family members told themselves he would never have to go to a nursing facility, it became necessary. This proved more difficult for them than for him. Ted adjusted quite well within three months. Sue visits daily, but it is rapidly taking its toll on her health. Tim and Becky live out of town and see him only about once a week.

Ted currently is in the severe Alzheimer's stage.

Spiritual History

Ted understood the need for forgiveness of his sins and trusted Christ as Savior when he was ten years old. He joined a Baptist church and was baptized. The church was small; therefore, few activities existed for children and young people. He faithfully attended church on Sunday mornings, sometimes on Sunday nights, but almost never on Wednesday evenings.

After marriage, Sue encouraged Ted to take a more active part in church life. He had greater opportunity to do so because they had joined a larger church in a nearby town. It was Methodist—her denomination. They both sang in the choir and taught Sunday school. From time to time, Ted served in other leadership positions. They had many friends within the congregation.

He was one of those people—always ready to help anyone in need. Yet, he was a humble worker who never did anything for recognition or personal gain.

In addition to the normal grief issues associated with Alzheimer's, Ted had a major grief experience around ten years ago when John was killed suddenly in an automobile accident. At first, he seemed to accept his son's death as well as could be expected. From time to time, he had bouts with depression even though the tragedy brought him "closer to the Lord." Now, he sometimes cries uncontrollably thinking John died today.

Spiritual Assessment

It is impossible for Ted to resolve his grief due to the nature of Alzheimer's and the fact that one never gets over the death of a child. However, it may be helpful when he cries to encourage him to talk about the good times he shared with John.

As Ted needed reassurance of God's love and presence following John's death, he needs it now, too, while living in the nursing facility and experiencing mental impairment caused by Alzheimer's.

Ted's favorite Bible verse, ". . . I will never leave thee, nor forsake thee" (Hebrews 13:5), comforts and sustains him as nothing else does. He finds reassurance when someone reminds him that God loves him and will never leave him. Ted also finds it meaningful when his favorite song ("Because He Lives") is sung. At times, he will even sing portions of the song by himself.

Ted usually attends worship services in the facility. The highlight for him is prayer time. He always wants to pray aloud. Sue tries to arrange her visits so she can worship with Ted. This is an excellent time for them to reaffirm their love for God and for each other.

Even though Ted cannot verbally express his need for meaning and purpose in life, he gives clues. When he paces aimlessly, this may indicate he is restless and wants to do something. Nursing facility staff seek ways for him to feel useful by helping. Because he enjoys praying, some of the employees ask Ted to pray for them and other residents.

Spiritual Care Goals

1. To assist Ted in finding meaning and purpose in life
2. To facilitate Ted's expression of grief
3. To reassure Ted of God's love

Spiritual Care Plan

1. Arrange a visit by pastor at least monthly.
2. Arrange at least two additional monthly pastoral visits by members of the congregation.
3. Arrange at least four monthly telephone calls by members of the congregation.
4. Listen.
5. Reminisce about the good times.
6. Encourage Ted to sing a hymn if he is able to do so.
7. Find an activity within Ted's ability and encourage him to do it with you.
8. Encourage Ted to talk about his grief when he cries.
9. Take a gift occasionally to be enjoyed during the visit.
10. Provide opportunities for Ted to marvel at the beauty of God's creation by watching a sunset, looking at a flower, and so on.
11. Share appropriate Bible verses.
12. Pray for Ted and his family—let him voice a prayer if he is able to do so.

CARE FACILITY WORSHIP SERVICE

Soft instrumental background music: "Count Your Blessings" (while residents gather in worship area). Worship leader greets each person by name and shakes hands.

SOLOIST: "Count Your Blessings." *[Invite everyone to sing chorus.]*

WORSHIP LEADER: Good morning [or evening]. I am Pastor Bill from Cherry Hill Church. It is so good to be here today [tonight] for our worship time. *[Reinforce words with nonverbal cues by wearing a cross or collar, carrying a Bible, etc.]* Let us say the Apostles' Creed together.

SOLOIST: "Gloria Patri." *[Invite everyone to sing.]*

WORSHIP LEADER: Although the Thanksgiving season is approaching, giving thanks *[fold hands and bow head]* to God should be part of our everyday lives. Sometimes we thank God for a good night's rest when we awaken in the morning. Sometimes before we eat our food, we say a blessing. Before we go to sleep at night, we may thank God for the good day He gave us. And, of course, any time we can thank Him for our family and friends, the beauty of His creation, and many other blessings. The Bible *[hold up Bible]* says, "Every good gift and every perfect gift is from above, and cometh down from the Father . . ." [James 1:17]. Let us take a moment now to thank God for the good things He gives us. God is so good to us. He is the One Who gives us all good things. Can someone tell me what is God's greatest gift to us? Yes, it is His Son, Jesus. The Bible *[hold up Bible]* also tells us, "For God so loved the world, that he gave his only begotten Son, that whosoever believeth in him should not perish, but have everlasting life" [John 3:16]. Let us all say that beautiful verse again.

CHORUS: "God Is So Good."

WORSHIP LEADER: Many of the songs we sing are "praise" or "thank you" songs to God. Singing is one way we worship Him. He alone is worthy of our praise. God wants us to thank Him for all He does for us. We can sing our thanks or pray. Prayer is talking to God. Let us talk to God *[fold hands, bow head, close eyes]* and thank Him for loving us. Would anyone like to talk to God aloud now? *[If not, voice prayer.]* Dear God, Thank You so much for loving me, Pastor Bill, and *[name all worshippers]*. It is good to be here today [tonight] to remember Your love for us. Help us to love You, too. In Jesus' name, I pray. Amen.

SOLOIST: "Thank You, Lord." *[Invite everyone to sing.]*

Worship leader bids each worshipper "good-bye" and again shakes hands. Soft instrumental background music: "Count Your Blessings."

WORSHIP VIDEO SUGGESTIONS

- Base video on a spiritual theme, liturgy, or holiday.
- Present the video as a gift to patient at Thanksgiving, Christmas, Easter, birthday, patriotic holidays, and other occasions.
- Create worshipful setting by videotaping outside of church building and religious symbols inside sanctuary.
- Play instrumental background music at beginning and ending of tape—"How Great Thou Art."
- Utilize soloist rather than duet, trio, quartet, or choir to avoid distraction.
- Use family member or friend who is recognized by patient as soloist, if possible.
- Include appropriate denominational liturgy and well-known music.
- Repeat patient's name frequently to hold and maintain attention.
- Clergyperson stands behind pulpit when speaking and soloist when singing.
- Clergy and soloist should wear Sunday morning vestments.
- Reinforce words with nonverbal cues.
- Cross or stained glass window should be visible behind and above minister and soloist.
- If desired, additional music by soloist or instrumentalist could be recorded.

SCRIPT FOR WORSHIP VIDEO

PASTOR: Hello, Ted. *[Refrain from saying "Good morning" or "Good evening" since patient may view video at various times of day or night and become confused.]* I am Bill Kerry, your pastor at Cherry Hill Church. It is wonderful that we have this opportunity to worship God now together. *[Pastor sits down and camera focuses on the Cross.]*

INSTRUMENTALIST: *[Plays]* "Jesus Loves Me."

SOLOIST: Daddy Ted, I am Becky, your daughter-in-law. Please listen as I sing "Jesus Loves Me." *[Sing all verses.]* Now, Daddy Ted, I would like for you to sing the first verse and chorus with me as I sing it again. Thank you for singing along. *[Soloist is seated and pastor returns to pulpit.]*

PASTOR: Ted, it is wonderful that Jesus loves us. The Bible *[hold up Bible]* says, "For God so loved the world, that he gave his only begotten Son, that whosoever believeth in him should not perish, but have everlasting life" [John 3:16]. Ted, God so loved the world—that includes you and me. God loves Ted Adams *[point outward]* and Bill Kerry *[point toward self]*. In fact, the Bible *[hold up Bible]* also says, "Behold, what manner of love the Father hath bestowed upon us, that we should be called the sons of God . . ." [I John 3:1]. We are children of God. At this time, Becky will sing another song about God's love for us.

SOLOIST: Daddy Ted, please listen as I sing "O How He Loves You and Me." *[Use motions. When singing "He" point upward; "loves" cross hands over chest; "you" point outward; and "me" point toward self.]* Daddy Ted, would you like to sing with me this time? I will not ask you to do the motions. That could be confusing. It is difficult to sing and do the motions at the same time. So, just sing with me. All right?

PASTOR: Ted, now I want to read a few more verses found in the Bible *[hold up Bible]*. "Who shall separate us from the love of Christ? Shall tribulation, or distress, or persecution, or famine, or nakedness, or peril, or sword? . . . Nay, in all these things we are more than conquerors through him that loved us. For I am persuaded, that neither death, nor life, nor angels, nor principalities, nor powers, nor things present, nor things to come, Nor height, nor depth, nor any other creature, shall be able to separate us from the love of God, which is in Christ Jesus our Lord" [Romans 8:35, 37-39]. Ted, let us talk to God and thank Him for loving us so much. Talking to God is praying. Can you close your eyes, bow your head, and fold your hands as we pray? *[Demonstrate these motions as you say the words.]* Dear God, Although we cannot understand how and why You love us so much, we simply say, "Thank You." Thank You for loving Ted and his dear family—Sue, Tim, and Becky. Lord, I thank You for the love they share with one another. We love You because You first loved us. Help us to show our love for You by the words we say and the deeds we do. In Jesus' name, we pray. Amen. God is good all the time. All the time, God is good. I will ask Becky to sing a praise song, "The Doxology." We sing it every Sunday in church. When you hear it, Ted, you may remember it. You have sung the "Doxology" many times in church.

SOLOIST: *[Sings]* "Doxology."

PASTOR: Let's pray the Lord's Prayer. "Our Father which art in heaven, Hallowed be thy name. Thy kingdom come. Thy will be done in earth, as it is in heaven. Give us this day our daily bread. And forgive us our debts, as we forgive our debtors. And lead us not into temptation, but deliver us from evil: For thine is the kingdom, and the power, and the glory, forever. Amen" [Matthew 6:9-13].

SOLOIST: *[Sings]* "God Be with You Till We Meet Again."

INSTRUMENTALIST: *[Plays]* "Jesus Loves Me."

SAMPLE FUNERAL SERMON I

PRELUDE: "Eternal Life."

SOLOIST, CHOIR, OR CONGREGATION: "Great Is Thy Faithfulness."

"To everything there is a season, and a time to every purpose under the heaven: A time to be born, and a time to die; . . ." [Ecclesiastes 3:1-2].

God, in His love and Providence, allowed the earthly life of Ted Adams to span seventy years.

[Read obituary.* A creative and personal way to honor the deceased is to relate the meaning of his or her first name and spiritual connotation. One's name often amazingly characterizes how the person lived.]

On behalf of Ted's family, I want to thank You for truly being the Church of Jesus Christ during these past days, months, and years. What a testimony! Only God knows how many prayers have been prayed, visits and calls made, cards sent, gifts given, and other expressions of love extended.

Our most eloquent human words are empty at times like this. But, please hear these words from God's Holy Word to strengthen our souls and comfort our hearts:

"If in this life we only have hope in Christ, we are of all men most miserable. But now is Christ risen from the dead, and become the firstfruits of them that slept. For since by man came death, by man came also the resurrection of the dead. For as in Adam all die, even so in Christ shall all be made alive" [I Corinthians 15:19-22].

"In hope of eternal life, which God, that cannot lie, promised before the world began" [Titus 1:2].

"Therefore being justified by faith, we have peace with God through our Lord Jesus Christ: By whom also we have access by faith into this grace wherein we stand, and rejoice in hope of the glory of God. And not only so, but we glory in tribulations also: knowing that tribulations worketh patience; And patience, experience; and experience, hope: And hope maketh not ashamed; because the love of God is shed abroad in our hearts by the Holy Ghost which is given unto us" [Romans 5:1-5].

"Be of good courage, and he shall strengthen your heart, all ye that hope in the Lord . . . the Lord will be the hope of his people . . . Christ in you, the hope of glory . . . Thou art my hiding place and my shield: I hope in thy word" [Psalms 31:24; Joel 3:16; Colossians 1:27; Psalms 119:114].

"Blessed be the God and Father of our Lord Jesus Christ, which according to his abundant mercy hath begotten us again unto a lively hope by the

---

*Be sensitive to families' needs and wishes. Generally, it is best not to make reference to "Alzheimer's disease" during the funeral unless you know the family would not be embarrassed or offended. If you are in doubt about this, ask them their preference.

resurrection of Jesus Christ from the dead, To an inheritance incorruptible, and undefiled, and that fadeth not away, reserved in heaven for you, Who are kept by the power of God through faith unto salvation ready to be revealed in the last time. Wherein ye greatly rejoice, though now for a season, if need be, ye are in heaviness through manifold temptations: That the trial of your faith, being much more precious than of gold that perisheth, though it be tried with fire, might be found unto praise and honor and glory at the appearing of Jesus Christ: Whom having not seen, ye love; in whom, though now ye see him not, yet believing, ye rejoice with joy unspeakable and full of glory: Receiving the end of your faith, even the salvation of your souls" [I Peter 1:3-9].

May we pray?

Heavenly Father: We thank You for the life of Ted Adams and for allowing his life to touch each of our lives. Thank you for all You taught us through him and for what you taught him through us. Because of Who You are, Your Word, Your death and resurrection, we have hope. Our hope provided strength in days past, comforts us in this moment, and offers assurance for the future. In Jesus' name, we pray. Amen.

SOLOIST: "He Giveth More Grace."

Tears are normal when someone we love dies because we will miss them and the good times we shared. Even Jesus cried when His friend Lazarus died. Remember the story?

When Lazarus was sick, his sisters, Mary and Martha, sent for Jesus because they knew He could heal their brother. But, Jesus was not in any hurry to get there and stayed two days longer where he was even after he learned of Lazarus' illness. In fact, by the time He arrived in Bethany, Lazarus had been dead four days. Many Jews tried to comfort Mary and Martha. As Jesus approached their house, Martha went out to meet him. She told Jesus that Lazarus would not have died if he had been there.

"Jesus saith unto her, Thy brother shall rise again. Martha saith unto him, I know that he shall rise again in the resurrection at the last day. Jesus said unto her, I am the resurrection, and the life: he that believeth in me, though he were dead, yet shall he live: And whosoever liveth and believeth in me shall never die. Believest thou this? She saith unto him, Yea, Lord: I believe that art the Christ, the Son of God . . ." [John 11:23-27].

Mary also ran out to meet Jesus later. She and the Jews with her were weeping. Jesus asked where Lazarus' body was. He wept. At the grave, Jesus told Martha to take away the stone. Then he commanded Lazarus to come forth.

If our loved ones confessed their sins, repented, sought forgiveness, and put their faith in Jesus to save them, we grieve but we do not grieve as those who have no hope.

The Bible says, "But I would not have you to be ignorant, brethren, concerning them which are asleep, that ye sorrow not, even as others which have no hope. For if we believe that Jesus died and rose again, even so them also which sleep in Jesus will God bring with him. For this we say unto you by the word of the Lord, that we which are alive and remain unto the coming of the Lord shall not prevent them which are asleep. For the Lord himself shall descend from heaven with a shout, with the voice of the archangel, and with the trump of God: and the dead in Christ shall rise first: Then we which are alive and remain shall be caught up together with them in the clouds, to meet the Lord in the air: and so shall we ever be with the Lord. Wherefore comfort one another with these words" [I Thessalonians 4:13-18].

"Blessed be God, even the Father of our Lord Jesus Christ, the Father of mercies, and the God of all comfort; Who comforteth us in all our tribulation, that we may be able to comfort them which are in any trouble, by the comfort wherewith we ourselves are comforted of God" [II Corinthians 1:3-4].

God comforts us in our troubles not just to comfort us. He comforts us so that we can be His channel of comfort to others. Life has been, and will be, changed for each of us because Ted lived and died. After we experience a hardship or tragedy, we tend to know what similar circumstances are like for others. We are able to empathize because of what we experienced.

Someday you may have a friend who loses a husband, father, or father-in-law through death. Tell that person how God helped and comforted you when your husband, father, or father-in-law died. Let your friend know that you did not have to bear your burdens alone—God came to be with you.

". . . be ready always to give an answer to every man that asketh you a reason of the hope that is in you . . ." [I Peter 3:15].

May we pray?

Heavenly Father: Thank You for allowing us to share life, love, and laughter with Ted. As You comfort us, let us comfort those You bring into our lives as we await . . . "Looking for that blessed hope, and the glorious appearing of the great God and our Savior Jesus Christ;" [Titus 2:13]. "Now the God of hope fill you with all joy and peace in believing, that ye may abound in hope, through the power of the Holy Ghost" [Romans 15:13]. In Jesus' name, Amen.

SAMPLE FUNERAL SERMON II

SOLOIST: "O Love That Wilt Not Let Me Go."

[Read obituary.]
You, Ted's family, have been known as caregivers for many years now. You have sacrificed in countless ways to try to meet his needs. Maybe there were times you wanted to eat but were interrupted to feed him. Maybe there were times you wanted and needed to sleep but you were awake doing something for him. Maybe you wanted to get away and have some fun but stayed home with him to keep him safe.

A designation I prefer for you, though, is "love-givers." You went beyond the duty of caregivers. You did what you could for Ted because you loved him—not because you had to! You lovingly cared for Ted.

Yet, as much as we have loved Ted through the years, there is One Who loved him and each of us longer and better than we can ever imagine. God is that "Love-Giver." His love tank never runs dry.

The Bible says, ". . . God commendeth his love toward us, in that, while we were yet sinners, Christ died for us" [Romans 5:8].

It is easy to love someone if that person is good to us and does good things for us. But, notice . . . God loved us while we were His enemies: ". . . all have sinned, and come short of the glory of God" [Romans 3:23].

We deserved to die because of our sins, but God made it possible for us to be forgiven and live with Him eternally in heaven: ". . . the wages of sin is death; but the gift of God is eternal life through Jesus Christ our Lord" [Romans 6:23].

"For God so loved the world, that he gave his only begotten Son, that whosoever believeth in him should not perish, but have everlasting life" [John 3:16].

But, in order for us to be forgiven and to have a mansion in heaven, we must confess our sins, repent, seek forgiveness, and put our faith in Jesus to save us. Please hear these words from God's Holy Word:

"If thou shalt confess with thy mouth the Lord Jesus, and shalt believe in thine heart that God hath raised him from the dead, thou shalt be saved. For with the heart man believeth unto righteousness; and with the mouth confession is made unto salvation . . . For whosoever shall call upon the name of the Lord shall be saved" [Romans 10:9-10, 13].

An unknown author penned these words:

To the artist, the Lord Jesus Christ is the One Altogether Lovely,
To the architect, He is the Chief Cornerstone.
To the baker, He is the Living Bread.

To the banker, He is the Hidden Treasure.
To the biologist, He is the Life.
To the builder, He is the Sure Foundation.
To the carpenter, He is the Door.
To the doctor, He is the Great Physician.
To the educator, He is the Great Teacher.
To the engineer, He is the New and Living Way.
To the farmer, He is the Sower and the Lord of the Harvest.
To the florist, He is the Rose of Sharon and the Lily of the Valley.
To the geologist, He is the Rock of Ages.
To the horticulturist, He is the True Vine.
To the judge, He is the Righteous Judge, the Judge of all men.
To the juror, He is the Faithful and True Witness.
To the jeweler, He is the Pearl of Great Price.
To the lawyer, He is the Counselor, the Lawgiver, the Advocate.
To the newspaper man, He is the Good News of Great Joy.
To the philanthropist, he is the Unspeakable Gift.
To the philosopher, He is the Wisdom of God.
To the sculptor, He is the Living Stone.
To the servant, He is the Good Master.
To the statesman, He is the Desire of all Nations.
To the student, He is the Incarnate Truth.
To the theologian, He is the Author and Finisher of our Faith.
To the laborer, He is the Giver of Rest.
To the sinner, He is the Lamb of God that taketh away the sin of the world.
To the Christian, He is the Son of the Living God, the Savior, the Redeemer and Lord.

"When Jesus came into the coasts of Caesarea Philippi, he asked his disciples, saying, Whom do men say that I the Son of man am? And they said, Some say that thou art John the Baptist: some Elijah; and others, Jeremiah, or one of the prophets. He saith unto them, But whom say ye that I am? And Simon Peter answered and said, Thou art the Christ, the Son of the living God. And Jesus answered and said unto him, Blessed art thou, Simon Barjona: for flesh and blood hath not revealed it unto thee, but my Father which is in heaven" [Matthew 6:13-17].

Because Ted died, we are confronted with the reality of death. Each of us will die one day unless Jesus returns to earth first. So, we are faced with that same solemn question Jesus asked His disciples, ". . . Whom say ye that I am?" [Matthew 16:15].

". . . at the name of Jesus every knee should bow, of things in heaven, and things in earth, and things under the earth; And that every tongue should confess that Jesus Christ is Lord, to the glory of God the Father" [Philippians 2:10-11].

Have you made Him Lord of your life by confessing your sins, turning from them, asking for forgiveness, and putting your faith in Jesus to save you? If you have never made the most important decision of your life, you can invite Jesus into your heart right now. Today can be the day of salvation for you.

May we pray?

Loving Father: We thank You for being Who You are—our Love-Giver. You love us with an everlasting love. You desire that each of us spends eternity with You in heaven and that we have life abundantly on earth. You have done all You can to make this possible. We must do our part by confessing our sins, turning from them, asking for forgiveness, and trusting Jesus to save us. Like Simon Peter, may our testimony also be that Jesus is "the Christ, the Son of the Living God." In Jesus' name, Amen.

DECLARATION OF FREEDOM FROM GUILT*

I, _____ (name), hereby trust that with

God's help you, _____

_____

_____

_____

(names of family members or other designated persons), will prayerfully do your best to provide for my physical, mental, emotional, and spiritual well-being, if I become unable to do so. Furthermore, regardless of the decisions you make or do not make in my behalf, I hereby make this declaration that I do not want you to ever feel guilty.

Signed _____

Dated _____

---

*This declaration does not take the place of medical, legal, and financial instruments including advance directives, wills, powers of attorney for health care, etc. It is an acknowledgment that others should not feel guilty for decisions made in an individual's behalf regardless of the outcome of those decisions.

Notes

Chapter 1

1. Elvin T. Eberhart, *Burnt offerings: Parables for 20th century Christians* (Nashville: Abingdon, 1977), pp. 14-15. Reprinted by permission.
2. Hani Raoul Khouzam, Charles E. Smith, and Bruce Bissett, "Bible therapy: A treatment of agitation in elderly patients with Alzheimer's Disease," *Clinical Gerontologist,* 15(2) (1994): 72.

Chapter 2

1. Alzheimer's Association (2005), *Basics of Alzheimer's disease: What it is and what you can do* (Chicago, IL: Alzheimer's Association), pp. 8, 15-16.
2. From "Medical aspects of dementia" by J. Thomas Hutton and Jerry L. Morris in *Caring for the Alzheimer patient: A practical guide* (Third edition) edited by Raye Lynne Dippel and J. Thomas Hutton (Amherst, NY: Prometheus Books, 1996), pp. 28-40. Copyright 1996. Reprinted by permission of publisher.
3. Alzheimer's Association, *Basics of Alzheimer's disease,* p. 12.
4. Ibid., pp. 12-13.
5. Liesi E. Hebert, Paul A. Scherr, Julia L. Bienias, David A. Bennett, and Denis A. Evans, "Alzheimer's disease in the U.S. population: Prevalence estimates using the 2000 census," *Archives of Neurology,* 60(8) (August 2003): 1119.
6. Denis A. Evans, Harris Funkenstein, Marilyn S. Albert, Paul A. Scherr, Nancy R. Cooke, Marilyn J. Chown, Liesi E. Hebert, Charles H. Hennekens, and James O. Taylor, "Prevalence of Alzheimer's disease in a community population of older persons: Higher than previously reported," *JAMA,* 262(18) (1989): 2551.
7. Lisa P. Gwyther, *Caring for people with Alzheimer's disease: A manual for facility staff* (Second edition) (Washington, DC: American Health Care Association and Chicago IL: Alzheimer's Association, 2001), pp. 8, 110-112. Used by permission.

Chapter 4

1. Kevin Ruffcorn, "Caring for the confused," *Leadership* (Winter 1993): 93.

Chapter 7

1. Thomas St. James O'Connor, "Ministry without a future: A pastoral care approach to patients with senile dementia," *Journal of Pastoral Care,* 46(1) (1992): 5, 7-12.
2. Naomi Feil, *The validation breakthrough: Simple techniques for communicating with people with "Alzheimer's-type dementia"* (Baltimore, MD: Health Professions Press, 1993), pp. 27, 30.
3. Alzheimer's Association (2005). *Communication: Best ways to interact with the person with dementia* (Chicago, IL: Alzheimer's Association), pp. 4-5.
4. Ibid., pp. 6-9.
5. Ibid., p. 10.
6. Ibid., p. 11.

Chapter 8

1. Thomas E. Bollinger, "The spiritual needs of the ageing" in *The need for a specific ministry to the aged* [conference proceedings] (Southern Pines, NC: Bishop Edwin A. Penick Memorial Home, 1969), p. 49.
2. Lisa P. Gwyther, *You are one of us: Successful clergy/church connections to Alzheimer's families* (Durham, NC: Duke University Medical Center, 1995), p. 39.

Chapter 9

1. James W. Ellor, John Stettner, and Helen Spath, "Ministry with the confused elderly," *Journal of Religion and Aging,* 45(2)(1987):22, 48-30.
2. Alzheimer's Association. *Alzheimer's Association Safe Return* ® [fact sheet] (Chicago IL: Alzheimer's Association, 2006), p. 1.
3. Robert Munsch, *Love you forever* (Willowdale, Ontario, Canada: Firefly Books Ltd, 1986).
4. David P. Wentroble, "Pastoral care of problematic Alzheimer's disease and dementia affected residents in a long-term care setting" in Larry VandeCreek, ed., *Spiritual care for persons with dementia: Fundamentals for pastoral practice* (Binghamton, NY: The Haworth Press, 1999), pp. 70-71.
5. Ibid., p. 69.

Chapter 11

1. Stephen Sapp, *When Alzheimer's disease strikes!* (Fifth edition) (Palm Beach, FL: Desert Ministries, 2002), p. 15.

Chapter 15

1. Grayce Bonham Confer, *Alzheimer's: Another opportunity to love* (Kansas City, MO: Beacon Hill Press, 1992).
2. Teresa R. Strecker, *Alzheimer's: Making sense of suffering* (Lafayette, LA: Vital Issues Press, 1997).
3. Hester Tetreault in *Stories for the heart,* compiled by Alice Gray (Sisters, OR: Questar Publishers, 1993), pp. 56-59. Reprinted by permission.

Conclusion

1. Ron Mehl, *The cure for a troubled heart: Meditations on Psalm 37* (Sisters, OR: Multnomah Books, 1996), pp. 128-129.

Bibliography

Articles

Abramowitz, Leah (1993). Prayer as therapy among the frail Jewish elderly, *Journal of Gerontological Social Work* 19(3/4):69-75.

Agostino, Joseph N. (1987). Religiosity and religious participation in the later years: A reflection of the spiritual needs of the elderly, *Journal of Religion & Aging* 4(2):75-82.

Alzheimer's Association National Newsletter (1995). Spirituality and Alzheimer's, Fall, p. 3.

Aronson, Miriam K., and Elaine S. Yatzkan (1984). Coping with Alzheimer's disease through support groups, *Aging* 347(3):5-9.

Barrett, John J. (1993). Counseling those who care for a relative with Alzheimer's disease, *Pastoral Psychology* 42(1):3-9.

Batz, Jeannette (1997). How do we know what they know? Decision to withhold Communion from Alzheimer's patients questioned, *National Catholic Reporter* 33(13):16.

Bell, Virginia, and David Troxel (2001). Spirituality and the person with dementia—A view from the field, *Alzheimer's Care Quarterly* 2(2):31-45.

Burgener, Sandy C. (1994). Caregiver religiosity and well-being in dealing with Alzheimer's dementia, *Journal of Religion and Health* 33(2):175-189.

——— (1999). Predicting quality of life in caregivers of Alzheimer's patients: The role of support from and involvement with the religious community, *Journal of Pastoral Care* 53(4):433-446.

Carlson, Dosia, and Sam Seicol (1990). Adapting worship to changing needs, *Generations* (Fall):65-66.

Chappell, Neena L., and R. Colin Reid (2002). Burden and well-being among caregivers: Examining the distinction, *Gerontologist* 42(6):772-780.

Clayton, Jean (1991). Let there be life: An approach to worship with Alzheimer's patients and their families, *Journal of Pastoral Care* 45(2):177-179.

Daire, Andrew P. (2002). The influence of parental bonding on emotional distress in caregiving sons for a parent with dementia, *Gerontologist* 42(6):766-771.

Dempsey, Marge, and Sylvia Baago (1998). Latent grief: The unique and hidden grief of carers of loved ones with dementia, *American Journal of Alzheimer's Disease* (March/April):84-91.

Elliott, Hazel (1997). Religion, spirituality and dementia: Pastoring to sufferers of Alzheimer's disease and other associated forms of dementia, *Disability and Rehabilitation* 19(10):435-441.

Ellor, James W., John Stettner, and Helen Spath (1987). Ministry with the confused elderly, *Journal of Religion & Aging* 4(2):21-33.

Farran, Carol J., and Eleanora Keane-Hagerty (1989). Twelve steps for caregivers, *American Journal of Alzheimer's Care and Related Disorders & Research* 4(6):38-41.

Farran, Carol J., Baila H. Miller, Julie E. Kaufman, and Lucille Davis (1997). Race, finding meaning, and caregiving distress, *Journal of Aging and Health* 9(3):316-333.

Gross, Joe (1994). A model for theological reflection in clinical pastoral education, *Journal of Pastoral Care* 48(2):131-134.

Hawkins, David G. (1987). Understanding and managing Alzheimer's disease, *Journal of Religion & Aging* 4(2):35-45.

Hellen, Carly R. (1994). The confused worshipper with dementia, the clergy and the caring congregation, *Aging & Spirituality: Newsletter of ASA's Forum on Religion, Spirituality & Aging* 6(1):1, 4, 8.

Hilmer, Ron (1997). Dealing with Alzheimer's: A spiritual approach to coping, *Northeast Texas Chapter Newsletter* 9(10):1, 3.

Hirschman, Karen B., Colette M. Joyce, Bryan D. James, Sharon X. Xie, and Jason H.T. Karlawish (2005). Do Alzheimer's disease patients want to participate in a treatment decision, and would their caregivers let them? *Gerontologist* 45(3): 381-388.

Justice, William G. (1991). A survey report of nursing home ministry and perceived needs with implications for pastoral care, *Journal of Religious Gerontology* 8(2):101-111.

Kaye, Judy, and Karen M. Robinson (1994). Spirituality among caregivers, *Image: Journal of Nursing Scholarship,* 26(3):218-221.

Khouzam, Hani, Charles Smith, and Bruce Bissett (1994). Bible therapy: A treatment for agitation in elderly patients with Alzheimer's disease, *Clinical Gerontologist* 15(2):71-74.

Kuhn, Daniel R. (1994). The changing face of sexual intimacy in Alzheimer's disease, *American Journal of Alzheimer's Care and Related Disorders & Research* (September/October):7-14.

Lapsley, James N. (2002). The clergy as advocates for the severely demented, *Journal of Pastoral Care & Counseling* 56(4):317-325.

Lenshyn, John (2005). Reaching the living echo: Maintaining and promoting the spiritual in persons living with Alzheimer's disease, *Alzheimer's Care Quarterly* 6(1):20-28.

Lieberman, Morton A., and Lawrence Fisher (2001). The effects of nursing home placement on family caregivers of patients with Alzheimer's disease, *Gerontologist* 41(6):819-826.

Marshall, Jan (1997). Using spirituality to visit a nursing home, *Northeast Texas Chapter Newsletter* 9(10):3.

Martin, Mike (2005). Prayer and church may slow Alzheimer's disease, *Science & Theology News* 5(10):7-8.

McFadden, Susan H., and Maryellen Hanusa (1998). Nourishing the spirit in long term care: Perspectives of residents and nursing assistants on sources of meaning in residents' lives, *Journal of Religious Gerontology 10*(4):9-24.

Meiburg, A.L. (1983). Pastoral communication with the confused, *Pastoral Psychology 31*(4):271-281.

Meuser, Thomas M., and Samuel J. Marwit (2001). A comprehensive, stage-sensitive model of grief in dementia caregiving, *Gerontologist 41*(5):658-670.

O'Connor, Thomas St. James (1992). Ministry without a future: A pastoral care approach to patients with senile dementia, *Journal of Pastoral Care 46*(1):5-12.

Oglesby Jr., William B. (1984). Biblical perspectives on caring for carers, *Journal of Pastoral Care 38*(2):85-90.

Picot, Sandra, Sara Debanne, Kevan Namazi, and May L. Wykle (1997). Religiosity and perceived rewards of black and white caregivers, *Gerontologist 37*(1):89-101.

Post, Stephen G. (2004). Alzheimer's and grace, *First Things 142:*12-14.

Reisberg, Barry, Steven H. Ferris, Mony J. de Leon, and Thomas Crook (1982). The global deterioration scale for assessment of primary degenerative dementia, *American Journal of Psychiatry 139:*1136-1139.

Richards, Marty (1990). Meeting the spiritual needs of the cognitively impaired, *Generations* (Fall):63-64.

Richards, Marty, and Sam Seicol (1991). The challenge of maintaining spiritual connectedness for persons institutionalized with dementia, *Journal of Religious Gerontology 7*(3):27-40.

Ries, Daryl T. (1993). Caregivers and the ministry in Alzheimer's disease, *American Journal of Alzheimer's Care and Related Disorders & Research 8*(6):31-36.

Robinson, Karen M., Sarah Ewing, and Stephen Looney (2000). Clergy support and caregiver expectations for support: A replication study, *American Journal of Alzheimer's Disease 15*(3):180-189.

Robinson, Karen M., and Judy Kaye (1994). The relationship between spiritual perspective, social support, and depression in caregiving and noncaregiving wives, *Scholarly Inquiry for Nursing Practice 8*(4):375-389.

Rohlfs-Young, Stephanie (1997). Research update: The physical effects of spirituality, *Northeast Texas Chapter Newsletter 9*(10):4.

Ronch, Judah L. (1996). Mourning and grief in late life Alzheimer's dementia: Revisiting the vanishing self, *American Journal of Alzheimer's Disease* (July/August):25-28.

Ruffcorn, Kevin (1993). Caring for the confused, *Leadership* (Winter):91-93.

Ryan, Ellen B., Lori Schindel Martin, and Amanda Beaman (2005). Communication strategies to promote spiritual well-being among people with dementia, *Journal of Pastoral Care & Counseling, 59*(1/2):43-55.

Sapp, Stephen (1988). The dilemma of Alzheimer's: Valuing autonomy and acknowledging dependence, *Second Opinion* (November) *9:*90-107.

——— (1998). Living with Alzheimer's: Body, soul and the remembering community, *Christian Century* (January 21):54-57, 59-60.

Schmall, Vicki L. (1984). It doesn't just happen: What makes a support group good? *Generations* (Winter) *9:*64-67.

Sligar, Sam J. (1987). A funeral that never ends: Alzheimer's disease and pastoral care, *Journal of Pastoral Care 41*(4):343-351.

Smith, Angela I. (2001). The stages of caregiving: The spiritual connection for the journey with Alzheimer's, *American Journal of Pastoral Counseling 4*(3): 19-40.

Smith, Marion Roach, and Jonathan Currier, presenters (October 1993). Spirituality for patients with dementia. Presentation at annual meeting of the American Association of Homes for the Aging. San Diego, CA: Alzheimer's Association, Capital District Chapter, 85 Watervliet Avenue, Albany, NY, 12206.

Stolley, Jacqueline M., Kathleen Buckwalter, and Harold G. Koenig (1999). Prayer and religious coping for caregivers for persons with Alzheimer's disease and related disorders, *American Journal of Alzheimer's Disease 14*(3):181-191.

Stuckey, Jon C. (1998). The church's response to Alzheimer's disease, *Journal of Applied Gerontology 17*(1):25-37.

Taylor, Sarah (1989). Clergy and church/synagogue: Special support for Alzheimer's caregivers, *Caregiver: Newsletter of the Duke Family Support Program 9*(13): 11-12.

Tornatore, Jane B., and Leslie A. Grant (2002). Burden among family caregivers of persons with Alzheimer's disease in nursing homes, *Gerontologist 42*(4): 497-506.

Upton, Rosemary J. (1999). Alzheimer's: Caring for the second victim, *Christian Counseling Today 17*(4):23-25.

Werner, Steve (2002). Worship with a twist, *Journal of Pastoral Care & Counseling 56*(2):165-168.

Wiser Now Newsletter (1995). Using spirituality to cope with Alzheimer's, *4*(3):1-4.

Woodman, Charles E. (2005). Seeking meaning in late stage dementia, *Journal of Pastoral Care & Counseling* (Winter) *59*(4):335-343.

Vogelsang, John D. (1983). A psychological and faith approach to grief counseling, *Journal of Pastoral Care 1*:22-27.

Weaver, Glenn D. (1986). Senile dementia and a resurrection theology, *Theology Today, 42*(4):444-456.

Whitlatch, Ann M., Dorothy I. Meddaugh, and Kristen J. Langhout (1992). Religiosity among Alzheimer's disease caregivers, *American Journal of Alzheimer's Disease and Related Disorders & Research* (November/December):11-20.

Wright, Scott D., Clara C. Pratt, and Vicki L. Schmall (1985). Spiritual support for care givers of dementia patients, *Journal of Religion and Health 24*(1):31-38.

Booklets

Alzheimer's Association (2006). *Lighting the path for people affected by Alzheimer's: African-American clergy guide.* Chicago, IL: Alzheimer's Association.

Alzheimer's Disease and Related Disorders Association (2000). *Alzheimer's disease: A guide for clergy.* Chicago, IL: Alzheimer's Association.

——— (1998). *Residential care: A guide for choosing a new home.* Chicago, IL: Alzheimer's Association.

Alzheimer Outreach Center, Alzheimer's Disease Research Center, and Alzheimer's Association Greater Pittsburgh Chapter (1995). *"Even these may forget, but God remembers": A resource guide for the clergy.* Pittsburgh, PA: Alzheimer's Association.

American Association of Retired Persons (n.d.). *The clergy: Gatekeepers for the future.* Washington, DC: American Association of Retired Persons.

——— (1989). *Guidelines for pastoral care of older persons in long-term care settings.* Washington, DC: American Association of Retired Persons.

American Bible Society (1992). *God's love for us is sure and strong: Comfort from God's Word for caregivers of persons with Alzheimer's disease.* New York: American Bible Society.

Ballard, Edna L. (2006). *"Hit pause": Helping dementia families deal with anger.* Durham, NC: Duke Family Support Program and Bryan Alzheimer's Disease Research Center, Duke University Medical Center.

Ballard, Edna L., and J. Whitney Little (2005). *Holiday visiting tips: A message for the faith community and friends of Alzheimer's families.* Durham, NC: Duke Aging Center Family Support Program and the Education Core, Bryan Alzheimer's Disease Research Center Duke University Medical Center, pp. 1-14.

Dunn, Hank (2001). *Hard choices for loving people* (Fourth edition). Herndon, VA: A&A Publishers.

East Central Iowa Chapter (n.d.). *Helping individuals and families face Alzheimer's disease through spirituality: A guide for clergy.* Cedar Rapids, IA: Alzheimer's Association.

Fazio, Sam (1995). *Respite care guide.* Chicago, IL: Alzheimer's Disease and Related Disorders Association.

Gwyther, Lisa P. (1995). *You are one of us: Successful clergy/church connections to Alzheimer's families.* Durham, NC: Duke University Medical Center.

National Family Caregivers Association (n.d.). *Model Catholic caregiving service.* Based on Interfaith Family Caregiving Service held on November 16, 1998, at St. John's Episcopal Church in Washington, DC, to celebrate National Family Caregivers Month.

——— (n.d.). *Model interfaith caregiving service.* Based on Interfaith Family Caregiving Service held on November 16, 1998, at St. John's Episcopal Church in Washington, DC. Kensington, MD: National Family Caregivers Association.

——— (n.d.). *Model Protestant caregiving service.* Based on Interfaith Family Caregiving Service held on November 16, 1998, at St. John's Episcopal Church in Washington, DC. Kensington, MD: National Family Caregivers Association.

Pohlmann, Elizabeth, and Gloria Bloom, compilers (n.d.). *Worship services for people with Alzheimer's disease and their families: A handbook.* Troy, NY: Eddy Alzheimer's Services.

Books

Adams, Martha O. (1986). *Alzheimer's disease: A call to courage for caregivers.* St. Meinrad, IN: Abbey Press.

Armstrong, Mary Vaughan (1990). *Caregiving for your loved ones.* Elgin, IL: David C. Cook Publishing Company.

Aronson, Miriam K., ed. (1988). *Understanding Alzheimer's disease.* New York: Charles Scribner's Sons.

Bagnull, Marlene, ed. and comp. (1994). *My turn to care: Affirmations for caregivers of aging parents.* Nashville, TN: Thomas Nelson Publishers.

Ballard, Edna L., Lisa P. Gwyther, and T. Patrick Toal (2001). *Pressure points: Alzheimer's and anger.* Durham, NC: Duke University Medical Center.

Ballard, Edna L., and Cornelia M. Poer (1993). *Sexuality and the Alzheimer's patient.* Durham, NC: Duke University Medical Center.

Ballard, Edna L., Cornelia M. Poer, and participants of Duke University Alzheimer's Support Groups (1999). *Lessons learned: Shared experiences in coping.* Durham, NC: Duke Family Support Program, Duke University Medical Center.

Barton, Julie, Marita Grudzen, and Ron Zielske (2003). *Vital connections in long-term care: Spiritual resources for staff and residents.* Baltimore, MD: Health Professions Press.

Bell, Sherry M. (2000). *Visiting Mom: An unexpected gift.* Sedona, AZ: ELDER Press.

Bell, Virginia, and David Troxel (2002). *A dignified life: The best friends approach to Alzheimer's care.* Deerfield Beach, FL: Health Communications.

Bollinger, Thomas E. (1969). "The spiritual needs of the ageing," in *The need for a specific ministry to the aged* [conference proceedings]. Southern Pines, NC: Bishop Edwin A. Penick Memorial Home.

Bresnahan, Rita (2003). *Walking one another home: Moments of grace and possibility in the midst of Alzheimer's.* Liguori, MO: Liguori/Triumph.

Bryden, Christine (2005). *Dancing with dementia: My story of living positively with dementia.* Philadelphia, PA: Jessica Kingsley Publishers.

Burchett, Harold (2002). *Last light: Staying true through the darkness of Alzheimer's.* Colorado Spring, CO: NavPress.

Cain, Danny, and Bob Russell (1995). *Blessed are the caregivers: A practical and spiritual guide for caregivers of Alzheimer's patients.* Prospect, KY: NB Publishing & Marketing.

Carroll, David L. (1989). *When your loved one has Alzheimer's: A caregiver's guide.* New York: Harper & Row, Publishers.

Carson, Verna Benner, and Harold G. Koenig (2004). *Spiritual caregiving: Healthcare as a ministry.* Philadelphia, PA: Templeton Foundation Press.

Carter, Rosalynn, with Susan K. Golant (1994). *Helping yourself help others: A book for caregivers.* New York: Crown Publishing Group.

Chapin, Shelley (1992). *Counselors, Comforters, and Friends: Establishing a Caregiving Ministry in Your Church.* Wheaton, IL: SP Publications, Inc.

Childress, Ellen, as told to Paulette ErkenBrack (2001). *Shattered lives: Finding hope in the midst of Alzheimer's and other related dementia.* Pittsburgh, PA: Dorrance Publishing Company.

Clemmer, William Michael (1993). *Victims of dementia: Services, support and care.* Binghamton, NY: The Haworth Pastoral Press.

Cohen, Donna, and Carl Eisdorfer (2001). *The loss of self: A family resource for the care of Alzheimer's disease and related disorders* (Revised and updated edition). New York: W.W. Norton and Company.

Confer, Grayce Bonham (1992). *Alzheimer's: Another opportunity to love.* Kansas City, MO: Beacon Hill Press.

Coste, Joanne Koenig (2003). *Learning to speak Alzheimer's: A groundbreaking approach for everyone dealing with the disease.* New York: Houghton Mifflin Company.

Coughlan, Patricia Brown (1993). *Facing Alzheimer's: Family caregivers speak.* New York: Ballantine Books.

Dash, Paul, and Nicole Villemarette-Pittman (2005). *Alzheimer's disease.* New York: Demos Medical Publishing and St. Paul, MN: American Academy of Neurology.

Davis, Patti (2004). *The long goodbye.* New York: Alfred A. Knopf.

Davis, Robert (1989). *My journey into Alzheimer's disease: A story of hope.* Wheaton, IL: Tyndale House Publishers.

DeBaggio, Thomas (2002). *Losing my mind: An intimate look at life with Alzheimer's.* New York: Free Press.

DeHaan, Robert F. (2003). *Into the shadows: A journey of faith and love into Alzheimer's.* Grand Haven, MI: FaithWalk Publishing.

Dippel, Raye Lynne, and J. Thomas Hutton (1996). *Caring for the Alzheimer patient: A practical guide* (Third edition). New York: Prometheus Books.

Doka, Kenneth J. (2001). Grief, loss, and caregiving. In Kenneth J. Doka and Joyce D. Davidson, eds., *Caregiving and loss: Family needs, professional responses.* Washington, DC: Hospice Foundation of America, pp. 215-230.

Doka, Kenneth J., and Joyce D. Davidson, eds. (2001). *Caregiving and loss: Family needs, professional responses.* Washington, DC: Hospice Foundation of America.

Eby, David W., Lisa J. Molnar, and Jean T. Shope (2000). *Driving decisions workbook.* Bethesda, MD: American Occupational Therapy Association. Available: www.aota.org/olderdriver/docs/assessumi/pdf.

Entwistle, Charles C. (1994). *"I'm just not myself anymore": A family guide to Alzheimer's disease.* Salt Lake City, UT: Northwest Publishing.

Everett, Deborah (1996). *Forget me not: The spiritual care of people with Alzheimer's.* Edmonton, Canada: Inkwell Press.

Ewing, Wayne (1999). *Tears in God's bottle: Reflections on Alzheimer's caregiving.* Tucson, AZ: WhiteStone Circle Press.

Fasano, Marie A. (1986). *Creative care for the person with Alzheimer's.* Englewood Cliffs, NJ: A Brady Book.

Fazio, Sam, Dorothy Seman, and Jane Stansell (1999). *Rethinking Alzheimer's care.* Baltimore, MD: Health Professions Press.

Feil, Naomi (1993). *The validation breakthrough: Simple techniques for communicating with people with "Alzheimer's-type dementia."* Baltimore, MD: Health Professions Press.

Fish, Sharon (1996). *Alzheimer's: Caring for your loved one, caring for yourself.* Wheaton, IL: Harold Shaw Publishers.

Fish, Sharon, and Judith Allen Shelly (1988). *Spiritual care: The nurse's role.* Downers Grove, IL: InterVarsity Press.

Fitchett, George (1993). *Assessing spiritual needs: A guide for caregivers.* Minneapolis, MN: Augsburg Fortress.

Gilhooly, Mary Ney (2000). *When memories go missing: My mother and Alzheimer's disease.* Dallas, TX: Maryvale Press.

Goldsmith, Malcolm (1996). *Hearing the voice of people with dementia.* London, England and Bristol, PA: Jessica Kingsley Publishers.

Gray-Davidson, Frena (1999). *The Alzheimer's sourcebook for caregivers: A practical guide for getting through the day* (Newly revised third edition). Chicago, IL: Lowell House.

Greenblat, Cathy Stein (2004). *Alive with Alzheimer's.* Chicago, IL: University of Chicago Press.

Grollman, Earl A., and Kenneth S. Kosik (1996). *When someone you love has Alzheimer's: The caregiver's journey.* Boston, MA: Beacon Press.

Gruetzner, Howard (2001). *Alzheimer's: A caregiver's guide and sourcebook* (Third edition). New York: John Wiley & Sons.

Hale, W. Daniel, and Richard G. Bennett (2000). *Building healthy communities through medical-religious partnerships.* Baltimore, MD: Johns Hopkins University Press.

Hale, W. Daniel, and Harold G. Koenig (2003). *Healing bodies and souls: A practical guide for congregations.* Minneapolis, MN: Augsburg Fortress.

Hall, Elizabeth T. (2000). *Caring for a loved one with Alzheimer's: A Christian perspective.* Binghamton, NY: The Haworth Pastoral Press.

Haugk, Kenneth C. (2004). *Don't sing songs to a heavy heart: How to relate to those who are suffering.* St. Louis, MO: Stephen Ministries.

Hellen, Carly R. (1998). *Alzheimer's disease: Activity-focused care* (Second edition). Boston, MA: Butterworth-Heinemann.

Hendershott, Anne (2000). *The reluctant caregivers: Learning to care for a loved one with Alzheimer's.* Westport, CT: Bergin & Garvey.

Hoffman, Stephanie B., and Constance A. Platt (2000). *Comforting the confused: Strategies for managing dementia.* New York: Springer Publishing Company.

Holder, Jennifer Sutton, and Jann Aldredge-Clanton (2004). *Parting.* Chapel Hill, NC: University of North Carolina Press.

Holy Cross Family Ministries (2006). *Pray with me still: Rosary meditations and spiritual support for persons with Alzheimer's, their caregivers, and loved ones.* Notre Dame, IN: Ave Maria Press.

Jones, Moyra (1999). *Gentlecare: Changing the experience of Alzheimer's disease in a positive way.* Point Roberts, WA: Hartley & Marks.

Justice, William G. (2005). *Training guide for visiting the sick: More than a social call.* Binghamton, NY: The Haworth Pastoral Press.

Keck, David (1996). *Forgetting whose we are: Alzheimer's disease and the love of God.* Nashville, TN: Abingdon Press.

Kimble, Melvin, and Susan H. McFadden, eds. (2003). *Aging, spirituality, and religion: A handbook* (Volume 2). Minneapolis, MN: Augsburg Fortress.

Kimble, Melvin A., Susan H. McFadden, James W. Ellor, and James J. Seeber, eds. (1995). *Aging, spirituality, and religion: A handbook*. Minneapolis, MN: Augsburg Fortress.

Kinast, Robert L. (1996). *Let ministry teach: A guide to theological reflection*. Colledgeville, MN: Liturgical Press.

Kirkland, Kevin, and Howard McIlveen (1999*). Full circle: Spiritual therapy for the elderly*. Binghamton, NY: The Haworth Pastoral Press.

Klapp, DeeAnn (2003). A practical theological model for worship with Alzheimer's patients: Using the validation technique. In Derrel Watkins, ed., *Practical theology for aging*, Binghamton, NY: The Haworth Pastoral Press, pp. 153-170.

Koenig, Harold G., and Andrew J. Weaver (1997). *Counseling troubled older adults: A handbook for pastors and religious caregivers*. Nashville, TN: Abingdon Press.

Kriseman, Nancy (2005). *The caring spirit approach to eldercare: A training guide for professionals and families*. Baltimore, MD: Health Professions Press.

Kübler-Ross, Elisabeth (1969). *On death and dying*. New York: Macmillan Publishing Company.

Kuhn, Daniel (2003). *Alzheimer's early stage: First steps for family, friends and caregivers* (Second edition). Alameda, CA: Hunter House Publishers.

Lovette, Katie (1999). *Loving care for Alzheimer's patients: Practical solutions for caregivers and their families*. Los Angeles, CA: Health Information Press.

McCall, Junietta Baker (1999). *Grief education for caregivers of the elderly*. Binghamton, NY: The Haworth Pastoral Press.

McKim, Donald K. (1997). *God never forgets: Faith, hope, and Alzheimer's disease*. Louisville, KY: Westminster John Knox Press.

McQuilkin, Robertson (1998). *A promise kept*. Wheaton, IL: Tyndale House Publishers.

Mace, Nancy L., and Peter V. Rabins (2006/1981). *The 36-hour day: A family guide to caring for persons with Alzheimer's disease, related dementing illnesses, and memory loss in later life*. New York and Boston, MA: Warner Books. Originally published Baltimore, MD: Johns Hopkins University Press.

Manning, Doug (1999). *Share my lonesome valley: The slow grief of long-term care*. Oklahoma City, OK: In-Sight Books.

———— (2006). *When love gets tough: The nursing home decision*. Oklahoma City, OK: In-Sight Books.

Markin, R.E. (1992). *The Alzheimer's cope book: The complete manual for patients and their families*. Secaucus, NJ: Carol Publishing Group.

Mayo, Mary Ann (2003). *Twilight travels with Mother: How I found strength, hope, and a sense of humor living with Alzheimer's*. Grand Rapids, MI: Fleming H. Revell.

Miller, Sue (2003). *The story of my father*. New York: Alfred A. Knopf.

Moberg, David O. (1971). *Spiritual well-being*. Washington, DC: White House Conference on Aging.

Murphey, Cecil (2000). *My parents, my children: Spiritual help for caregivers*. Louisville, KY: Westminster John Knox Press.

———— (2004). *When someone you love has Alzheimer's: Daily encouragement.* Kansas City, MO: Beacon Hill Press.

Nelson, James Lindemann, and Hilde Lindemann Nelson (1996). *Alzheimer's: Answers to hard questions for families.* New York: Doubleday.

Noyes, Lin E. (2002). Loss and Alzheimer's disease. In Kenneth J. Doka, ed., *Living with grief: Loss in later life.* Washington, DC: Hospice Foundation of America.

Oliver, Rose, and Frances A. Bock (1987). *Coping with Alzheimer's: A caregiver's emotional survival guide.* New York: Dodd, Mead & Company.

Parrent, Joanne (2001). *Courage to care: A caregiver's guide through each stage of Alzheimer's.* Indianapolis, IN: Alpha Books.

Payne, Franklin E., Jr. (1985). *Biblical/medical ethics: The Christian and the practice of medicine.* Milford, MI: Mott Media.

Petersen, Ronald (2002). *Mayo clinic on Alzheimer's disease: Practical answers on memory loss, aging, research, treatment and caregiving.* Rochester, MN: Mayo Clinic Health Information.

Piepenbrink, Linda, ed. (2002). *Caring for aging loved ones.* Wheaton, IL: Tyndale House Publishers.

Pohlmann, Elizabeth, and Gloria Bloom, comp. (n.d.). *Worship services for people with Alzheimer's disease and their families: A handbook.* Troy, NY: Eddy Alzheimer's Services.

Post, Stephen G. (2000). *The moral challenge of Alzheimer's disease* (Second edition). Baltimore, MD: Johns Hopkins University Press.

Powell, Lenore S., with Katie Courtice (2002). *Alzheimer's disease: A guide for families and caregivers* (Third edition). Cambridge, PA: Perseus Publishing.

Price, David M. (2001). Hard decisions in hard times: Helping families make ethical choices during prolonged illness. In Kenneth J. Doka and Joyce D. Davidson, eds., *Caregiving and loss: Family needs, professional responses.* Washington, DC: Hospice Foundation of America, pp. 271-286.

Purtilo, Ruth B., and Henk A.M.J. ten Have, eds. (2004). *Ethical foundations of palliative care for Alzheimer's disease.* Baltimore, MD: Johns Hopkins University Press.

Rain, Mary Summer (2002). *Love never sleeps: Living at home with Alzheimer's.* Charlottesville, VA: Hampton Roads Publishing Company.

Ramshaw, Elaine (1987). Ritual and pastoral care. Philadelphia, PA: Fortress Press.

Rau, Marie T. (1993). *Coping with communication challenges in Alzheimer's disease.* San Diego, CA: Singular Publishing Group.

Reisberg, Barry (1981). *A guide to Alzheimer's disease: For families, spouses, and friends.* New York: Free Press.

Richards, Marty (1999). *Caregiving: Church and family together.* Louisville, KY: Westminster John Knox Press.

Robbins, Jerry K. (1993). *Carevision: The why and how of Christian caregiving.* Valley Forge, PA: Judson Press.

Roche, Lyn (1996). *Coping with caring: Daily reflections for Alzheimer's caregivers.* Forest Knolls, CA: Elder Books.

Roberts, D. Jeanne (1991). *Taking care of caregivers: For families and others who care for people with Alzheimer's disease and other forms of dementia.* Palo Alto, CA: Bull Publishing Company.

Roberts, Joan D. (1991). *Caring for those with Alzheimer's: A pastoral approach.* New York: Alba House.

Ronch, Judah L. (1989). *Alzheimer's disease: A practical guide for those who help others.* New York: Continuum Publishing Company.

Samples, Pat, Diane Larsen, and Marvin Larsen (2000). *Self-care for caregivers: A twelve step approach.* Center City, MN: Hazelden Foundation.

Sands, Daniel (1987). Philosophy of care. In Anne Kalicki, ed., *Confronting Alzheimer's disease.* Owings Mills, MD: National Health Publishing, in cooperation with the American Association of Homes for the Aging, pp. 43-45.

Sapp, Stephen (2002). *When Alzheimer's disease strikes!* (Fifth edition). Palm Beach, FL: Desert Ministries.

Shamy, Eileen (2003). *A guide to the spiritual dimension of care for people with Alzheimer's disease and related dementia: More than body, brain and breath.* London, England: Jessica Kingsley Publishers.

Shelly, Judith Allen (2000). *Spiritual care: A guide for caregivers.* Downers Grove, IL: InterVarsity Press.

Shelly, Judith Allen, and Sharon Fish (1988). *Spiritual care: The nurse's role* (Third edition). Downers Grove, IL: InterVarsity Press.

Shelp, Earl E., and Ronald H. Sunderland (2000). *Sustaining presence: A model of caring by people of faith.* Nashville, TN: Abingdon Press.

Shenk, David (2003). *The forgetting Alzheimer's: Portrait of an epidemic.* New York: Anchor Books.

Shimer, Porter (2002). *New hope for people with Alzheimer's and their caregivers.* Roseville, CA: Prima Publishing.

Simmons, Henry C., and Mark A. Peters (1996). *With God's oldest friends: Pastoral visiting in the nursing home.* Mahwah, NJ: Paulist Press.

Simpson, Robert, and Anne Simpson (1999). *Through the wilderness: A guide in two voices.* Minneapolis, MN: Augsburg Fortress.

Smith, Patricia B., Mary Mitchell Kenan, and Mark Edwin Kunik (2004). *Alzheimer's for dummies.* Hoboken, NJ: Wiley Publishing.

Snowdon, David (2001). *Aging with grace: What the nun study teaches us about leading longer, healthier, and more meaningful lives.* New York: Bantam Books.

Stone, Howard W., and James O. Duke (2006). *How to think theologically* (Second edition). Minneapolis, MN: Augsburg Fortress.

Strauss, Claudia J. (2001). *Talking to Alzheimer's: Simple ways to connect when you visit with a family member or friend.* Oakland, CA: New Harbinger Publications.

Strecker, Teresa R. (1997). *Alzheimer's: Making sense of suffering.* Lafayette, LA: Vital Issues Press.

Syverson, Betty Groth (1987). *Bible readings for caregivers.* Minneapolis, MN: Augsburg Fortress.

Upton, Rosemary J. (1990). *Glimpses of Grace: A family struggles with Alzheimer's.* Grand Rapids, MI: Baker Book House.

VandeCreek, Larry, ed. (1999). *Spiritual care for persons with dementia: Fundamentals for pastoral practice.* Binghamton, NY: The Haworth Pastoral Press.
Wall, Frank A. (1996). *Where did Mary go? A loving husband's struggle with Alzheimer's.* Amherst, NY: Prometheus Books.
Warner, Mark L. (2000). *The complete guide to Alzheimer's-proofing your home* (Revised and updated edition). West Lafayette, IN: Purdue University Press.
White, Debra (2007). *She touched my heart.* Mustang, OK: Tate Publishing & Enterprises.
Yale, Robyn (1994). *Early stage Alzheimer's patient support groups: Research, practice and training materials.* San Francisco, CA: Special Projects Press.
Yearwood, Mary Margaret Britton (2002). *In their hearts: Inspirational Alzheimer's stories.* Victoria, Canada: Trafford Publishing.

CD

Zucker, David J. (2006) *The way we were: Rituals for families coping with dementia.* Association of Professional Chaplains Annual Conference Presentation. Available for purchase through Veranda Communications: (502) 485-1484.

Manuals

Ballard, Edna L., and Lisa P. Gwyther (1988). *In-home respite care: Guidelines for training respite workers serving memory-impaired adults.* Durham, NC: Duke University Center for the Study of Aging Family Support Program.
East Central Iowa Chapter, Alzheimer's Association (n.d.). *Helping individuals and families face Alzheimer's disease through spirituality: A guide for clergy.* Cedar Rapids, IA: Alzheimer's Association.
Gwyther, Lisa P. (2001). *Caring for people with Alzheimer's disease: A manual for facility staff* (Second edition). Washington, DC: American Health Care Association and Chicago, IL: Alzheimer's Association.
Gwyther, Lisa P., and Edna L. Ballard (1988). *In-home respite care: Guidelines for programs serving family caregivers for memory-impaired adults.* Durham, NC: Duke University Center for the Study of Aging Family Support Program.
Lawson, Judy, ed. (2002). *Male caregivers' guidebook: Caring for your loved one with Alzheimer's at home* (Revised edition). Des Moines, IA: Greater Iowa Chapter, Alzheimer's Association.
McCormick, Tom, and Penny McCormick (1982). *Nursing home ministry: A manual.* Philadelphia, PA: Great Commission Publications.
Miller, Joan E. (1998). *Circle of hope resource manual: A guide for congregations assisting dementia families.* Charlotte, NC: Carolina Piedmont Chapter, Alzheimer's Association.
Murphy, Judith K. (1986). *Sharing care: The Christian ministry of respite care.* New York: United Church Press.

Ver Hoef, Judi, and Diana Findley (1993). *Building a volunteer respite program: A "how to" manual especially for churches.* Des Moines, IA: Des Moines Alzheimer's Association.

Pamphlets

Alzheimer's Association (2006). *About clinical studies and participating in research* [fact sheet]. Chicago, IL: Alzheimer's Association.

———— (2007). *About the Alzheimer's Association* [fact sheet]. Chicago, IL: Alzheimer's Association.

———— (n.d.). *African-Americans and Alzheimer's disease: The silent epidemic.* Chicago, IL: Alzheimer's Association.

———— (2006). *Alzheimer's Association 24/7 helpline* [fact sheet]. Chicago, IL: Alzheimer's Association.

———— (2006). *Alzheimer's Association Safe Return®* [fact sheet]. Chicago, IL: Alzheimer's Association.

———— (2004). *Alzheimer's disease growth: U.S. will see average 44 percent increase in Alzheimer's disease 2025* [fact sheet]. Chicago, IL: Alzheimer's Association.

———— (2006). *Alzheimer's disease statistics* [fact sheet]. Chicago, IL: Alzheimer's Association.

———— (2005). *Basics of Alzheimer's disease: What it is and what you can do.* Chicago, IL: Alzheimer's Association.

———— (2005). *Behaviors: What causes dementia-related behavior like aggression, and how to respond.* Chicago, IL: Alzheimer's Association.

———— (2007). *Caregiver stress: Respect your well-being.* Chicago, IL: Alzheimer's Association.

———— (2005). *Communication: Best ways to interact with the person with dementia.* Chicago, IL: Alzheimer's Association.

———— (2005). *Depression and Alzheimer's disease* [fact sheet]. Chicago, IL: Alzheimer's Association.

———— (2006). *Disaster preparedness from the Alzheimer's Association* [fact sheet]. Chicago, IL: Alzheimer's Association.

———— (2006). *Driving* [fact sheet]. Chicago, IL: Alzheimer's Association.

———— (2005). *Early-onset Alzheimer's: I'm too young to have Alzheimer's disease.* Chicago, IL: Alzheimer's Association.

———— (2006). *End-of-life decisions: Honoring the wishes of the person with Alzheimer's disease.* Chicago, IL: Alzheimer's Association.

———— (2006). *Ethical considerations: Issues in death and dying* [fact sheet]. Chicago, IL: Alzheimer's Association.

———— (2006). *Ethical considerations: Issues in diagnostic disclosure* [fact sheet]. Chicago, IL: Alzheimer's Association.

———— (n.d.). *Ethical issues in Alzheimer's disease: Assisted oral feeding and tube feeding.* Chicago, IL: Alzheimer's Association.

Alzheimer's Association (n.d.). *Ethical issues in Alzheimer's disease: End-of-life care.* Chicago, IL: Alzheimer's Association.

—— (n.d.). *Ethical issues in Alzheimer's disease: Genetic testing.* Chicago, IL: Alzheimer's Association.

—— (n.d.). *Ethical issues in Alzheimer's disease: Telling the truth in diagnosis.* Chicago, IL: Alzheimer's Association.

—— (2006). *Feelings* [fact sheet]. Chicago, IL: Alzheimer's Association.

—— (2006). *Genes and Alzheimer's disease* [fact sheet]. Chicago, IL: Alzheimer's Association.

—— (2006). *Grief, mourning, and guilt* [fact sheet]. Chicago, IL: Alzheimer's Association.

—— (2006). *Hallucinations* [fact sheet]. Chicago, IL: Alzheimer's Association.

—— (2006). *Holidays* [fact sheet]. Chicago, IL: Alzheimer's Association.

—— (2006). *Hospitalization* [fact sheet]. Chicago, IL: Alzheimer's Association.

—— (2005). *If you have Alzheimer's disease: What you should know, what you should do.* Chicago, IL: Alzheimer's Association.

—— (2006). *Incontinence* [fact sheet]. Chicago, IL: Alzheimer's Association.

—— (1998). *Just for children: Helping you understand Alzheimer's disease.* Chicago, IL: Alzheimer's Association.

—— (n.d.). *Just for teens: Helping you understand Alzheimer's disease.* Chicago, IL: Alzheimer's Association.

—— (2005). *Late-stage care: Providing care and comfort during the late stage of Alzheimer's disease.* Chicago, IL: Alzheimer's Association.

—— (2005). *Legal plans: Assisting the person with dementia in planning for the future.* Chicago, IL: Alzheimer's Association.

—— (2005). *Money matters: Helping the person with dementia settle financial issues.* Chicago, IL: Alzheimer's Association.

—— (2006). *Parents' guide: Helping children and teens understand Alzheimer's disease.* Chicago, IL: Alzheimer's Association.

—— (2007). *Respite guide: How to find what's right for you.* Chicago, IL: Alzheimer's Association.

—— (2006). *Safe Return®: Guide for Law Enforcement.* Chicago, IL: Alzheimer's Association.

—— (2005). *Safe Return® Wandering: Who's at Risk?* Chicago, IL: Alzheimer's Association.

—— (2006). *Safe Return® Wandering Behavior: Preparing for and Preventing It* [fact sheet]. Chicago IL: Alzheimer's Association.

—— (2006). *Safety* [fact sheet]. Chicago, IL: Alzheimer's Association.

—— (2005). *Safety at home: Adapting the home to support the person with dementia.* Chicago, IL: Alzheimer's Association.

—— (2006). *Sexuality* [fact sheet]. Chicago, IL: Alzheimer's Association.

—— (2006). *Stages of Alzheimer's disease* [fact sheet]. Chicago, IL: Alzheimer's Association.

—— (2006). *Telling the person, family and friends* [fact sheet]. Chicago, IL: Alzheimer's Association.

———— (2006). *Ten ways to help a family living with Alzheimer's.* Chicago, IL: Alzheimer's Association.

———— (2006). *Understanding early-onset Alzheimer's disease: A guide for health care professionals.* Chicago, IL: Alzheimer's Association.

———— (2005). *Understanding early-stage Alzheimer's disease: A guide for health care professionals.* Chicago, IL: Alzheimer's Association.

———— (2006). *Vacationing* [fact sheet]. Chicago, IL: Alzheimer's Association.

———— (2006). *Visiting* [fact sheet]. Chicago, IL: Alzheimer's Association.

———— (n.d.). *What is happening to Grandpa?* Chicago, IL: Alzheimer's Association.

———— (2006). *What's being done about Alzheimer's?* Chicago, IL: Alzheimer's Association.

National Family Caregivers Association (2000-2005). *Supporting caregiving families: A guide for congregations and parishes.* Kensington, MD: National Family Caregivers Association.

National Institute on Aging and National Institutes of Health (2006). *Alzheimer's disease* [fact sheet]. Bethesda, MD: National Institute on Aging and National Institutes of Health.

———— (2003). *Alzheimer's disease: Unraveling the mystery.* Bethesda, MD: National Institute on Aging and National Institutes of Health.

———— (2004). *Alzheimer's disease genetics* [fact sheet]. Bethesda, MD: National Institute on Aging and National Institutes of Health.

———— (2005). *Depression: Don't let the blues hang around.* Bethesda, MD: National Institute on Aging and National Institutes of Health.

———— (2004). *Getting your affairs in order* [AgePage]. Bethesda, MD: National Institute on Aging and National Institutes of Health.

———— (2006). *Home safety for people with Alzheimer's disease.* Bethesda, MD: National Institute on Aging and National Institutes of Health.

———— (n.d.). *Hospitalization happens: A guide to hospital visits for loved ones with memory disorders.* Bethesda, MD: National Institute on Aging and National Institutes of Health.

———— (2003). *Long-term care: Choosing the right place* [AgePage]. Bethesda, MD: National Institute on Aging and National Institutes of Health.

———— (2004). *Older drivers* [AgePage]. Bethesda, MD: National Institute on Aging and National Institutes of Health.

Rosalynn Carter Institute of Caregiving (2004). *12 tips for caregivers: Caring for yourself while helping a loved one with Alzheimer's disease.* Americus, GA: Rosalynn Carter Institute of Caregiving.

Professional Project Report

Otwell, Patricia Anne (1986). *A chaplain-led ministry to families of Alzheimer's disease patients through the development and utilization of a support group.* Fort Worth, TX: Southwestern Baptist Theological Seminary.

Videos

O'Neill Foundation for Community Health (2004). *Alzheimer's disease.* DeLand, FL: O'Neill Foundation for Community Health.

University of Alabama Center for Public Television (1995 and 1997). *Pastoral care, Part I and Part II.* Tuscaloosa, AL: University of Alabama Center for Public Television.

University of Pittsburgh Alzheimer's Disease Center (1991). *Even these may forget (A pastoral challenge: Training program for clergy).* Pittsburgh, PA: University of Pittsburgh Alzheimer's Disease Center.

World Wide Pictures (1999). *A vow to cherish.* Minneapolis, MN: World Wide Pictures.

Index